AN INTRODUCTION TO

DEMOCRATIC THEORY

H. B. Mayo

NEW YORK | OXFORD UNIVERSITY PRESS

© 1960 by Oxford University Press, Inc.
Library of Congress Catalogue Card Number: 60-7063

Tenth Printing, 1977

Printed in the United States of America

335.42
N45i
120752
mar 1982

Preface

It is only too painfully obvious that there are a number of theories of democracy in circulation. Some of them are extremely vague, few if any of them are fully worked out, and some of them contradict one another. Nor, in view of the popularity and importance of democracy, has there been very much serious writing on the subject, strange as this may seem.

Historians and political scientists in large numbers could be cited to make the same points. One typical comment will suffice:

> ... there are very few books to which we can turn, and particularly few by Americans, that seriously try to enlighten us about the nature of democracy. If on the contrary we want expositions of the nature of dictatorship we can find them aplenty. Thousands of books have been written about its various forms ... but you will find a scant handful of books that offer enlightenment on the principles of democracy.[1]

One sometimes hears it said that times of stress and strain, of rapid social change, always generate political theory. Yet despite the stimulus to political theory in our troubled times, one may reasonably doubt that great constructions in political theory have been made. Until the classic work comes along, we must make do with more modest efforts such as this essay. And anyone who makes even a small effort at a comprehensive theory of democracy must be brash: he must ignore the kind of advice given by Lord Acton to persons about to write History:—Don't.

The method adopted in this essay is not to present and analyze the medley of democratic theories, noting their differences and

[1] R. M. MacIver, *The Ramparts We Guard*, New York, 1950, p. 4.

points of agreement. I tried this method at first but it led only to confusion, and there seemed no end to the undertaking. Instead therefore the method chosen is to set up a consistent and coherent theory of democracy which I hope may command wide—though not, of course, unanimous—agreement, and to show here and there how other theories differ from it. The theory is in the form of a few closely connected principles of operation of a democratic political system, principles which may be cast in both operational and normative terms, to explain the system and to justify it. Only a few of the problems arising from the theory are dealt with; some are scarcely mentioned let alone fully explored. I hope that others, much better qualified, will go on to explore them. Confusion over 'democracy' is not likely to end in my lifetime, but it may be reduced, and we may move close to agreement over what it is that we disagree about. Then we can move on from linguistic disputes to more interesting and important arguments.

It is scarcely possible to keep personal bias out of an inquiry such as this, so mine is stated openly. I have a bias in favor of the theory which I set forth; but I hope this has not prevented my explaining, as fairly as possible, any different views that are examined. This essay is written in simple, non-technical language since it is my belief that political theory, like the writing of history, should communicate with the layman.

My special thanks are due to Professor Douglas N. Morgan whose collaboration and criticisms have been of inestimable value on many points; to Henry F. Angus who gave a most helpful reading of the manuscript; to the Social Science Research Council of Canada which gave me a grant in order to buy leisure time—that scarcest of all commodities in academic life; and to the University of South Carolina for its generous typing assistance. Thanks are also due to Dr. John H. Hallowell of Duke University who allowed me to reprint material from the *Journal of Politics;* and to E. E. Weaver of the University of Utah for permission to quote from Volume X, No. 1 of the March 1957 issue of the *Western Political Quarterly.*

H. B. M.

Columbia, South Carolina
March 1960

Contents

ONE | *On the Nature of Politics and Political Theory*

WHAT DO WE MEAN BY 'POLITICS' AND 'POLITICAL'?

Many writers, when dealing with their subjects—psychology, economics, biology, and so forth—start by saying what the subject is about. I shall follow this useful custom and try first of all to identify the usual subject matter of the political studies. It is particularly important to do so, because works on politics all too often neglect this elementary inquiry.

Traditionally, the political studies have been chiefly concerned in one way or another with the 'state' as the central concept, a practice for which there are understandable reasons—among them that the ancient Greeks started the fashion, and that today the state is a universal type of organization. But there can be government and politics without a state, as in primitive societies or the feudal world; and it is more enlightening, I think, to begin not with an entity such as the state but with the governing function, which is performed somehow in every human society of which we have any knowledge.

We may as well admit that it is not at all an easy thing to mark off the field of the political from the fields of other social studies. The boundary lines between the functions of different social institutions, and hence between the social studies, are always shifting and partly arbitrary. A useful start may be made by noting that we occasionally speak of the politics of any kind of society—whether a state, a primitive tribe, or the 'society of nations,' or we refer to the politics of a club, a church, a university, or other private organization. Some persons go so far as to speak of both public and 'private' government, a usage found, for instance, in several of the works of Charles E. Merriam. What we seek are some criteria which will distinguish the public from the private meaning of politics, and the political studies from other social studies.

The *first* step is traditional enough, even trivial. By general usage, the political includes the governmental, and those activities closely related to the formal government of states. But this is to take an institutional approach, and it is better to think in terms of function, and behind function, purpose. It is the reference to policies—their complex formation and execution—that gives content to the governing function of a society. The political or public policies *par excellence* are most commonly thought of as made by government and embodied in statutes—the decisions of legislators. But this is not of course the only form which public policies can take. Often on matters of high policy, the decisions may be made by judges. The policy-making of judges is especially common in constitutional matters, and in that large part of the common law dealing with—among other things—the family, property, civil damages, and many aspects of commerce. Instead of being resolved in the legislature, the conflicting claims and opinions are mediated and decided in a courtroom. Policies may also be made by the executive and administrative branches of government, and many of them take the form of ordinances, orders, decrees; or they may emerge in the daily operation of the executive departments, as in the conduct of foreign policy. And—a most important point—since policies may be of many levels of generality, they may be made at any level in the administrative hierarchy, or in the whole complex of legislative-executive-administrative relationships. The political, then, includes the governmental, or even in simple societies, what we may call the governing function. And the heart of the governing function, however performed, is the policies which are reached and carried out.

The *second* point about those policies which are called political is that they are normally regarded as binding on all the members of the society. The focus of political studies has generally been upon these policies of formal government which are binding because law enforcement is there in the background if it should be required. As Locke put it: 'Political power, then, I take to be a right of making laws with penalties of death, and consequently all less penalties...' Yet to treat only of laws and the monopoly of force behind them is to narrow the scope of the political to the legal, and—much worse—it gives rise to misunderstanding of the sanctions for all public policies, including laws themselves.

In many common instances, the sanctions behind policies are not legal penalties but arise from custom and usage: for instance, in the case of decisions made outside of the formal machinery of government, as by a party caucus or convention. The same is true (but less obviously) of some formal decisions, say legislative or Cabinet resolutions. Locke himself expected rulers and subjects alike to be bound in conscience by his version of the 'laws of nature.' Force and legal penalties alone seldom, if ever, make a policy binding. Indeed, force and law are usually quite ineffective unless policies are also enforced by other social institutions and assented to on grounds of their 'legitimacy.' The sanctions of the legally enforcible decisions are those of 'law plus' while those of many, perhaps most, political policies are not legal sanctions at all, but rest simply upon the common agreement to regard them as binding, which in turn rests upon moral, customary, religious, or other obligation. These are the 'bonds and ligaments of the Commonwealth, the pillars and sustainers of every written statute.' In this sense, a political settlement of disputes—in caucus or party, for instance—is an alternative to a legally enforcible settlement.

The point can be made in another way by asking: in what sense do we look upon politics as supreme or paramount, and upon economic, literary, or ecclesiastical decisions, or those dealing with women's fashions, as *not* supreme? The usual answer is to say that the political can fall back upon the legal penalties, the monopoly of force held by government—'in the last resort.' But this answer, I am suggesting, is insufficient and hence partly misleading, since it does not distinguish the political from the legal. It is equally true, and of much more importance in understanding politics, that 'in the last resort' popular obedience (roughly, acceptance, or regarding political policies and agreements as binding) is forthcoming for other reasons or sanctions than law, even where law is concerned. The sense in which the political-governmental is supreme is in its comprehensive function of finally reconciling and arbitrating social disputes—a function which in turn rests upon the sanction of 'law plus,' and often, indeed, upon the 'plus' alone without the law.

The *third* meaning or characteristic of political policies is that they connote conflict and dispute. This is possibly the most misunderstood aspect of what is usually meant by politics and the political. The very language of 'policies,' 'decisions,' and 'agreements,' carries the implication of choice and alternatives, of conflicts to be settled, at least for the time being. Policies are inevitably hammered out of dispute not only because conflict, as well as cohesion, is endemic in any society but also because policies refer to courses of action for the future: they contain the notion of time and novelty and hence of expectation and estimate; of contingent circumstances as well as general principles. 'Decision is choice under uncertainty.'[1] Proof or demonstration is impossible beforehand since no one knows the future or the full consequences of any act; general principles alone can never settle a particular dispute, and hence there is always room for disagreement over policies.

Relations between individuals may be regarded as the fundamental concept of any study of society (that is why psychology is not a *social* science), and although not all such relations are political (e.g. those between lovers or friends), yet political relations involve at least two persons. Robinson Crusoe is much beloved of economic theory, but he is of no use at all to political theory until Friday comes on the scene. Political relations arise when men agree on some things and disagree on others, when there is some compatibility and some conflict, both common and conflicting interests, both partnership and competition, out of which a binding policy is to be shaped. We may say then that the function of politics is to compromise, to mitigate, and sometimes to transcend the conflicting interests and loyalties.

[1] Cf. G. L. S. Shackle, *Time in Economics*, Amsterdam, 1958.

... every society has its political aspect, *in so far as* discussion of policy and of desirable change goes on, and there is some recognized procedure for making decisions. Under 'politics' we may include not only methods of bringing pressure to bear on the making of decisions, but the discussion and procedures by which decisions are made.[2] [My italics]

No political problem in this third sense arises when there is only harmony and unanimity, and so we say that matters on which we are unanimous or virtually so are 'beyond politics.' There is in fact an ambiguity here in the ordinary usage of 'political.' Of any matter that is 'beyond politics,' we may mean either or both of two things: (a) it may be left entirely alone by government, as with the rules of etiquette and cooking, or the many social disputes which are always going on (and which politicians may, for example, regard as too 'hot' to handle) ; (b) it may be related to government, but be virtually beyond dispute, such as the principle of adult suffrage or of compulsory school education or of a nationalized postal system, or the American decision to declare war on Japan after Pearl Harbor. A distinction may thus be drawn between government and 'political' government, although by long tradition the political studies concern themselves with non-political government as well, and will no doubt continue to do so. If they did not, there would be no such subject as public administration.

Politics, then, is not only controversy but also a method by which disputes are settled and conflicts resolved in arriving at policies that are binding and related to government. But the political method is not used in making the absolutely best policy after the manner of Plato's ideal republic, or when decisions are made by a dictator, or when we are unanimous, although in all these cases there may be much or little government. Neither— although I cannot argue the case here—is politics very much like the scientific enterprise. Political problems are of a different order from those of science or technology and so technical knowledge is not particularly qualified to settle them, though it is of course relevant. How to make the H Bomb is a technical matter,

2 Dorothy M. Emmett, *Function, Purpose and Powers,* London, 1958, p. 132.

but whether to make it, how much money to divert to it from other uses, whether or when it should be dropped—are all political and governmental questions of the highest order.

The subject matter of the political studies, then, is the governing function, which is performed by means of those policies which are (a) related to formal government and (b) normally binding on all members. To this, if the governing is performed in a political manner—the third sense outlined above—may be added (c) that the policies emerge from conflict and dispute, whether openly conducted as in a free society, or suppressed and driven underground as in a despotism.[3]

Now this is admittedly a somewhat vague threefold criterion of what makes up politics and the political.[4] What does 'related to' formal government mean? How far from the formal machinery must we get to reach the limit of the political? Where can we stop in considering policies—their origin, formation, execution, or sanctions? But to set any more precise limits in advance would exclude a great deal of the existing political studies; while any broadening would make the political synonymous with *all* social policies and *all* methods of social control, and the political studies would become swallowed up by sociology.

What actual disputes are regarded as political, and so within the scope of political studies, will vary from time to time and place to place. Matters may move into and out of the sphere of politics. (The wisdom of having particular matters tossed into the political arena and the traditional question of the 'proper' functions of government are not being discussed here. Libraries

---

[3] We know more now of the kind of underground palace politics that went on in Hitler's Germany, thanks to such books as Trevor-Roper's *The Last Days of Hitler*. We know little, however, of the 'suppressed politics' that goes on in the Soviet Union in the absence there of recognized channels of politicking.

[4] Merriam suggests that it is not one, but the accumulation of characteristics that is more helpful in marking off the political from other aspects of society. He lists the reference to the territorial organization (the state), the generality of its purposes (in contrast to the specific purposes of other organizations), the penalties or sanctions, and the finality of the decisions (for the time being). C. E. Merriam, 'Political Power,' Chapter 1 in *A Study of Power* by Lasswell, Merriam, Smith; Glencoe, Illinois, 1950.

of books have been written around that theme.) If anyone drags anything into the sphere of public dispute related to government it becomes *ipso facto* political. What else could we label it without debasing our language of communication? Yet there is an absurd and dangerous tendency in some quarters to take debatable and debated policies out of politics by trying to shut off debate, and worse, to make of elected persons that monstrous contradiction known as 'non-political' politicians.[5] In the modern world all countries appear to be growing increasingly regulated by governments, and our best hope in the democracies seems to me to be that public policy-making should always remain political. It will not have escaped notice that the third sense of political noted above does in fact best fit democratic politics, though politics is always a matter of degree, taking place in any country in the proportion that political liberties and channels for politicking exist. The idea of government emerged at a comparatively late stage in man's history; the idea of politics, as legitimate dispute about public policies, is still emerging.

The search for a rigorous definition of subject matter seems to be a late and sophisticated stage in the growth of many disciplines, taking place only when their pursuit has become self-conscious and critical and is seething with 'creative' activity (or at any rate with discontent). Each of the social studies, as it has grown and become specialized, has tried to define more closely the aspect of life in society which it examines; aspects which, although not purely arbitrary, are marked off from one another only by definition and abstraction, and the shifting interests of the discipline. But neither human beings nor societies can be chopped into pieces, and so it is hard to isolate the political or the moral or the economic or any other single aspect of life. Each of the social studies selects as the object of its attention—its sub-

---

[5] A monarch or president can be 'beyond' or 'above politics' only if he has no political power: give him power to make policies and he will become embroiled in dispute. The yearning for a Patriot King or President with power but beyond politics is at its best an inferior kind of Platonic notion. Even Bolingbroke, whose name is inevitably associated with the Patriot King as a remedy for a corrupted nation, was shrewd enough to see that a Patriot King 'is himself a sort of standing miracle.'

ject matter—a different aspect of society. Consequently each is incomplete as a general theory of society, since none deals with the entire social 'system.' There are no water-tight compartments in personal life or in society. (In primitive societies the political, the legal, the religious, and other aspects may be so fused together that no distinction between them may be possible.)

Nevertheless, what is joined together in society may be put asunder in thought for purposes of study, and the separate aspects may be studied by specialists, if only because the whole is too much for any one person to handle. In these respects, the social studies are like the natural sciences, which are also pursued by specialists and between whose territories also there are no sharp boundary lines. It is the hard core, not the periphery, by which any subject is defined. Differences of degree are everything in separating the social studies, as they are in politics itself, e.g. in distinguishing domestic and foreign policy, or policy and administration.

Since there is not, as yet anyway, an agreed framework of unifying theory, comparable to scientific or even economic theory, by which to explain and order political data, the best we can do is to organize theoretical and practical inquiries around some center or focal point. It is only the focus, or selective interest, as MacIver once said, which divides the various social studies. I have suggested for the political studies the focus of public policy, or the binding decisions relating to government and arising from dispute.

In putting governmental and political policy at the center of the inquiry, I am implying that to do so is more enlightening (will advance more our understanding and knowledge) than to concentrate on the state, or law, or power, or equilibrium, or control, or other unifying concepts which have been put forward from time to time. There is some confirmation for the view expressed here in the fashionable emphasis today on the policy 'sciences.' [6]

Moreover, this view of what the political studies are centered

[6] These are all the sciences which assist in policy-making (by governments). They are, however, science as 'means' and make no pretense of assessing different ends or goals. The choosing of goals (values) is disclaimed, as in such disparaging remarks as 'the higher abstractions from which his [man's] values are derived.' Harold D. Lasswell and Daniel Lerner eds., *The Policy Sciences*, Stanford, 1951, p. 12.

upon is not merely personal and stipulative. The governing function of society has always been in one way or another the subject of political studies, and the traditional inquiries of political philosophy can be accommodated to this focus upon policy by adding the notion of politics as controversy and as a method of settling disputes. The next question which arises is: what kind of knowledge do we seek, in political *theory*, about our subject matter?

WHAT DO WE MEAN BY A POLITICAL 'THEORY'?

The significance of the governing function lies in the making and executing of public policies for the society concerned. In sophisticated societies the function is performed by a specialized set of social institutions which, taken collectively, we may fairly enough call the 'political system.'

Now it is well known that political or economic systems may be classified in different ways. Economic systems differ from one another in how they make the economic decisions, i.e. in how they satisfy man's economic wants, and they are usually studied from this point of view. Political systems may be approached in a similar manner, classified and studied by their treatment of the political, i.e. by how the binding policies relating to government are made in the political conflict. Each type of political system presumably has a theory appropriate to it, a more or less cohesive body of principles on which it operates, and a body of normative beliefs to justify it. A complete political theory, then, we may say explains and justifies a political system.

Regarded in this way, anarchism is a political system (nowhere in existence) which dispenses with government in all ordinary meanings of the word. At the other extreme is a totalitarian system where politics in the sense of legitimate public controversy are submerged but virtually everything is assimilated to the governmental. Between these logical opposites an almost infinite variety of political systems is possible; history and the literature of political philosophy are full of them.

A democratic system—which is our quarry here—is, in common usage, one that is marked by many popular disagreements and disputes about policies, where all policies are made in a context of political freedoms, and where the final decisions of government are made by representatives freely elected on a wide, usually universal, suffrage. A democratic system is not only governmental and administrative—all systems, except anarchism, are that—but it is also the most political of all systems, in that disputes are open and continuous, going on between elections as well as during campaigns, and often being settled for the time being without reference to the arbitrament of law. It is also, I think, the most complicated of systems both to explain and to justify, and this helps to account for the almost endless confusions in the many theories of democracy.

Not all political theories are so wide as to embrace an entire political system; the minor strains—for instance, Protestant or existentialist political thought or the Single-Tax scheme of Henry George—are not complete theories which outline alternative political systems and explain and justify them. They cover a narrower range of political data and for the most part are content to advocate particular policies, or else they are concerned with the general principles underlying such policies. Other minor strains of theory deal with only one or a few empirical generalizations, e.g. that political parties tend to be oligarchical. These minor or less comprehensive theories may all fairly be described as *partial* political theories.

All theories, whether partial or complete, have some common ground. For one thing political systems overlap and are never found as 'pure types,' all mutually exclusive. For another, a case for government is shared by all theories except that of anarchism.

Political theories, whether partial or complete, typically contain a number of standard ingredients. These may be classified into three groups. First, they all have a purely factual and descriptive component, just as history, no matter how interpretative, has its purely chronological and descriptive elements. The second component, shading imperceptibly out of the first, is made up of the generalizations which reduce to order the huge mass of political data and the complications of policy-making. Such empirically-based generalizations aspire to the neutrality if not the precision of science, and at their most ambitious in reliability and generality, are sometimes called laws or principles. It is these empirical generalizations and hypotheses that we chiefly have in mind when we think of the function of a political theory as that of explaining a political system by laying bare its operating principles.[7]

Third, there is the moral component. The economist usually thinks of his task as a science of means: how to maximize the community values. But the values themselves he takes as 'given.' Political philosophers have seldom worked within these self-imposed limits, but have usually been more concerned with the goals than with the political means to reach them, with legitimatizing political rule in moral terms as well as with neutral explanation. That is, they have been philosophers (in the older sense) openly moral in their approach, occasionally going so far as to sketch ideal states, as in Plato's *Republic*. Sometimes political philosophers have gone beyond the moral to more general philosophy or metaphysics, or even to theology and revealed religion, into which they have fitted their political prescriptions. In Plato's political theory it is plain that both the purposes and forms of government are thought to follow logically (or at any rate to be inseparable) from the first principles of his world outlook, his Forms of the Good and the True. In other theories there may not be the same close connection betweeen fundamental philosophical or religious beliefs and their political application. The relation between philosophy and political theory is much debated and sadly confused, but cannot be explored here.

The mixture of description, neutral generalization, and moral principle is not of course found in the same proportion in all political theories. As a rule, the older the theory the more broadly ethical it is, and the more subordinate is the purely descriptive and neutral. Plato and Aquinas are at this extreme, both being openly moral in the very basis of their theory and in the prescrip-

[7] The difficulty of doing empirical research on important general principles often leads to large expenditures of energy and money on the easy and the trivial; as someone has said, what is found out may not be important, but at least it will be well documented, and it might even be true.

tions which they make, while the factual and causal elements are mostly implied or incidental. At the other end of the scale are men such as Hobbes, Machiavelli, Bentham, and Marx, with the factual and 'scientific' elements to the fore, while the morality is mostly implied and occasionally not even recognized. The apparent absence of the moral element, where it has not been explicit or on occasion even recognized, has lent a spurious air of science to what in fact is disguised moral philosophy, as in the theories of Comte and Marx.

All complete political theories, then, consist of this mingling of description, generalization merging into causal theory, and justification which is, whether knowingly or not, moral in its basis. Some theories emphasize one element more than another, and hence theories are occasionally classified into the empirical and the prescriptive. Even the more modest attempts at partial theories, which go by the name of political 'thought' or 'ideas' have these same ingredients; and so too, pre-eminently, have the everyday political disputes over particular policies within any one political system.

Now if we wish to examine a contemporary political theory such as that of democracy, where do we look to find it? The *first* and more direct approach is to take note of the theories corresponding to the different political systems—those theories, often called 'isms' or 'ideologies,' by which they are explained and defended. But the same system may give rise to conflicting theories, since theories can both explain and denounce as well as explain and defend a system. The Marxist theory of 'capitalist democracy' is for instance quite irreconcilable with that of most democrats. Even the apologists do not always expound the same doctrine of democracy, as we shall see later.

Consequently, we must resort to a *second* source of political theory: the political system itself. We must try to deduce or disentangle the operative principles and ideals from the actual working of a political system; we cannot rely on the consciously held ideology, which may be quite different and contain many fashionable fictions. The implicit, whether neutral or normative, is difficult to disentangle from practice, because it consists of the unexpressed assumptions underlying the practical art; operative beliefs are often inarticulate, embedded with the values they contain in the political system itself.

Third, since any political system and its theory contains elements from the past, we may go to the classics. For democracy we go to Locke, Rousseau, Mill and others—perhaps as far back as the Athenian democrats—although present theory may have much that we cannot find in the classic thinkers.

Finally, in the contemporary world—or in those parts where politics and inquiry are not suppressed—we must also go to the academic researchers, not only for much of the descriptive material but also for many hypotheses. Here, then, is a fourth rich source of theory—the original constructions arising from or tested by current empirical research. In a sense it is a source which may also be highly personal, so that everyone is his own political theorist, finding and offering evidence for his own hypotheses, as all political philosophers have attempted to do, however crudely, from time immemorial.

Conscious theory is never a mere photograph of the data. It aims at abstraction and generalization, and consequently never describes the particular and the unique. Because political theory has, however, usually aimed at being useful for policy decisions, it has seldom proceeded by the method of building analytical models after the fashion of economic theory, and consequently is less often subject to the charge of being 'remote' or 'useless.' On the other hand, it is often accused of being 'apologetics'; a charge which must certainly stand in the case of ideologies.

But a political theory nevertheless aims at consistency and coherence, in spite of the fact that political life is sprawling, untidy, and inconsistent when judged by canons of strict logic. It is the business of theory to precipitate out the anomalies and solecisms which are held in solution in our everyday actions and beliefs. Theory always tends to grow self-conscious, critical, and analytic in any reasonably free society, and consequently there is always 'a strain to consistency.' As anomalies are exposed, they tend to be removed.

Now if political theories have the characteristics mentioned, and more besides, some consequences seem to follow for 'methodology'—or methods of pursuing and assessing political theory. Because a political outlook, however ostensibly untidy, is somehow fused together in the person and in society, an effort of sympathetic imagination must be made to understand the fusion or coherence which is made in the complexities of a political system and its ideology. 'History, logic, experiment, insight, intuition, invention—none of these is foreign to the search for truth in the study of government.'[8] Whether a theory challenges an ideology or supports a system, it cannot rely on the empirical approach alone; like all social theory it will consist, too, of conceptual analysis, of a wide variety of methods of practical and theoretical construction and testing, each of them valid, none alone sufficient.

APPRAISING A POLITICAL THEORY

Why should we want to study political theory at all? Apart from cultural reasons (which are in themselves perfectly valid), or possibly disciplined thinking (a reason seldom given nowadays for any study because claimed for all), there are three reasons usually put forward.

The first of these is to assist in the disinterested understanding either of the past or of the contemporary political scene. It is impossible to understand any historical period, including our own, without knowing its political systems, the principles upon which they operate, and their official purposes or ideals.

The second reason is perhaps more common: political theory is influential.[9] Instead of being useless, political theory has the

8 Charles E. Merriam, *Systematic Politics*, Chicago, 1945, p. ix. Because political studies like other social studies are something of an art, like medicine, they require insight, sensitivity, and sympathy, as well as scientific method. That is why some social research strikes us as blundering or unenlightening—it lacks the diagnostic qualities which a good practitioner displays.

9 A justification for teaching political science to large numbers of university students lies in the value this study is alleged to have in building better citizens. 'The training of citizens is one of the major goals of American political science.' *Goals for Political Science*, Report of the Committee for the Advancement of Teaching, A.P.S.A., New York, 1951, p. 24. 'Training for citizenship' is a highsounding but woolly and in some respects repellent ideal.

most far-reaching political effects both in undermining and in supporting political systems. Students in an ivory tower, like Marx in the British Museum, can upset the world. We study theory so that it may illuminate and guide behavior with respect to our own political system. This, too, was the aim of all the classic thinkers in political theory. 'Knowledge for what?'

The third reason, while not entirely separable from the first two, may be distinguished for purposes of discussion. It is a reason of paramount concern to many in this day of 'isms' and ideologies: to assess the different systems and theories offered for inspection, to find out which of them is better or truer. Many people come to the study of philosophy for the same reason: to find out what they can believe and build their lives around.

Regarded in this manner, a political theory is studied in order to appraise a political system as well as to understand it. Indeed, the crowning achievement in the study and construction of political theory is to assess: that is what gives point to the whole undertaking. There is, in simple fact, no avoiding judgment and commitment, since we must adopt attitudes every day toward political systems and their theories no matter how unaware we may be of doing so. At once, however, a serious obstacle confronts us. Everyone would grant that we may, in principle, apply empirical tests to the factual and explanatory part of a theory, but what criteria do we use to test the prescriptive elements— their truth and validity as well as their feasibility?

To deal at all adequately with this great question would require a minor treatise on moral philosophy, so that a brief statement of the position adopted here must suffice. My position is that we can and do appraise and judge political theories, both their empirical and moral components. On the other hand, I do not claim that one can 'prove' or demonstrate every political belief, whether neutral or moral—and still less a whole theory— beyond any shadow of doubt.

The view that one must have either demonstrable certainty or sheer skepticism about political or other beliefs is nonsense,

---

which I cannot discuss here. Political science also has a more humdrum vocational aspect—especially in training for government and university employment.

and poses two quite unrealistic alternatives. Most of the continuing controversy between the 'absolutist' and the 'relativist' is a waste of time except as it clears the air somewhat. Human life would be quite impossible if all we had to go by was either certainty or doubt. There are degrees of reliability in all our beliefs—the simple factual, the empirical, the moral, or whatever they may be. Political beliefs, and a whole theory, can then be judged or justified, and some theories can emerge better from a battery of tests than others; that is, better justification can be offered for some than for others.[10]

Neither a political system nor a theory can be judged by its origins; nor is the truth of beliefs affected by the personal motives of those who hold them. Discussing truth and error is not the same as attributing sin. Beliefs can be explained in a genetic and historical manner but they are not thereby explained away, since origins neither validate nor invalidate our present values.[11]

The first test of a good theory is that it fit the system which it purports to explain, i.e. it must present the operative principles and norms by which the system actually operates, as well as take note of the official ideology. A good political system is, alas, sometimes justified by reference to a poor theory. Second, the empirical generalizations must be distinguished from the normative principles in a theory—often no easy task—and the case for each must be weighed. Neither the explanatory principles nor the justification of the moral elements is ever conclusively established; nor is a political theory in its entirety like a well-established scientific theory. We do not 'defend' the laws of gravitation: we point to evidence which shows them to be true, evidence which is capable of 'convincing the Gods themselves.'

Third, principles must be traced back to their 'ultimates,' a process which cannot go on indefinitely since somewhere faith,

[10] Cf. D. N. Morgan, 'Is Justification Scientifically Impossible?', in *Ethics*, vol. LXIX, Oct. 1958, pp. 19-48.

[11] No doubt there is a common tendency to invent noble origins for our values, as for our ancestry, but to do this is to run the risk of disillusion when the origins turn out to be lowly. Think of Soames Forsyte. It was, I think, the deeply cherished mistake of linking origins and values which caused so much hostility to the theory of evolution in the last century and to the theories of psychoanalysis in this century.

like time, must have a stop, whether in moral, epistemological, or metaphysical ultimates. Fourth, there is the opposite process to that of tracing principles back to their ultimates: the tracing of them forward, by deduction and other means, to the practical consequences or implications which flow from them, since only by showing their consequences can we understand, let alone judge their full meaning. Again, no ideal can be judged or understood in isolation from the means and conditions necessary for its achievement. Neither can we judge a political system and its theory apart from some of the historical context, or some historical 'explanation'—a respect in which a political theory is unlike scientific truth, which is universal and a-historical.

Other tests, mixing the formal and empirical, are both possible and necessary: what are the values inherent in the system as a whole, as distinct from those in the separate component principles? How feasible or realistic is the system or policy advocated? How plausible is the theory in today's climate of opinion which is so heavily secular and scientific? What of the logical rigor and coherence and interdependence mentioned in the preceding section? Is the theory compatible with what is known in other fields of modern knowledge? How broad and inclusive is the range of data brought within its scope? Above all, the best way to test a theory is to attempt to refute it—a procedure well-known in science where the 'force of the negative instance is the greater.' But to discuss such criteria further would be out of place here.

When the whole battery of possible tests has been applied, it will still be impossible to put Q. E. D. after one theory and turn all others out of court. After laying bare and examining a contemporary theory of democracy we shall come out with a theory for which a case has been made—a defense, a justification. No rational and empirical case is finally verified, or must of necessity be believed. We ought therefore to carry our theories lightly, in face of the ignorance of even the wisest among us.

Political ideologies always combine, more or less felicitously, factual propositions and value judgments. They express an outlook on the world and a will orientated towards the future. They cannot be described as literally true or false, nor do they belong to the same category as taste and colour. The ultimate philosophy and the hierarchy of preferences invite discussion rather than proof or refutation . . . [12]

A final point. Even if our theory of democracy turns out to be reasonable and justified, that in itself is not what gives a theory or system popular support. We are born into a political system, we absorb its ethos, we learn the appropriate beliefs and attitudes. Our convictions, especially those with a moral component, get their vitality from many sources which we may sum up as the experiences we meet in life. Reason may be 'the crown of life . . . but it is not the most powerful of all human forces.' [13] In order to generate enthusiasm, beliefs do not need demonstration, but faith or hope or hate or other strong emotions. As Newman put it, 'many a man will live and die upon a dogma; no man will be a martyr for a conclusion.' All this may be granted, but our commitment to truth compels us to submit our theories to the tests which the intelligence can devise. Only if these can be passed can we safely call upon other supports as well—will, imagination, historical tradition, and the like.

[12] Raymond Aron, *The Opium of the Intellectuals*, London, 1957, p. 236.
[13] Morris Cohen, *A Dreamer's Journey* (Autobiography), Boston, 1949, p. 190.

TWO | *The Problem of Defining Democracy*

INTRODUCTORY

At first glance, democracy appears to be an immensely popular political theory nowadays, far more popular than it was twenty years ago. At that time two large European countries—Germany and Italy—proclaimed their adherence to theories that were elitist, authoritarian, and violently anti-democratic. Occasionally, it is true, Hitler called his system 'real' democracy, and Mussolini once described Fascism as 'an organized, centralized, and authoritarian democracy,' but these atypical remarks need not confuse us; for the most part the Nazis and Fascists rejected democracy, and boasted of doing so. Today nearly all the world, including a number of communist countries, has kind words for democracy.

After the Second World War, UNESCO sponsored a study which obtained the views of more than a hundred scholars, both East and West, on democracy. Surprisingly enough:

> ... there were no replies adverse to democracy. Probably for the first time in history, democracy is claimed as the proper ideal description of all systems of political and social organisation advocated by influential proponents.[1]

All this praise and prevalence of democracy appears very reassuring. If spokesmen for countries of all kinds—capitalist, communist, Christian, Hindu, Muslim, and Jewish—profess their belief in democratic principles, where is, then, the 'conflict of

[1] *Democracy in a World of Tensions*, UNESCO, Paris, 1951, p. 527.

ideologies' of which we hear so much? Is the conflict merely over the use of words, a trivial semantic dispute, behind which there is a fundamental agreement on the methods and purposes of politics and government? Alas, no. Although the label of 'democracy' is used by all parties, the conflict of political theories, as of political systems, is real and deep enough. Although we are all (or nearly all) in favor of 'democracy,' we are not on that account in favor of the same political theory or system.

The different schools of thought, calling themselves democratic, are arguing about fundamental questions: about how public policies are and should be made in a political system, and often about what they should *be*. Some indeed are also arguing that democracy is a social and economic, as well as a political system and theory. Some are defending what they regard as more basic philosophic beliefs—moral or metaphysical or theological—on which their theories of democracy are built, or thought to be built. This sort of confusion, with apparent agreement on the surface but deep disagreement underneath, is nothing unusual among men. The word 'Christian,' for instance, is used in common by more than two-and-seventy jarring sects, many of them quite irreconcilable. Much the same holds of a great many ambiguous or portmanteau words in common use: love, goodness, justice, religion, decency, liberty, equality, and so on.

Since there is then a considerable number of theories bearing the label 'democracy,' to find a generally acceptable method of arranging, if not of disentangling, them is of some importance.

THE MEANING OF MEANING

As a preliminary clearing of the ground, it may be helpful to distinguish several different kinds of meaning or definition which words may have, limiting our comment to those relevant to our purpose here. The most common kind of meaning is that given to words by ordinary usage and reported in the dictionaries. Some confusion is, of course, possible even here, since words sometimes have more than one such meaning, and meanings alter through time. The common or lexicographic meaning of 'democracy' which it has had since the days of Athenian greatness is 'government or rule by the people.' It refers, that is, to a method of governing, and does so by specifying who rules, or makes the binding policy decisions in a state. Any contemporary attempt at a definition will cause less confusion if it keeps close to this original meaning of 'democracy,' given to it by long historical usage.

A related kind of meaning is the technical definition of a word, given to it by the authority and agreement of specialists such as biologists or physicists, who habitually use it in a fixed sense in their technical discourse. Again, some confusion may arise, in this case because the popular usage may differ from the technical meaning. Although there are, in the political studies, a number of technical words with fixed meanings, unfortunately 'democracy' is not one of them. The technical sense of meaning therefore need concern us no longer.

A third type of meaning is often met with, which leads to far more confusion than the first two types put together. This is where persons or whole schools of thought give a word a special meaning to suit themselves. Lewis Carroll's Humpty Dumpty is the patron saint of all those who use words with this personal, particular, and unique kind of meaning.

'Democracy' is much abused in this private and stipulative fashion. To one, 'democracy' means a Christian society; to another, a society 'with liberty and justice for all'; to still others, an economic system of private enterprise or of socialism; while to others it may stand for an attitude toward life, or even something called a 'way of life.' In all these usages 'democracy' may or may not have anything to do with a specific type of government or method of arriving at public policies. There is hardly any end to the special and personal meanings which are given to 'democracy,' until it is no wonder that public discussion of 'democracy' is almost a complete Babel, or that much of the writing is inspirational in character, generating vague feelings of uplift about nothing in particular.

People who define 'democracy' in this stipulative way often use the words 'true' or 'real' as prefixes. Thus: 'Democracy is commonly taken to mean government by the people, but of course "true" democracy is . . .' and then follows the rest of the unique and persuasive definition. It is a sound rule to suspect all definitions that include 'real' or 'true.' These prefixes are signs which show the alert listener that a word is not being used in its ordinary (lexicographic) or technical senses. When used with 'democracy,' they tell us a good deal about the political beliefs of the speaker, but they do not tell us what most other people mean by 'democracy.'

There is one other great source of confusion in meaning. It is the idea that words have some intrinsic or essential meaning waiting to be discovered; that there is some metaphysical essence or quintessence behind the word, having nothing to do with ordinary usage or technical definition by agreement, so that if we analyze a word long enough we shall arrive at its inner, 'real,' 'true' meaning, or essence. This was Plato's way of looking at meaning or definition, 'the account of the essence of the thing.' Whatever the faults of the linguistic analysts, in their 'battle against the bewitchment of our intelligence by means of language,' they have at least emancipated millions from this ancient and erroneous doctrine. (The linguistic analysts were not the first to show the error and futility of seeking 'true' meanings or essences in words. Locke, for instance, did the same.)

Finally, to end this simple preamble, words like 'democracy' are often used not so much to convey information as to persuade and arouse emotions, whether favorable or unfavorable. Advertisers and orators are the professional experts in this emotive and persuasive art of definition. Many if not all words have a general drift or 'aura.' Words which have strong emotive meaning are sometimes known as 'boo' words, or 'hurrah' words, the latter being what Veblen used to call 'honorific.'

HISTORICAL REACTION TO DEMOCRACY

The emotions and attitudes aroused by democracy have changed several times in the course of history. When Pericles spoke of democracy in his speeches to the Athenians he spoke with pride, as anyone may see who reads his wonderful Funeral Oration, and he was applauded by his listeners. There is probably no better statement in the world which so captures the spirit of a political ideal. But to Plato, shortly afterward, 'democracy' was a word that generally stirred only unfavorable reactions. In Aristotle, the feelings aroused were more mixed, but one must say that on the whole they tended to be unfavorable. To them both, though perhaps not always to Aristotle, 'democracy' stood for rule by the many, and since the many were mostly the poor and the ignorant, it seemed to them that such rule would be quite unenlightened, as well as likely to prove oppressive for the rich.[2]

It is scarcely too much to say that the word stood for much the same beliefs, and aroused similar unfavorable emotions, for the next two thousand or so years. 'Democracy' began to be used again, with favorable connotations, in 17th-century England, for example by the Levellers, although there is no doubt that the original idea of rule by the people (or its near relative, the idea of a popular share and influence in government, or more distant relative, the idea that all legitimate authority is derived from the people) had been raised from time to time, with approval by some, during the intervening two millennia. Yet even as late as the latter part of the 18th century, democracy was not thought well of by most people, and certainly not by most of the educated or ruling classes. For the most part, it was also used with disapproval by the Founding Fathers of the American Constitution, who preferred republicanism as a word and a theory of government, though some of them occasionally gave the name 'republicanism' to what would often be called 'democracy' today. But during the 19th century, democracy—both the word and the political system it stood for—largely overcame its ill repute, and grew rapidly in public esteem.

A tidal wave of popularity for democracy swept around the world during and after the First World War.[3] This was to be

2 Some attempt has been made—unsuccessfully, I think—'to demonstrate that Plato and Aristotle believed fundamentally in the essence of democracy.' W. K. Prentice, *The Greek Political Experience*, Princeton, 1941, pp. 193 ff.

3 Thus Viscount Bryce (although he had doubts of the prospects of democracy) could write in 1920 of: '...the universal acceptance of democracy as the normal and natural form of government. Seventy years ago—the word Democracy awakened dislike and fear. Now it is a word of praise. Popular power is welcomed, extolled, worshipped. The few whom it repels or alarms rarely avow their sentiments.' James Bryce, *Modern Democracies*, New York, 1921, vol. I, p. 4.

the century of the common man, of popular influence upon government, and of the self-determination of nations. Even Mussolini, in the early 1920's, joined in this paean of praise to democracy. There was a fall away from the high peak of enthusiasm, especially during the thirties, but today democracy is almost universally popular again. A mention of democracy will generally arouse a favorable if vague reaction, and hence the widespread use of the word in political speeches, on ceremonial occasions, and in daily life. 'Democracy' is an honorific and persuasive word even within the Soviet Union, although when it is used there, two or three kinds of 'democracy' are distinguished: the bourgeois or 'sham democracy' of the capitalist world, their own proletarian or 'real democracy,' and the 'people's democracies' of the East European satellites and China. That is, the Soviet Communists have appropriated the label 'democracy' because it arouses so many favorable feelings, but have cleverly given it quite different meanings. Elsewhere in the world too, dozens of other groups do the same, until we may well wonder—half sadly, half cynically—whether language is not more useful at hindering rather than helping the communication of ideas.

Even when democracy has been most popular, there has always been an undercurrent of disapproval and dislike for it. This dislike has manifested itself not only in that some countries have at one time or another rejected a democratic system—as in Italy or Argentina—but also in the continuing stream of criticism from within the western democracies themselves, by Fascists, Communists, cynics, spokesmen for many elitist theories, and others. W. H. Lecky, Sir Henry Maine, Thomas Carlyle, John Ruskin, and to some extent Macaulay were all severe and sometimes quite angry 19th-century critics of democracy. H. L. Mencken never mentioned the word without a sneer and about the best he could say, in a comment that sounds like an echo of Plato, was:

> I do not believe in democracy, but I am perfectly willing to admit that it provides the only really amusing form of government ever endured by mankind.[4]

[4] *A Mencken Chrestomathy*, New York, 1953, p. viii.

Tocqueville, on the other hand, while pointing out the defects of 'Democracy in America,' did accept its inevitability and also took note of some of its virtues—points often forgotten by those who copy out Tocqueville's criticisms more or less accurately and take them for the whole truth.

Today, too, there is a substantial and perhaps increasing flow of criticism which often combines nostalgia for the earlier, less democratic times with peevishness and disillusionment.[5] The emotive meaning of democracy is thus not uniformly favorable. And wherever it is not favorable, it usually carries with it the ancient connotation of rule by the many—interpreted to mean the masses and the mob, both of which are 'boo' words.[6] In the case of many others, as of Lecky, the dislike of democracy is plainly enough derived from the fear on behalf of property.

Where democracy is regarded favorably, however, it is given a wide variety of meanings that steadily increase in number the more popular democracy becomes. Clearly, it is not going to be easy to give any precise definition of democracy which would be (a) generally agreed upon, even in the western democracies, and (b) definite enough to mark off democracy from other political theories and systems. (We can hardly say that one definition is correct and all the others improper, or we shall end up in 'true' meanings or essences.) It must now be our task to salvage something more specific from the all-inclusive and ambiguous meanings of 'democracy.'

APPROACH TO DEMOCRACY AS A POLITICAL SYSTEM AND ITS THEORY

The approach taken here is to confine 'democracy' first of all to its ancient and still common usage as standing for a *political* theory and system. That is, I shall exclude all the wider mean-

5 The nostalgia is clearly evident in some of the contributions to *Parliament: A Survey*, by Lord Campion and others, London, 1952. The disillusioned tone is evident in such works as that of Walter Lippmann, *Essays in the Public Philosophy*, Boston, 1955; while the peevish and sometimes shrill note is sounded by some crusaders for the new style of American 'conservatism.'

6 The exception to this strain of criticism is the Marxist, which criticizes democracy (of the bourgeois type) precisely because it is *not* rule by the masses.

ings at first—the philosophical or 'way of life' aproach, the reference to social and economic arrangements, and the like—and concentrate only upon the reference to politics and government. If we cannot give democracy a core of agreed meaning in political terms, the prospects of finding a meaning somewhere else are dim indeed.

The old method of classifying governments or states which was invented by the Greeks gave three simple types in terms of the numbers of those who made the political decisions. If the assembled citizens as a whole (or a majority of them) made the final decisions, then the system was said to be a democracy; if at the other extreme one person made the decisions, then it was a monarchy (or in its bad form, a tyranny); if an intermediate number, a few, then it was an aristocracy (or in its bad form, an oligarchy). The Greeks were sensible enough to know that the pure form of any type was seldom if ever found in real life, but that most governments mixed the three types in varying proportions. A monarch was inevitably forced to delegate some decisions; some members of an oligarchy might influence decisions more than others; while even the whole citizen body delegated some authority to officials and relied in some degree upon the relatively few, whether politicians or technical experts.

The fundamental question, then, around which to organize this study of democracy is: how are public policies made in a democratic political system and what justification may be given for such a method? The assumptions are that different political systems employ different methods of political policy-making, and that one of these—which we call the democratic—has identifiable and characteristic features.

In more traditional language the question has usually been put as: who rules, or who should rule? The answer has often been phrased in terms of 'sovereignty'—and many and subtle are the discussions of 'sovereignty' in the literature of political theory.[7] The controversies have been interminable and inconclusive: is

---

[7] An analysis of the various meanings which have historically been given to 'sovereignty' is contained in *Philosophy, Politics, and Society,* ed. Peter Laslett, Oxford, 1956. A simple discussion is contained in the first-rate little book by G. C. Field, *Political Theory,* London, 1956, pp. 58 ff.

'sovereignty' inalienable, indivisible? Where does it reside? Where should it reside? What is its 'essence'? How many kinds are there? I do not propose to get entangled in that briarpatch, nor do I think it necessary to do so in order to formulate a political theory. It may be by-passed, and everything necessary may be put in terms of public policies which are normally obeyed or binding. From the point of view of the rulers, or decision-makers, this may be called 'sovereignty' (for those who prefer the older terminology), and from the point of view of the ruled it may be called obedience or perhaps consent (although consent is a more ambiguous notion).

To say that a political system is concerned with public policy-making allows for the fact that some decisions may be made by one authority (e.g. the legislature) and some by another (e.g. the courts); that decisions may be at all levels of generality, from the broad outlines of policy in a statute down to the smallest decision made by the lowest civil servant on the totem pole; and that in a federal system the decision-making is further dispersed and obedience further distributed; while some decisions are not made in the formal machinery of government at all, and do not rely on legal sanctions. It is not a matter of looking for the essence of 'sovereignty,' for something mysterious in the very 'nature of things.' It is the more mundane inquiry of identifying the principles on which a political system operates, those principles of organization according to which the political decisions are made, together with the moral and other justification offered on behalf of the separate principles and of the system as a whole. In answering the question of how policies are made in a democracy we shall also answer the traditional question of who *should* make the decisions and receive the obedience. Democracy is then one answer to the question of how the political policy decisions are made and should be made. It is both a political system and a theory to explain and justify it.

METHOD AND CONTENT

To make a method the chief distinguishing mark of a political system and its theory may strike many people as odd. Is it not more natural to be interested in *what* decisions are made? In the substance, rather than the procedures which are followed? Should not a political theory begin by setting up ends to be pursued by a political system—such as order, national security, justice, the 'good life,' and the like—and only then descend to the practical and show how they may best be achieved? After all, some may say, what does the procedure matter so long as the right results are obtained? The common attitude of indifference to methods is well expressed in the lines of Pope:

> O'er forms of government let fools contest,
> Whate'er is best administered is best.

If we are to judge by history, it seems to be well established that people have been far more interested in the substance of political and governmental decisions than in the niceties of the procedure by which they are reached. They have been concerned with peace, taxation, employment, justice; with grievances such as liability to military service, excessive bail, general warrants, harsh legal penalties, ex post facto laws, and so forth. When life has grown hard, or chaotic, it has always been tempting to sigh for a benevolent despot to reform, to ameliorate, to bring justice and order, i.e. to make 'wise' policies. It seems clear today, too, that the average Russian for example is not concerned greatly with the political liberties and a share in making public policy. He may distrust his governors, but his more vocal wants are specific: more consumer goods, leisure, economic opportunity, and less interference in his private life. He expects the state to provide these things, and if it does so he may well remain indefinitely contented with narrowly circumscribed political freedoms.

The same preference for results rather than methods may be something that we are all inclined to. At any rate, obedience to a system is rarely if ever unconditional, i.e. always given regardless of the results turned up by the system. The problem raised here is of the first magnitude for any political theory, and Bertrand de Jouvenel's recent book *Sovereignty* (Chicago, 1957) is devoted entirely to this question. More is said on this point later.

For the moment it is enough to illustrate the nature of the problem. Would we prefer (let us ask ourselves) an improper court decision or income-tax ruling in our favor, or a fair trial with a decision that went against us? A democracy that was anti-Semitic, imperialist, given to injustice, or an aristocratic system that was tolerant, peaceful, just, and promoted 'true religion'? [8] A democracy with a low standard of living or a benevolent despotism with a high one? These are obviously leading questions, they tend to play down our civilized concern with 'due process,' and we do not need to seize either horn of the dilemma; but no one ought to put 'democracy' as another name for Utopia, or take for granted that it will necessarily promote the aims which many individuals and groups would like to promote.

A definition of democracy is usually an attempt to find, in the sphere of government, the ideal state of things, or the best constitutional means of approaching the ideal, it being already agreed that this ideal includes or involves a large participation of the common people in the forming of public policy.[9]

But to define democracy in ideal terms at the start as 'good' government or a 'good" political system and to read into it all of our ideal ends, in all their diversity and conflict, is to rob the theory of all operational or empirical content. In short, communication on the subject of democracy will not only be confused (as it is already) but will also become virtually impossible (which it is not quite, yet).

This always seems to be a hard lesson for democrats to learn, for there is a strong tendency to identify democracy, by definition, with everything that is good, i.e. with the 'good' laws, policies, etc., which we want. The distinction between democracy and good government must, however, be made for purposes of analysis (and also to forestall personal disillusion in real life). The tendency to identify the real and the ideal is a quite under-

---

8 Similar 'mental experiments' are given in J. A. Schumpeter, *Capitalism, Socialism, and Democracy*, New York, 3rd ed. 1950, pp. 240 ff.

9 Richard Robinson, *Definition*, Oxford, 1949, p. 166.

standable one and is common in other fields than political theory. The process is something like this: we approve and give our loyalty to a theory ('democracy'), and then we read into it—and still worse, into the working system ('democracy')—our own highest personal ideals. It is very much like attributing to a friend or hero all the virtues which we think a friend or hero should have. Or again it is like our partisanship in games or national patriotism: having chosen our side, our loyalty leads us to identify *our* side with everything that is good, often in the face of the most discouraging evidence to the contrary.

Further, it can hardly be denied that for the most part political philosophers have started their inquiries with a consideration of the ends of the state—what government should do, or aim at—and only then have devised the form of government which seemed best calculated to promote these ends. Plato and Aristotle set the fashion, and they have been copied by most philosophers since. The ends which men have thought government should promote are legion; from vague and ultimate objectives such as the 'good life,' happiness, the 'development of personality,' justice, and the rights of man, to more apparently specific ends such as the preservation of domestic tranquillity, private property, national security, or a particular religion or economic system.

Now it has often been assumed in the past that the theory of democracy, too, should specify certain ends which democracy as a political system should pursue (other than those ends such as order and security which *all* governments by definition do pursue). Some folk approach the theory of democracy from this standpoint today, so that broadly speaking, all theories of democracy, like theories of other political systems, divide themselves into two classes. One class refers chiefly to the form or method of government, what we are calling the system of political policy-making; the other kind to the 'quality of life,' the moral purposes, or the content of the political policies. Although the two classes have been closely intertwined, it is possible to separate them for purposes of analysis; and as I have suggested, they must be separated if we are to understand the working of any existing democratic system, and if we are to avoid getting bogged down in innumerable, stipulative definitions of 'democracy.'

Democracy is a political method, that is to say, a certain type of institutional arrangement for arriving at political—legislative and administrative—decisions and hence incapable of being an end in itself, irrespective of what decisions it will produce under given historical conditions. And this must be the starting point of any attempt at defining it.[10]

Consider the analogy of an economic system. The chief social function of an economic system is to provide goods and services to satisfy human wants, and economic systems are distinguised from one another by how the economic decisions are made. One system may rely upon principles of competition and free pricing in the market; in others the decisions of what to produce, in what quantities, and at what prices may be made by immemorial custom or by a central authority. But the economic systems are not distinguishable by what goods and services are produced, and economic analysis never approaches them from that direction. Economic theory starts by examining how the economic decisions are made, how the economic problems are solved, and in doing so it identifies principles and lays bare their assumptions and their implied consequences. It does not start with philosophic discussions on the content of particular decisions, or the ideal standard of living.

The analogy of the political and the economic breaks down at some points—vital points—but I am suggesting that at this one point, namely, the approach via a method of decision-making, political theory may usefully follow economic theory. Instead of starting from the kind of public policies enacted, the content of the laws, or the 'proper' ends of the state, we may most usefully start with how the policies are made. We can then tentatively agree to call a democratic political system one which has characteristic principles of operation, both descriptive and normative. And a complete theory of democracy will be one which lays bare and justifies the separate principles of both kinds, and the system as a whole.

One cannot, of course, legislate on these things. No doubt 'democracy' will continue to be used by the public in vague and

---

10 Schumpeter, op. cit. p. 220.

ambiguous senses. Professional discourse can, however, set a good example, once political scientists reach general agreement or consensus on the kind of political system and theory they label 'democracy.' And the approach suggested here appears to me the only one at all likely to lead to general agreement in the profession.

THREE | *The Athenian Direct Democracy*

INTRODUCTORY

Throughout all the contemporary confusion over democracy one thing seems plain: the ancient Greeks were the first to give a democratic answer to the question of how to organize a political system. Or, at the very least, it is the Athenian example which is best known and has chiefly influenced political thought; and we have some obligation to understand the system. In considering the Athenian example we shall be keeping close to the original, historical, political meaning given to democracy and close also to common (though not universal) usage today; and so we shall reap the inestimable benefit of avoiding at the beginning all fancy stipulative meanings.

Athenian democracy was practiced in a small city-state, where the citizens themselves or a large sample of them could and did actually make many of the political decisions directly. Athens thus provides a working model of something close to the pure or extreme case of democracy, and we are saved the trouble of abstracting from contemporary democratic systems, of laboriously constructing a model after the fashion of the economists. With the simple model, it should be relatively easy to draw out implications, to lay bare principles and assumptions. Then again, Athenians such as Plato and Aristotle were philosophers—genuine and incomparable philosophers, not merely logical positivists, pragmatists, or instrumentalists—and we can make use of their analysis of the democracy of their time to help us understand it and pass judgment upon it. In doing so, we must remember, however, that Plato and Aristotle were critics, not supporters, of

Athenian democracy, and we must look to more sympathetic interpretations if we are to do Athens justice. We must remind ourselves too that Athens was not a small scale model of modern representative democracies, nor can we transplant Athenian institutions and thinking into the modern world. Yet it would be odd if there were no family likeness of principles whatever between ancient and modern democracies.

OPERATING PRINCIPLES OF THE ATHENIAN DEMOCRATIC SYSTEM

No attempt can be made here to sketch in the background, history, or cultural flowering of the Greek city-states. All that is given is a bare outline of those features or operating principles of the Athenian political system in the fifth century B.C. which the Athenians themselves regarded as making their state democratic, together with the chief theoretical ideas associated with the system and offered in its defense.[1]

In the first place, the citizens themselves made some of the political decisions directly, and controlled others, in contrast with other types of city-state where policy was both made and controlled by a few rulers or by one. 'Our constitution,' said Pericles, 'is named a democracy, because it is in the hands not of the few but of the many.' It was not merely that the citizens exercised some *influence* upon political policies, or merely that the General Assembly of citizens existed. All governments, whether in ancient Greece or in the modern world, admit some influence of public opinion and pay some deference to it. Other Greek city-states besides Athens had the General Assembly, but in those, instead of making effective decisions, the Assembly merely pro-

---

[1] A few of the most useful and readily available works are: Werner Jaeger, *Paideia: The Ideals of Greek Culture,* translated by Gilbert Highet, 3 vols., New York, 1939; Alfred E. Zimmern, *The Greek Commonwealth,* Oxford, 1931; W. K. Prentice, *The Greek Political Experience,* Princeton, 1941; Ernest Barker, *Greek Political Theory,* London, 4th ed. 1941; T. A. Sinclair, *A History of Greek Political Thought,* London, 1951. A good short account is that in G. C. Field, *Political Theory,* London, 1956, Appendix, pp. 275 ff. On the theoretical side the most illuminating work is Eric A. Havelock, *The Liberal Temper in Greek Politics,* London, 1957.

vided, so to speak, an audience for the rulers. The comparison is with totalitarian states of today, which sometimes have all the trappings of democracy but nothing of the substance—as in Hitler's use of the Reichstag and the electoral machinery, or in the Soviet Parliament and elections.

In the second place, there was a political and legal equality of all citizens in voting upon issues, in public debate, and in eligibility for public office. But this was not accompanied by economic equality, any more than in modern democracies, and the Athenian democracy stood firmly for the protection of private property. A citizen had all his 'kingly dignity' even though he was utterly destitute. Nor did the term 'citizen' cover all residents of the city-state, but in this respect we differ from Athens in that modern democracies have broadened the category of citizens entitled to vote and to hold office. Estimates of the number of adult citizens in fifth-century Athens differ a great deal, but the general opinion of many scholars puts the number at roughly 30,000 to 40,000.

Poor citizens were not excluded from office-holding, and to ensure the reality of equal eligibility for office (except for criminals), most offices were paid, and attendance at the Assembly itself was paid in the later period.[2] A feature more unfamiliar to us today was that offices such as those of magistrates and Council members were filled by lot from panels of elected candidates, in order to ensure that all citizens had an equal chance at office, and that no one should be tempted by the heady wine of power. Other rules also ensured the wide distribution of office and obedience to the popular will; for instance, an office could

---

[2] So many people were on the public payroll at times that a serious financial problem arose. But the bulk of these 'employees' was usually the armed forces. Aristotle thought, perhaps mistakenly, that payment for Assembly members had to be introduced in order to secure substantial attendance. If political equality was to be realistic for the poorer citizens, payment for public duties in Assembly and 'juries,' at least at subsistence rates, was in fact the only logical policy. The picture given by critics of the democracy—of public apathy and public pay for the mass of the citizens—is, in general, quite wrong. Cf. A. H. M. Jones, *Athenian Democracy*, Oxford, 1957, pp. 50 ff. Cf. also Barker, op. cit. p. 30: '... the Periclean system was intended to attract into politics, and succeeded in attracting into politics, those whose time was worth money and could not be had for nothing.'

not normally be held more than once by the same person, and a term was usually restricted to one year. A few officials were, however, elected directly from the Assembly by a show of hands, among them the generals, of whom Pericles is the best known. These were usually eligible for re-election, and from them, and the Assembly orators, came most of the leadership.

In the third place, there was widespread political and civic freedom. Freedom of discussion was the usual feature in the Assembly, the Council, and other political institutions, and decisions were taken after canvassing all arguments. The wide latitude of viewpoint and criticism extended even to the criticism of the basic principles of Athenian democracy itself, as in the writings of Plato. Since Plato taught at the Academy, we may say that he enjoyed academic freedom of teaching and writing, probably to a greater extent than in some modern democracies.

The actual machinery of government was as follows. The General Assembly (*ecclesia*) of citizens (males, age 20 and over) meeting normally 10 times a year, and sometimes in special session, was the chief means by which the citizens controlled public affairs. The smaller Council which, with officials, performed the executive function, had to give an accounting before the Assembly (or the large 'juries,' see below). The main body of the law changed but slowly from the time of Solon, and when changes were made, they were approved by the Assembly (or the 'juries'), with proposals and the actual drafting—like the agenda for the Assembly—commonly coming from the Council, from a committee, or even from a single legislator. The Assembly itself did not so much 'make law' as discuss policy, and often made or revised specific decisions and executive decrees, especially those concerning the conduct of war, diplomacy, foreign trade, and finance; and it frequently struck down as well as confirmed many specific acts of the Council.

The Council of Five Hundred (*boule*), an elected body made up of 50 from each of the ten Athenian 'tribes,' acted in the name of the Assembly between meetings, but was itself too large to be powerful, and smaller parts of it composed ten executive committees or boards which supervised the execution of the

Assembly decrees, each committee being on duty for a tenth of the year and meeting daily. Most of the officials thus did not act as individuals, but as committees, and they were not supposed to make policy. As we should put it, the 'executive authority' of the Council was extremely weak.

A feature which strikes us as curious today is that the judicial function was also performed by the citizens themselves, either in the Assembly, which sometimes conducted a trial, or—more often —by a court made up of hundreds of citizens, who were both jurors and judges. These large courts or 'juries' (*heliaia*) were chosen by lot from a panel of thousands (6,000) elected each year. In that innocent world there were neither professional lawyers nor judges, though well-known orators often played conspicuous parts in prosecution and defense. (Even Roman law much later had no professional, permanent judges.) Anyone could launch a prosecution, and some smart people set up as self-styled guardians of the public interest and did rather well out of the rewards for bringing successful prosecutions. But they were never a popular class, since their vocation savored too much of the 'informer.'

The 'juries,' like the Assembly itself, were thought of as the people in action. They were amateurs, not professionals, and too much knowledge of the technicalities of the law was suspect. They exercised the fullest degree of popular sovereignty, and found plenty to exercise their talents since the Athenians were greatly addicted to litigation. The 'juries' even more than the Council were large samples of the citizens acting in the name of all, and it is not far-fetched to see in this a form of representation, since the panels of candidates were for convenience presented from what might roughly be called wards ('tribes,' subdivided into *demes* or non-contiguous local units) of the city-state.

There was not the modern distinction between legislative and judicial functions, and the 'juries' determined both fact and law. The 'juries' were much more political than we normally expect courts to be, but their record for fairness and freedom from corruption is excellent. The rough—very rough—parallel today would be a legislature acting also as a court, as sometimes happens, e.g. in impeachments.[3] They followed no principle of *stare decisis;* a session lasted only one day, and a vote was taken by secret ballot. There was no higher court and consequently no appeal, and here at least the Athenians saved themselves still further litigation. As with an American jury, there were often many emotional speeches to the jurors, often on irrelevant matters. The forensic orators who composed speeches for their friends and clients are sometimes regarded as the beginning of the legal profession.[4]

Finally, as the fourth principle of policy-making, when all the arguments were in, a question had to be settled by taking a vote; and both the Assembly and the large 'juries' took the majority vote as that of the whole, as most legislatures, Scottish juries, and the United States Supreme Court do today. To convince opponents freely, particularly in the Assembly, was, how-

[3] The trial of Socrates on a charge of impiety took place before one of these popular juries in 399 B.C. The democracy had recently been restored (403 B.C.) and the state was in great unrest and turmoil after its reverses in foreign affairs and the overthrow of its domestic tyranny. We have no full account of the trial and what we do have is strongly for the defendant, in Plato's *Apology*. In the end, Socrates was convicted by 281 votes in a court of 501. Dispute is unending about the fairness of the trial. Some judicial students have argued that had Socrates been tried anywhere else—even in England, a country rightly proud of its judiciary—he would have fared worse at any time up to the middle of the 19th century. (Cf. Sir John MacDonell, *Historical Trials*, London, 1937, p. 16.) To put the best face upon the trial, we may say that the people saw in him a threat to the authority of the state itself—a clash between 'the inward voice' and the state, or perhaps between the 'higher law' of Antigone and the man-made law of Creon, or possibly between the individual and the community. This, I think, is much too high-minded; a democracy can sometimes be as stupid as any other political system. The public of Athens was in fact alarmist at the time, and indulged in 'a fit of puritanism.' (Zimmern, op. cit. p. 33.) The modern comparison is with the public orgy of hysteria during World War I or the years of McCarthyism. 'It was one of the few instances of radical intolerance in the history of Athens.' (W. R. Agard, *The Greek Mind*, Princeton, 1957, p. 61). Even so, to do Athens credit, Socrates would have been acquitted had he not deliberately provoked the jurors by his 'arrogancy of speech.' After all, he had lived in the democracy honored and free to a ripe old age (as did Plato); had he been living in Plato's ideal state, he might have been put away at the first sign of his 'dangerous thoughts.' The best discussion of the subject known to me is in the lovely book by E. R. Dodds, *The Greeks and the Irrational*, Berkeley, 1951, pp. 189ff.

[4] R. J. Bonner, *Lawyers and Litigants in Ancient Athens*, Chicago, 1927. J. Walter Jones, *The Law and Legal Theory of the Greeks*, Oxford, 1956, Chapter VII.

ever, more important than to coerce, and to take the majority's decision and make it one's own, self-imposed, was no doubt the ideal. Yet it seems plain enough from Athenian history that a minority, though obeying the decision, frequently felt itself coerced.

Such, then, are the bare bones of the Athenian democratic institutions, as they may be seen during the changes of the fifth and early fourth centuries B.C. The principles which to the Athenians justified giving their system the name of democracy are plain enough: the direct control or making of the political decisions by the assembled citizens; the political equality of all citizens; the liberties, including the freedom to oppose; and the taking of decisions by a majority vote. The city had no master, no autocrat, to rule it, no 'ruler' to which a foreign envoy might address himself:

> No will of one
> Holdeth this land; it is a city and free.
> The whole folk year by year, in parity
> Of service is our king.[5]

Direct government by the citizens themselves was probably taken as far as it has ever gone or could go in any state. And even then, as we have noted, much of the Athenian democracy was indirect—in the large 'juries,' the Council, and officials, who acted in the name of the whole citizen body. The need for any continuing administration and for efficiency always rules out the full practice of direct democracy in any state, no matter how small.

IDEALS OF THE ATHENIAN SYSTEM

Has this working democratic system, so far removed from us in time and circumstances, any relevance today? Can any analysis of it throw light on the theory and working of contemporary democracies? Let us see where a cautious analysis and appraisal will take us.

Two preliminary comments may be made. To begin with, it

---

[5] Zimmern, op. cit. p. 125.

seems a safe enough conclusion that Athenian democracy was feasible only in a small state. Even so, complete self-government was not practicable if by that we mean that all the citizens take all the decisions. Probably less than one-tenth of the citizens ever attended the Assembly at one time. The only actual count which has come down to us shows 3515 in attendance.[6] The political function of the Assembly (and 'juries') was not only to make the decisions but also to scrutinize decisions of officials at the end of a term of office, the modern parallel—though not at all a close one—being the general election. The Athenian institutions have had little application throughout most of western history, with possible exceptions such as Uri and other small Swiss cantons. When the idea of democracy was revived again, in the sense of direct or face-to-face democracy, it was applied in Britain during the 17th century chiefly to church government where it was workable at the level of the local congregation. When it was extended to the state, it was modified almost beyond recognition by representative government, except in such rare instances of direct democracy as the celebrated New England town meeting.

Secondly, it is worth pointing out a common misconception regarding the existence of slavery in Athens: the idea that the citizens formed a leisure class, and that without slavery the Athenian democracy would not have been possible. The first part of the notion is simply false. The citizens were not gentlemen of leisure devoting their full time to public affairs. They were overwhelmingly people who worked for their living, especially in agriculture, and gave to the affairs of the *polis* such time as they could spare from their private pursuits. Most of them paid the price of this participation in a lower standard of economic living.[7] The modern parallel would be to imagine citizens willing

---

[6] Zimmern, op. cit. p. 164. A quorum of 6,000 was required for ostracism, and even for some unexciting issues, and 'it was perhaps on the latter occasions that the Scythian police literally roped people into the assembly.' A. H. M. Jones, op. cit. p. 109.

[7] The Athenians did not despise manual labor or commerce, as is commonly supposed: on this we have been misled by Plato and Aristotle. If they despised any ways of making a living, these were money-lending and retailing, though probably on this also we are too inclined to regard Aristotle's views as typical. One recent estimate states: '... out of a total population of

to shorten their working week and put up with the lower income so obtained to give the spare time so created to public business. The second part of the notion—that the democracy necessarily depended upon slavery—is equally a mistake. Slavery was of course a commonplace in the ancient world, although there were nearly always critics of it. Societies with all types of government contained slaves—the absolute monarchies of the East and the oligarchies and aristocracies of many Greek cities. But the fact that a given state had slaves did not determine its form of government. Athenian democracy *for the citizens* was compatible with slavery, with an agrarian society of free-holders, or an urban society of burgesses.[8] In the same way, all modern societies take for granted the wage system of the economy, but the wage system does not determine the political system and does not mean that we cannot distinguish democracies from dictatorships. Similarly, the democracy of Athens did not depend on empire, although the financial returns from the empire enabled Athens to live at a higher standard, and to erect the Parthenon and other magnificent public buildings.

The deeper distinction is that the Athenians held a conception of citizenship quite different from ours today. The resident foreigners (outlanders or *metics*), women, children, and slaves were all excluded. Citizenship was traditional, a matter of birth, only rarely something to be acquired, and its mark—its very definition almost—was a sharing in and control of civic affairs, not a set of legally guaranteed civil rights such as forms so much of the modern concept of citizenship (and which was characteristic of Rome). Nevertheless, we do have something of the Athenian

---

21,000 citizens [at that time] about 12,000, say 60%, earned their living by working on very small holdings of 5 acres downwards, or as skilled craftsmen or shopkeepers with five slave assistants downwards, or as casual labourers.... It is unlikely that any slaves were owned by two-thirds to three-quarters of the citizen population.' A. H. M. Jones, op. cit. pp. 17, 81. Zimmern (op. cit. p. 409) estimates adult males as follows: slaves 55,000, outlanders 24,000, citizens about 40,000, to a total of 119,000. The figures are for all Attica, i.e. Athens and the territory around it, say an area of some 1,060 square miles.

8 The Athenian democracy with slavery may be compared with a modern democratic state with a dependent colonial territory; or with a democratic organization whose staff of janitors and other servants does not share in the government by the membership.

in our own concept of citizenship, insofar as it implies political equality and the right to take part in politics and to vote. We have in most democracies, however, extended this right to all adults, and we should classify a system as more or less democratic depending on the extent of the franchise. (This is but one element of a modern democratic system.) We have too, I think, a somewhat wider conception than the Greeks about the responsibility of the state to others than its own citizens, especially to other states. The city-states were 'particularist,' thoroughly attached to their autonomy and imbued with ideas of self-sufficiency, and hence 'international' affairs were in principle extraordinarily difficult. The pan-Hellenic ideal came to the fore later, after the decline of Athens.

With these preliminary points out of the way, we now come a little closer to the theory of Athenian democracy, i.e. the ideals which inspired and actuated it. It is much easier to describe institutions than to capture their spirit and ideal, and yet, however difficult to put into words, something must be said of the Athenian political ideals.[9] Their flavor is best caught in the funeral oration which Thucydides put in the mouth of Pericles—a classic speech which is perhaps the world's best statement of a political ideal. The central idea was that the good life for the citizen could only be lived by active participation in the life of the city-state. The Athenian, like everyone else, had his private affairs of business and family, but he was not engrossed in them to the neglect of his civic affairs. The citizen who did not participate actively in public affairs would have been thought not only useless, as Pericles put it, but almost a danger to the state. There seems to have been little of the modern concept of a continual conflict of interest between public and private affairs. Individual interests were not supposed to take precedence (the Greeks had no doctrine of individualism). In a real sense, the higher interests were automatically assumed to be those of the city; the life of the citizen found a worthy expression only in service to the

[9] The Athenian ideal is sometimes summed up in *Isonomia* that 'most beautiful of words'—a set of ideas clustering around 'equality of law,' and meaning at least equal treatment by the law and an equal share in helping to make the law. Gregory Vlastos, 'Isonomia,' *American Journal of Philosophy*, vol. LXXIV, 4, 1952-53.

city, and by participation in its governing. (Service alone was not enough: a foreigner or a slave might serve the city in non-political ways.) Free and equal citizenship in a free state: if this was not all of the good life for an Athenian democrat, at least it was a large and essential part of it—the part that inspired the democratic institutions and made them workable.

There is no way of telling how widely this ideal was held among the citizens, but it seems to have been very widely assumed, even if not always expressed. It is, of course, not a simple ideal but a complex one, with several facets, and it may well be that one or other of the separate aspects of it were more familiar to most Athenians than any general statement of the overriding ideal.

A well-recognized part of the ideal was always the respect for law—for the law as handed down, for the decision once made, and for the procedures by which it was made known and applied to particular cases. The rule of law was Greek, they said, but barbarians had only arbitrary rulers. This is the kind of pride that lurks behind the phrase 'British justice.' In theory, too, law and morality were fused, with the law setting the standard of right and wrong, so that the distinction between the legal and moral—though often drawn—was nothing like so commonplace as ours. Inevitably, this respect for procedures and the law presupposed a willingness to abide by the decisions of the Assembly and of the 'juries' as the voice of the whole city, even when the decisions went against the individual citizen or a 'faction.' Respect for the due process of law is one of the more remarkable attitudes showing through the last speeches of Socrates.[10] It was also regarded as part of the character of the citizen, to be promoted by such means as education. Law was the 'soul of the city.' As Aristotle put it in his *Ethics*:

> And whereas we take offence at individuals who oppose our inclinations, even though their opposition is right, we do not feel aggrieved when the law bids us do what is right.

[10] It is a fallacy, however, to assume that equal justice and codified law came into the world only with Athenian democracy. They have sometimes existed also in monarchic and aristocratic states, no less in the ancient world than at later dates. Cf. Jaeger, op. cit. vol. I, p. 101.

There can be no doubt that this readiness to accept the decision of the majority was fostered by the free discussion, which meant that no decisions were entirely one-sided or arbitrary, but that all citizens had the chance to contribute to the common pool of information, and the chance afterward to alter or reverse decisions by the accepted procedures. (The other side of the freedom was that political 'factions' would be formed, especially those of rich and poor which so often plagued Athens.)

From a technical viewpoint, this may be regarded as the minimum consensus which was needed in the *polis:* the agreement to abide by the settled procedures—by majority decisions of the Assembly after a fair debate, and of 'juries' after a fair trial. Such procedural agreement could only be firmly based in a society whose citizens were bound together by tradition and ideals, perhaps unspoken assumptions or fundamental beliefs; where majorities were not patently abusing their strength of numbers against the interests of other citizens, i.e. so that minorities would not regard decisions as majority 'tyranny,' or would not become completely intransigent and refuse to abide by them.[11] The question of consensus is a tricky one, about which it is not easy to be specific. By definition, there must be enough consensus in any society to hold it together and to work its institutions. But what is 'enough'? Can it be tested or measured, apart from the crucial practical tests of disruption by civil war, conspiracy, rioting, or other signs of public discontent? There is also the point that in Athens religious ritual and popular entertainments at religious festivals formed a bond uniting the citizens. Religion was subordinated to government and community, so that Athenian citizens were not divided by a number of different and conflicting religions, as many modern democracies are.

UNDERLYING ASSUMPTIONS

Clearly the working principles and ideals of Athenian democracy rest upon assumptions that go a little deeper, some of which

[11] The democracy was sometimes regarded as majority 'tyranny,' e.g. when the rich and the farmers paid the cost of wars, and when a regular property tax was instituted; but this was in the declining stages of the imperial democracy.

may be made explicit. First is the assumption not only of political equality, but also of the rationality of the citizens, and their devotion to the *polis*. The citizens are assumed to have a special kind of character: they will not sacrifice the public welfare for their private interests; they also have the ability to absorb information and to make wise decisions about public affairs. The success of the whole enterprise was in a sense based on a hopeful view of human nature (though the Athenians were distrustful of officials). Alternatively, one may look upon it as the assumption that if the democratic procedures were followed, the content of decisions would in fact produce acceptable justice, together with policies which insured the survival and welfare of the *polis*.

Second, a particular view of politics is assumed—that the city's business is a kind that does not require, for the most part, expert knowledge in order to pass judgment. Hence the 'happy versatility' of the Athenian citizen, the idea—as Pericles put it—of all citizens 'being sound judges of policy,' as of music, poetry, and the other arts. Public affairs are not esoteric, and the good life insofar as it concerned sharing the art of government was something within the competence of all. Public policies are matters on which no one is more expert than his neighbor; 'not the cook, but the one who eats the dinner is the best judge of the food.' In this respect, the view is in striking contrast to Plato's *Republic,* which rests on quite different and almost certainly anti-democratic assumptions. The view of the competence of the average citizen to decide public policies in any detail may well have been more realistic in the *polis* (as it may be in a small town meeting) but is quite far-fetched in any modern state. And even in Athens the aristocracy provided much of the political leadership—as in the Periclean age, the most flourishing period of the democracy.

Third, the system presupposed on the part of the citizen a lively interest in the affairs of the city: '... the breath of life to Periclean Athens was political activity.' This constant interest was of course easier to maintain because of the relatively simple political system and its few functions (the city performed few welfare or economic services, though foreign trade, particularly in corn, was closely regulated), but even more important was the fact that the Athenians were a sociable, gregarious, and outdoor people, living an all-pervasive common life to which the meetings of the Assembly, the wide opportunities to serve on the Council, the large 'juries,' and the chance to hold other offices all contributed. The affairs of the *polis* were in fact what the Romans later called 'res publica,' or 'everybody's business.' At times, from a third to a half of Athenian citizens would be on public service of one kind or another, though many of these would be in the military.[12] The interest and participation went far beyond the equivalent of the modern glance at the newspaper headlines and the casting of a ballot every few years, and may be compared with the interest in politics shown by that small minority in every democracy today who are called the 'politically active.' Possibly, however, we tend to exaggerate and idealize the interest of the average Athenian in politics. It has been surmised that 'Doubtless the ordinary citizen then, as today, cared little about constitutional forms so long as his stomach and purse were not empty.'[13]

Fourth, the Greek notion of freedom was freedom in participation: only by and through civic activity was a man released to 'develop his personality,' to enlarge, not to restrict, his 'natural' self. The notion is quite far in spirit from the later Hebrew-Christian idea of freedom *from* the community, and even further from the narrower modern view of freedom from the government. Still less is there any suggestion of individualism, or individual rights, or the state as a necessary evil merely guaranteeing order while citizens are left alone to pursue their own interests in their own ways.

> The distinctive merit of the Athenian regime lay in the fact that each citizen directly and vitally and, it would seem, contentedly shared in communal services without impairment of individual freedom of action and thought.[14]

We are compelled to say, I think, that the Greek city-states—whether democratic or not—demanded an exclusive, even a kind of spiritual, loyalty as they succeeded to older exclusive tribal

---

[12] George M. Harper, Jr., in Prentice, op. cit. p. 45.
[13] Ibid. p. 31.
[14] Ibid. p. 49.

and village loyalties. There was little conception, in the relation of the individual to the state, of competing and perhaps higher group loyalties, or of 'pluralism': the state as merely one among a number of associations. 'The most sovereign and inclusive association is the *polis*, as it is called, or the political association.' [15] (To call the Greek *polis* a 'state' in the modern sense is always somewhat misleading.) How much this demand for undivided loyalty was a reaction against earlier narrower loyalties and internal dissension is hard to say, but part of it certainly goes much deeper—to the traditional fusing of law and morality, to the priority given to the community over the individual. It was, I think, this notion of an ethical community and its all-demanding loyalty that so captured the imagination of Hegel and other German admirers of ancient Greece who transmuted (or degraded) it into the jealous god of the ethical-nation-state.

THE ARGUMENTS FOR AND AGAINST THE SYSTEM

Now the Athenians, so far as we know, never subjected their democratic political system and beliefs to elaborate and persistent analysis. Much of the system was taken for granted, as were the specific values associated with it and justifying it. The case *against* the democracy was more fully thought out, or at any rate has been better preserved for us in the ancient documents which have survived—from Plato, Aristotle, Thucydides, Xenephon, and others. Very likely there were more philosophers of the democratic persuasion than we think. How different history might have been had more of the democratic philosophy been preserved and absorbed into Western culture! [16] The political achievement of Athens is often forgotten, naturally so perhaps in

---

15 *The Politics of Aristotle*, translated by Sir Ernest Barker, Oxford, 1948, p. 1. Alternative translation (Zimmern, op. cit. p. 76): 'The city is the highest of all forms of association and embraces all the rest.' Jaeger, (op. cit. vol. I, p. 101) puts the same idea as: 'The polis is the sum of all its citizens and of all the aspects of their lives.'

16 A more just appreciation of the Athenian democracy and of its philosophy is, I think, coming about. Two excellent recent works may be cited: Eric A. Havelock, op. cit., and A. H. M. Jones, op. cit.

view of the more dramatic and durable flowering of Greek art, philosophy, and science. Yet several arguments were put forward on behalf of democracy from time to time, some of which may be seen, for example, in Aristotle.

The best known of Aristotle's arguments is the simple one that the citizens, or the majority, are more likely to be right; there is a surer wisdom in the decision of the many because it is a collective decision, to which all could freely contribute. Proposals were subject to public scrutiny and debate and a decision drew upon the wisdom and experience of all. The decisions of one person, or of a few people, were without these salutary checks and the larger pool of opinion and judgment. In short, it is the familiar argument that many heads are wiser than one, and that people are better as a group than as individuals. (When the majority was confined to one class—the poor—Aristotle was less favorable to democracy.) The belief in the collective good judgment of the masses, over that of the expert, is sometimes suggested as having retarded the growth of representative government in Greece.[17]

A second argument was, I think, more basic. In one form it is scarcely more than a re-statement of the whole Athenian ideal: that free participation in the political life is the proper mark of a citizen, the thing that makes him fully a person; that to be a participating citizen is itself something of high value not only to the state but also to the individual citizen. It thus shades over into an argument for democracy because of its effects upon persons. The system is good because it encourages the development of certain good human qualities: of self-confidence and initiative yet also of self-mastery, of fraternity and amity yet also of eccentricity, of courage yet also of gentleness and human kindness—and these qualities carry over into the whole of social life. Even critics of Athenian democracy agreed that the system did indeed produce that type of man and society: its 'way of life' which Pericles praised so highly *was* different from that in other city-states. The state itself had hardly any other aim or purpose than to enable the citizens to lead the good life as they worked

[17] J. O. A. Larsen, *Representative Government in Greek and Roman History*, Berkeley, 1955, pp. 1, 14, 21.

it out together in political equality. There is nothing in this conception like Plato's dedication of the state to an Absolute Good or transcendental end, and not much that could be put in the teleological language of Aristotle. Whether a state was good or not depended on the quality of the citizens, and the character of the democratic citizen was judged good. The freedom, the equality, the cares of citizenship—all constituted a kind of moral education which ensured the development of the good man and good citizen, and made the two synonymous.[18]

> For a whole wonderful half-century, the richest and happiest period in the recorded history of any single community, Politics and Morality, the deepest and strongest forces of national and of individual life, had moved forward hand in hand towards a common ideal, the perfect citizen in the perfect state.[19]

There were, of course, other arguments in the case. It was, for instance, argued that democracy gave the best protection against abuse by officials, against misgovernment and injustice. While mistakes might sometimes be made, or the majority might now and then offend against an individual or a minority, yet even so there were safeguards: the equal entitlement to share in the law through open legal processes, and the opportunities of peaceful persuasion in the processes of political debate. What other system could provide these powerful safeguards against oppression? Since legal and peaceful means of persuading one's fellows were at hand for redress, what need was served, what advantage to be gained, by disobedience and violent overthrow? For that reason, the Athenian democrats were on the whole right when they thought the danger to their system was to be apprehended chiefly from conspirators and small factions of oligarchs (of whom they were always suspicious, with good reason) and not from the great body of citizens.

The distrust of human nature, the danger from men vested

---

[18] In one sense, Plato may be regarded as criticizing the democracy because it did not live up to its ideals, and so he wrote to restore the community as the moral agent, to re-establish standards in a period of decadence. Cf. Jaeger, op. cit. vol. III, pp. 237ff.

[19] Zimmern, op. cit. p. 426.

with irresponsible power, were practical lessons taught by experience, not arguments of philosophical subtlety, and so they were regarded as of lesser importance by the critics.

The philosophers are strangely blind to this danger, and are content to rely on the virtue of their usually hereditary or co-optative oligarchies of wise men.[20]

Again, at a practical level it was argued that democracy gave more stability of government, because the obedience would be willing and freely given on account of the widespread participation, and because democracy was more 'free from party strife than oligarchy.' In Solon's words: 'Equality breeds no revolution.' Even Plato thought there was something to this argument, though he also thought that 'excess of liberty' leads to tyrants. Too much liberty, not regimentation, was feared as the typical danger of the democracy, unlike today when every second citizen professes to fear regimentation and the loss of liberty.

Naturally, criticism of the system was not lacking, and it was put forcibly and cogently. Most of the criticisms are put best in the writings of Plato, who was the persistent outstanding critic although some of his anti-democratic attitude is possibly exaggerated; and when he speaks of democracy he almost always seems to assume that the majority would by definition be the 'mob,' forgetful of the fact that the majority will also have its share of leaders and wisdom. One of his arguments was on the strictly practical level. The mass meetings, he thought, were likely to be emotional, to lend themselves to demagogy and to decisions prompted by the brief and shortsighted interests of the mob. Assembly government would thus tend to be unpredictable, to waver, to reverse itself, with the result that there would be a lack of continuity of policy; and responsibility for decisions being so widely dispersed, no individual would feel responsible for any particular decision or for the state as a whole. How could wise decisions come out of this sort of mob rule if the majority consisted of only one class? And if the decisions were not wise, what kind of a state would it be, and how long could it last? The mob rule criticisms of Plato and others were

[20] A. H. M. Jones, op. cit. p. 61.

in fact sometimes valid for Athens, especially in the later period (though Socrates remarked on the shrewd judgment of the citizens), but have less relevance to democracies today, when the political and other decisions are made by legislators or judges or administrators, not by mass meetings of citizens.

The second and far the heavier of the guns which Plato trained upon the democracy rested upon the incompetence of the ordinary citizen. It was a complete denial of the ideal of 'happy versatility.' The assumption behind it was almost exactly the opposite view of politics and government to that held by the democrats. Instead of public affairs being simple, within the ability of the ordinary citizen, governing and policy making was a difficult art, or 'royal science,' requiring special knowledge, ability, and training. It was an expert skill, like medicine or navigation; something which could only be done well by the very highest talent after the most rigorous training, and as a full-time job undistracted by private interests of property and family ties. In the extreme case —in the *Republic*—the guardians alone could attain to the 'superknowledge' required. These, being the only people equipped to rule, should rule, or the state would always be making do with something below the best.

Plato's criticism went far beyond the idea that politics is a difficult art only to be grasped in detail by experts; he assumed that there is a 'supreme good,' that only some qualified people can know what it is, and the knowledge gives them a title to rule and to make what will always be the 'best' decisions. This is not merely a different view of social life and politics, but at bottom a quite different metaphysics concerning the nature of knowledge and of the 'good.' His philosophy implies a total rejection of what is commonly meant by politics and the political; it leads to government, but not to *political* government. In all this, Plato is not un-Greek, but he is entirely un-democratic, and for the very highest reasons.[21]

21 There is a large contemporary literature criticizing and defending Plato— it is in fact one of the more innocent academic diversions of our times—so I realize that anything at all said about Plato is bound to be questioned.

CONCLUSIONS

Through some two and a half millennia, these arguments in criticism of democracy have scarcely been improved upon. They are, with variations and more historical detail, the substance of many arguments still in use by critics today, although several others have also been invented, by Marxists and spokesmen for various types of elite rule. In a similar way, among the arguments for democracy today are those used in the Athens of Pericles (although again new ones have been added).[22] Yet unless the working principles and institutions of Athenian democracy are roughly identical with those of modern democracies, it would not seem that the same arguments either for or against could apply. Ancient Athens is not a miniature of our contemporary democracies, and its institutions cannot be copied in any modern state. Consequently the Athenian arguments pro and con are frequently misleading if used to judge modern democracies. How is this so?

From an institutional point of view, it will be recalled, the chief features of Athenian democracy were (1) the making of decisions directly by the Assembly itself—a relatively large sample of the citizens, (2) the control over decision makers (e.g. the Council and officials) by the Assembly, (3) the administration of justice directly by the large popular 'juries.' None of these is transferable to a modern state, by reason of the difference of scale alone. Instead, a democracy of today holds free popular elections and acts through a relatively infinitesimal number of representatives each of whom knows intimately only a tiny proportion of the country—his home constituency; while a powerful executive, an independent professional judiciary, and a large specialized bureaucracy are perhaps even further removed from

22 'Neither of two famous modern arguments for Democracy—i.e., the moral argument that all men have the right to govern themselves, and the sceptical argument that since men can never know what is right, they should be governed in accordance with their wishes—is much heard of as far as we know in antiquity.' R. Wollheim, 'Democracy,' *Journal of the History of Ideas,* April 1958, p. 227.

the primary assemblies of Athens. Neither is it feasible today that we should revert to the annual choice of office holders by lot— or there would be a good chance of an utter breakdown of the intricate machinery of government. Given these institutional differences, at once all the arguments against modern democracy based on the Athenian originals—of mob rule, demagogy and incompetence of the ordinary citizen—fall to the ground. And correspondingly, we cannot call upon the Athenian arguments in favor of their system without taking into account the differences in scale and institutions.

Despite these points of difference—and they could be extended greatly—there is a certain likeness of general principles, and a kinship of spirit and temper, between the Athenian democracy and a democracy of today. The Athenian democrat, if transported by magic into a 20th-century representative democracy, could recognize by an effort of imagination, in the popular choice of government at election times, in the legal and political equality of citizens, in the range of political liberties and activities, some faint resemblance to the political principles of his own times. He could recognize also in the varied life of modern democracies the spirit of curiosity and the free scientific and artistic enquiry which were so characteristic of his own times. He would not of course be entirely at home. The sheer size of our modern states would appall him. Our restless search for more and more material goods would be foreign to him as would our lavish spending on private wants and our niggardly spending on public services. Nor would he find every modern citizen keenly interested in politics and the common life. He would also miss the *homonoia*—the unison, the 'consonance of minds and hearts'—the concord, of his beloved *polis*.

The last point is I think sometimes misunderstood by those who stress the loyalty, unity, and participation of Athenian citizens, and so tend to equate the ancient democracy with the quasi-totalitarian state. The concept of citizenship did revolve around participation, but it was nevertheless critical participation, not an imposed uniformity; devotion to the *polis*, yes, but there was also privacy.

But if the essence of democracy was placed in the power of the people to do whatever it willed, it was also believed to guarantee to the individual citizen a sphere of action within which he was free to do as he thought fit, even against the wishes of the majority of his fellow-citizens unless these were expressed in constitutional form.[23]

The *polis* was so to speak held in common by kinsmen, was a co-operative undertaking, and was not looked upon as an authority over and above individuals, or as the private concern of a despot. One of the complaints of Plato in the *Republic* is that in the democracy there is too much individual freedom:

the city is full of liberty and free speech and everyone in it is allowed to do what he likes... each man in it could plan his own life as he pleases.

There is one really big difference between the Athenian democracy and our own democratic states. It lies in the Athenian mingling of the political, the cultural, the religious; and especially in the fact that in the Athenian the moral and the legal standards of the community were so mingled together (in the *nomoi*) that they appeared as one, whereas we have divided the two. The great reason for this of course is that our democracies have a very mixed ancestry. We are the heirs not only of Greece but also of the religious earnestness of the Hebrews, and of the Christian message.

Greek thought took for granted that the ideal of human conduct was static: that it was the business of the state to maintain and uphold that ideal: that therefore in the properly organized state legal and moral ideals would coincide. The Christian ideal of perfection implied that the morality recognized and enforced by law could not possibly be the high morality incumbent on the Christian.[24]

To this we must add the doctrines of individualism which have come from Roman law, the Renaissance, the Reformation, and

[23] J. Walter Jones, op. cit. p. 90.
[24] A. D. Lindsay, *The Modern Democratic State*, Oxford, 1943, p. 251. The Byzantine tradition is perhaps closer to the Greek conception—with the State

other sources. The result is that 'The citizen, in our Western heritage, is held to be both a public person and a private person, to be both in and yet also out of society.' [25] He is a member of many lesser groups including religious groups, which serve as centers of his loyalty and life, and which mediate between the state and the citizen.

---

responsible for morals, conduct and belief—though the Greeks were not so much concerned with religious *belief* as with reverence for the local gods and the ritual.

[25] H. Mark Roelofs, *The Tension of Citizenship*, New York, 1957, p. 155.

FOUR | *The Theory of Democracy Outlined*

INTRODUCTORY

As stated in Chapter 2, the approach taken in this study is to regard democracy as a political system with a theory to explain and justify it. The first problem is, then, to identify the working principles of the political system generally called democratic.

In order to arrive at these distinguishing principles, several starting points are possible. We could, for example, begin with some of the older classic statements of democracy, or with a contemporary definition, or with the institutions of one of the existing democratic systems. Although all these sources will be tapped from time to time, I shall take as the starting point the Athenian example analyzed briefly in Chapter 3. This need not be misleading if we do take it as no more than a starting point, and do not regard Athens and its unique institutional features as a small scale model of contemporary democracies.

The original democratic system of Athens could be described in one phrase as 'rule by the people,' if 'people' was construed narrowly to mean adult male citizens, comprising a small proportion of the total persons in a small state. This definitive operating principle, traced out into secondary principles and institutions, made it easy for Athenians—and for us—to distinguish the democracy from other ancient political systems. Such a principle was both accurately descriptive and quite workable, given the scale of operations. But the principle is neither descriptive of nor feasible in any modern state. It makes sense to say that one person rules, or that a few persons do, no matter how large the state; but it makes almost no sense to say that the people rule in any modern state, in any ordinary sense of the word 'rule.' (In this sense 'rule' means to make directly the binding political decisions—or the major ones, including the decision as to what is major—and to receive the obedience.) In Gladstone's words:

> No people of a magnitude to be called a nation has ever, in strictness, governed itself; the utmost which appears to be attainable, under the conditions of human life, is that it should choose its governors, and that it should on select occasions bear directly on their action.[1]

Or as MacIver was always concerned to put it:

> Democracy is not a way of governing, whether by majority or otherwise, but primarily a way of determining who shall govern and, broadly, to what ends ... The people, let us repeat, do not and cannot govern; they control the government.[2]

The only exception to this is the occasional use of 'direct democratic devices' such as the referendum.

Democracy, then, as a political system must have identifiable features other than the people's actually 'governing,' to distinguish it from other methods of making public policies. The problem is to separate the accidental features from the characteristic. Some political features, such as whether the government is federal or unitary, presidential or parliamentary, unicameral or bicameral, republican or monarchical, are by general agreement accidental variations from a common type. So, too, is the kind of economic system with which the political system is associated—although this is more debatable. These and other features are not necessarily related, either in logic or practice, with features of the political system ordinarily listed as democratic. Since one cannot analyze all of a system, except perhaps in a treatise on comparative democratic systems, we seek here only the differentiating features or principles of organization typical of all democracies and not typical of any other systems.

What, then, in any contemporary state corresponds to the

1 *Nineteenth Century Opinion*, ed. Michael Goodwin, Harmondsworth, Middlesex, 1951, p. 226.

2 R. M. MacIver, *The Web of Government*, New York, 1947, p. 198; *The Ramparts We Guard*, New York, 1950, p. 51.

'rule by the people' in the Athenian system? We are inevitably driven to conclude, I think, that such a corresponding factor lies in the effectiveness of the popular control over the rulers or decision-makers. In short, a political system is democratic to the extent that the decision-makers are under effective popular control. (One should perhaps add: to the extent to which decisions are *influenced* by the people, but this is a more amorphous concept, for which allowance will be made later.)

Plainly however, this, although in the spirit of the Athenian democracy, is a much vaguer test to apply than the Athenian. To distinguish ancient democracy from other types of the Greek *polis* was easy, and there could scarcely be dispute about it. But when the test is the extent of effective popular control, then the existence of democracy in any system is obviously a matter of degree. At one extreme will be the absolute ruler—a Hitler, a Stalin, a Peron—who, however despotic, must sometimes take popular sentiment into account (but who will endeavor, through education, censorship, propaganda, and other means, to engineer the popular sentiment which he wishes), and whose elections and plebiscites, if they are held at all, are carefully 'rigged.' At the other will be an elected government anxious to be re-elected, and an opposition anxious to become the government, both of them therefore sentitive to public opinion, with a wide range of political freedoms through which continuing influence as well as periodic control can be exercised.

Popular control of policy-makers is then the basic feature or principle, and political systems can be classified as more or less democratic according to a number of criteria associated with popular control and designed to make it effective; only if a particular system meets the tests of a substantial number of these criteria do we, by common consent, agree to call it democratic. But although the existence of democracy then becomes a matter of degree, the distinction is valid enough as we shall see, and the criteria will enable us to say in what respects and to what extent a system is democratic.

It must now be our purpose to try to make this somewhat vague language more precise. Accordingly I shall first sketch what I take to be a consistent and coherent theory of democracy in the form of the minimum number of distinguishing principles. At the same time, the outline will be reasonably close to contemporary usage, and is recognizably approximated by a number of existing democracies. The analysis and justification of these principles and of the system as a whole, together with the chief questions or problems which arise, will be given in later chapters.

DISTINGUISHING PRINCIPLES OF A DEMOCRATIC SYSTEM

Influence over decision-makers and hence over public policies may be exercised in many ways, even in a non-democratic system. The policies of an absolute ruler or of an oligarchy, for instance, may be affected by palace intrigue and court favorites, or by careful calculation of what the subjects will stand in the way of taxes and the like; it is possible to conceive of a benevolent autocrat who will in fact keep his ear to the ground and often graciously accede to public demands. But popular influence, although necessary, is not enough even if institutionalized to make a political system democratic.

1. *Popular control of policy-makers,* however, is a democratic stigmatum, and this is our first and most general principle. The one institutional embodiment of the principle universally regarded as indispensable in modern democracies is that of choosing the policy-makers (representatives) at elections held at more or less regular intervals. This is as close as we usually get—which is not very close—to imitating the making and control of decisions in the Athenian *ecclesia.*

Other methods of choosing and authorizing representatives—e.g. by lot or heredity—have died out, except for remnants of the lot such as are left in the choice of a jury. Even the Soviet type of 'democracy' pays tribute to the method of electing representatives, although their practice of it is quite different from that in other kinds of democracies. In this as in other respects, the Soviet Union has borrowed some of the forms and language of democracy and stripped them of their spirit and meaning.

Three riders must be added to our general principle at the outset in order to avoid misunderstanding:

(a) On the whole, no democratic system operates on the principle that voters directly decide public policies at elections. The control over policy is much more indirect—through the representatives. This will be made clear later (in Chapter 5), but if we accept provisionally that voters choose representatives at elections and do not normally decide policies, then the usual criticism aimed at modern democracies on grounds of the incompetence of voters to judge policies is wide of the mark, however true it may have been of Athens where the citizens did decide directly.

(b) The popular influence upon policies, as distinct from control over policy-makers, goes on all the time and may take many institutionalized and legitimate forms. The extent of such influence, however, cannot be reduced to any public test which can be incorporated at the present time into a general theory. The reason is that popular influence and consultation take such an infinity of forms—of which interest or pressure groups are perhaps the best known—that hardly any general principle can as yet be enunciated. What gives popular influence its sanction is that it can affect the chances of a representative at election time, or, more accurately, the representative's estimate of his chances.

(c) Popular control by means of modern elections has only a faint resemblance to the old principle that, in some sense, authority stems from the people, and to old practices such as an elective monarchy. The assumption or belief that authority *should* derive from the people—sometimes called the doctrine of popular sovereignty—does of course underlie the practice of popular elections, but our immediate concern is with the translation of the assumption into an operating principle or institutional practice.

2. The second principle of democracy is that of *political equality*, which in turn is institutionalized as the equality of all adult citizens in voting.

It makes little difference whether we think of this principle as co-ordinate with the first, or derivative—a widening of the meaning of 'popular.' Political equality is a principle common to Athenian and modern democracies. There is, of course, more to citizenship than voting, and hence other ways in which political equality or inequality can prevail, but it is not debatable today that in any democracy the principle of equality of voting is taken for granted.

Although the general principle may be cast in the Athenian form, the modern expression of it is quite different. For one thing, equality of voting is not, as in Athens, an equal share directly over the decisions; the share in the decisions is indirect—only the share in the control of the decision-makers is direct. For another, political equality today covers a wider range of citizens and voters than the Athenian, and in this respect we should call modern democracies more democratic than Athens.

Political equality is complex, like all general principles, and may be broken down into several elements, consisting at least of the following:

(a) Every adult should have the vote—the familiar device of the universal adult suffrage. Popular control defines the 'people' as all adult citizens, although there are of course minor differences in the definitions of an 'adult.'

(b) One person should have one vote—that is, there should be no plural voting.

(c) Each vote should count equally—that is, votes are not weighted in any way.

In terms of representation, the belief in equal voting is expressed in the old slogan of 'representation by population' or in Bentham's formula regarding happiness, that 'everybody is to count for one, nobody for more than one.' In terms of control over policy-makers, it is expressed by saying that every vote should have an equal share in that control.

(d) If every vote is to count equally, the corollary follows that the number of representatives elected should be directly proportional to the number of votes cast for them. If we assume, for simplicity of argument, a two-party system, then the number of representatives elected from each party will be proportional to the number of votes cast for that party. Thus, in a two-party system, if party A gets 60 per cent of the popular vote it will get

60 per cent of the seats, and party B will get 40 per cent. Any other result would not be counting each vote equally.[3] It is just at this point, however, as we shall see, that the practice of many democracies diverges from this aspect of political equality, and often does so for very good reasons.

A little reflection will show that equality of voting, even if followed to the letter, is not enough of itself to distinguish a democratic system from an elected dictatorship. The belief and indeed the practice of equal voting are both official in the Soviet Union. Equality of voting, with its corollary, may thus be regarded as a necessary, but not a sufficient, principle of democracy. Is there, then, anything else about political equality and the franchise to distinguish a democratic political system? The answer must lie in the fact that voting alone does not ensure the reality of popular control; the mechanism may be manipulated to prevent such control.

3. The third principle may be stated either in terms of the *effectiveness of the popular control* or in terms of *political freedoms.*

Again, it makes little difference whether we regard 'effectiveness' as part of the first principle (popular control) or as specifying the conditions of effective control. Can one set of decision-makers be turned out of office at elections and another set installed? Is there a free choice among alternatives, whether independent candidates or parties? That is, is the voting merely ritual, or does it effectively (freely) control the decision makers?

This again is a very general statement of what prevails in a democracy. To make the general standard specific enough to test in practice, we must once more break it into components.

(a) To say that the voting must be effective is to say that there must be free choice, without coercion or intimidation of the voters. This in turn drives us back upon the secrecy of the ballot, whether we draw the conclusion from reflecting on human nature—that we live in an imperfect world of imperfect people— or from reflecting upon the historical experience of many countries with open voting. Yet the condition of the secret ballot

---

[3] Note that the reference is in terms of actual votes, not in terms of eligible adults—a point to which fuller reference is made later.

alone is not enough to ensure free choice, since even a Soviet election may provide the voter with privacy in the voting booth.

(b) In order that voting may be effective, it must, then, be free in another sense, i.e. at least two candidates for each position must be able to come forward if they wish. This minimum in itself is also not enough, because it could be cleverly imitated even in the Soviet Union by the simple device of putting forward more official candidates than seats to be filled.

An effective choice for the voter entails freedom for candidates to stand for election outside of the single party, not deterred by legal obstacles. (The question of *de facto* obstacles such as poverty is explored later.) At this point we come close to the most characteristic feature of a modern democracy: the meaningful choice or control when candidates are free to run for office, when they and their supporters are free to press their claims publicly, to put forward alternative policies, to criticize the present decision-makers and other candidates; in short, when there is what Schumpeter has called a competitive bidding for votes.

The effectiveness of popular control thus entails a range of political freedoms. Among them are certainly the freedoms of speech, assembly, and organization, as well as the freedom to run for office. These widespread political liberties were characteristic of the Athenian form of democracy, and are likewise typical of all other historical versions, though lacking in the Soviet system.

These formal rules or conditions or devices of effective choice —secret ballot, freedom to run for office, and freedom to speak, assemble, and organize for political purposes—are procedural political freedoms, necessary if there is to be any meaningful choice at the polls, if the voters are to control the decision-makers at election times and through them indirectly to sanction the decisions. Or they may be looked upon as the rules which insure free competition for office, men being what they are and the world being what it is.

Among those political freedoms, that of organization leads almost inevitably (as we shall see later) to the formation of political parties, with different sets of candidates and sometimes with different outlooks and policy alternatives. The pure theory, of itself, will hardly tell us whether or not political parties will make their appearance in a democracy. They are not, so to speak, logically entailed as part of popular control, of effective choice in free and equal voting, and they do not always appear at local levels of government. Experience and history, however, give an enormous weight of evidence to show that political parties invariably do appear, despite the early, and mostly non-democratic, objection to 'factions.'

The existence and extent of these political liberties, as manifested above all in political opposition, is perhaps the most crucial test of the extent of democracy within a country. They are often summed up in the single concept 'freedom to oppose.' The touchstone of a democratic system is political freedoms, opposition, and parties. Not one of the indispensable freedoms, nor the open and legitimate opposition which is always the consequence of freedoms, is present, for example, in the Soviet Union, despite the noble language of liberty embalmed in the Soviet constitution of 1936. For that reason we are fully justified in saying there is no effective choice or popular control of the decision-makers in the Soviet Union.

The result of political activity taking place within these rules—equality of voting and political liberties—is to enable the effective choice of representatives to take place, i.e. to ensure the popular control of decision-makers at election time, and to keep the channels open to legitimate influence at all times. From the viewpoint of the individual voter, the vote is the formal means by which he takes his share in political power. It scarcely needs pointing out that other implications also follow, for instance that the outvoted citizens accept the verdict of the polls with fortitude if not with gladness.

Although equality of voting within the context of political freedoms is a basic part of a democratic system, it is not all. Another essential part, already implicit, is that the policy decisions are made by the elected representatives, since only these are susceptible to popular control. The policies are not made, for instance, by others behind the scenes—as Marxists allege—nor by any non-elected body, such as a hereditary upper house. Insofar as they are made elsewhere, to that extent we say democracy is lacking. (To say this, however, is not to ignore the political reality of executive or Cabinet leadership.)

It is plain that we cannot expect the representatives to be unanimous, any more than we can expect the electorate to be so. Political systems are devised *because* there is conflict and disagreement. There must, then, be a principle or rule according to which decisions are made among the representatives themselves.

4. The fourth principle is that *when the representatives are divided, the decision of the majority prevails.*

This is, in fact, the nearly universal rule for decision-making in all legislatures. Let us be clear how it links with the previous principles. Equality of voting, in a context of political freedoms, turns up representatives who are authorized to make the policies for the time being. This may be loosely called 'consent of the governed' in the sense that there is a choice and one set of representatives rather than another is chosen. But 'consent' is a slippery term, and it is better to think of election results as authorizing the successful candidates to make decisions, or in other words, as investing the government and its policies with legitimacy.

The common assumption is that with an electoral system based on equality of voting a majority of the representatives have been chosen by a majority of the voters, and hence the majority rule in the legislature yields decisions as legitimate 'as if' they had been made directly by a majority of the voters, and indeed by a majority of all the adult citizens. That is why this fourth principle is sometimes called 'majority rule.' In fact, however, if governments depended for their legitimacy on this strict relation of votes to representatives, half the democratic governments of the world could at times claim no rightful authority from the 'people.' (See Chapters 5 and 6.)

The principle of decision-making by a majority of representatives is much disputed, and is examined *in extenso* later (Chapter 8), particularly the justification for the majority principle. The case *against* may be put in a nutshell: that it is both necessary and feasible to maintain legal limits upon a majority of the decision-makers (and hence by implication upon a majority of the citizens), and by so doing we may achieve the best of all possible systems: a 'wise' minority veto of 'unwise' majority decisions. Democracy would then be identical with ideal government, and the historic search for a government with power to rule wisely, but powerless to do wrong, would be over. To state the case is almost enough to refute it.

From this method of policy-making there follow certain implications, which may be called the rules of the game for representatives.

First, the majority of the representatives makes the policy decisions within the framework of the political freedoms mentioned earlier. These freedoms are taken as given, as part of the formal principles or essential conditions of democracy. Whatever else the majority may do—and it may mete very ill treatment through some of its decisions—it does not shut up the opposition, the critics, the dissenters, whether these are within or without the legislature. Opponents may be coerced into obedience to law, but not abolished or silenced or shorn of their political liberties: this is the one inhibition upon the majority decisions so long as a democracy exists. When the political liberties and the legitimate opposition are gone, so, too, is democracy.

Second, the minority of representatives and their supporters among the public obey even though under protest, while working either to alter the policy to which they object or to dislodge the government and if possible to become a majority—by all peaceful political means, but only by these. No doubt it is often difficult to obey a law which is heartily disliked—and on this something more is said in Chapter 11—but for the moment it is enough to state the formal rule.

Third, when the opposition in its turn has grown into a majority and attains office, the play begins all over again with different actors in the roles of government and opposition. The minority also agrees beforehand that they, too, will extend the same political freedoms and follow the same rules of the game should they arrive in the seats of office. The problem which arises here is that created by the existence of a minority party which uses the political freedoms in order to abolish democracy. (On this, see Appendix to Chapter 8.)

Many social conditions are, of course, necessary if the majority principle is to work well, but those formal conditions just stated are the minimum rules of the game for majorities and minorities in the legislature if democracy is to work *at all*. Moreover, in any functioning democracy, regardless of the niceties of the electoral system, the rules apply in those common cases where the majority of representatives happens to be elected by the minority of voters. No identity of voters and representatives need be assumed as long as the unwritten constitution does not require it, although there is, I think, an obligation to reduce the likelihood of wide discrepancies by eliminating abuses from the electoral system and thus closely approximating the principle of political equality.

The foregoing is a simplified, formal, abstract sketch of a democratic political system—its essential principles of operation for political policy-making. It concentrates upon how the binding decisions, related to government and arising from conflict and dispute, are made in the context of political freedoms. In other terms, the outline concentrates upon the ways in which policy-makers get their power and authorization—their legitimacy, always a prime concern to any political theory. The principles are close enough to common usage, and to some political systems in existence, to warrant the description democratic.

Each of the principles can be cast in operational terms. This has the great advantage of giving us practical tests which, taken together, enable us to distinguish democratic from non-democratic systems, and also to identify democracies empirically as more or less democratic, in this or that respect. One need not attempt, however, to solve the impossible problem of exact summation—of trying to construct a single index number which will register all the tests for democracy. Some criteria are more important than others, and all are a matter of degree.[4]

Each of the principles can also be cast in normative (moral) terms—for example, that political equality *should* prevail—and

[4] See Russell H. Fitzgibbon, 'A Statistical Evaluation of Latin-American Democracy,' *Western Political Quarterly*, IX, September 1956, pp. 607ff., for an attempt to measure (in 'a crude and groping way,' as the author says) which countries of Latin America are more democratic. At that time, Uruguay, Costa Rica, and Chile were at the top of the list.

in this form they constitute the moral justification of a theory of democracy. They are moral beliefs for which a case can be made, and which may be traced further back until we lay bare the 'ultimates' or postulates to which the principles commit us.

Considered in both operational and normative terms, the principles may thus fairly be described as making up a democratic political theory which both explains and justifies a democratic political system.

A working definition may be constructed from the above: a democratic political system is one in which public policies are made, on a majority basis, by representatives subject to effective popular control at periodic elections which are conducted on the principle of political equality and under conditions of political freedom. The definition is hardly remarkable; others of a similar kind have frequently been constructed.[5]

I am aware that the bare outline bristles with questions, as any model does when it is made up of an abstraction of formal principles. Moreover, even when the skeleton has been given flesh and blood, there are a number of other far-reaching queries which at once suggest themselves, among them: what values (if any) inhere in a political system operating on such principles? What case can be made for the system as a whole other than that involved in the justification of the separate principles?

Again—and this will be the question of chief concern to many —what of the kind or quality of decisions thus made and authorized? Must we assume that the content of democratic decisions will take care of itself, or has the theory any implicit purposes to which the system is committed? What kind of case can be made against such a system and against its theory by the critics? What of the social, economic, and other conditions which may be needed in order that a democratic system may work at all, or work well? What are the prospects for such a system in the world

5 For instance, John Morley's: Democracy is 'the name for a form of government by which the ultimate control of the machinery of government is committed to a numerical majority of the community.' *Oracles on Man and Government*, London, 1923, p. 29. Or again: Democracy is 'government of the whole, by the majority, generally through representatives elected by secret ballot of adults.' E. F. Carritt, *Ethical and Political Thinking*, Oxford, 1957, p. 150.

today? What application has the theory to international politics? For the time being, these wider questions will be put aside for later consideration, and I turn now to an examination of the empirical and the normative beliefs involved in the principles listed, and of how existing democracies deviate from the practice of these principles. This will take us as far as Chapter 8 and the problem of legal limits on the majority principle.

FIVE | *Popular Control and the Meanings of Elections*

INTRODUCTORY

I have stipulated a meaning, close to everyday usage, of democracy as a political system, with a few formal principles by which it may be distinguished from other systems. The first and broadest of these principles is comprised in the phrase: popular control of policy-makers; and the mechanism is that of free elections. Sometimes popular control is loosely referred to as popular government, self-government, popular sovereignty, and rule of the people. The looser phrases may do no harm if we do not take them literally, but unfortunately they are often so taken, to the great confusion of the theory of democracy.

We fall into the trap of literal interpretation, mistaking control for governing, for two reasons. One, because of our inveterate tendency to keep before our mind's eye the Athenian example, or the New England town meeting, where the assembled citizens did actually make decisions, or govern; and the other, because with equal stubbornness we tend to think of small democratic voluntary organizations (say sports clubs), where decisions are made by the members at an annual meeting. The psychological and other experimental work on small 'groups,' though useful in some respects, tends, when used to provide examples for political theories, to perpetuate misunderstandings about the political system. Democratic decision-making in small groups is quite unlike democratic politics. Neither the small political unit nor the small voluntary association is an institutional model for a large-scale operation. To talk as though the people actually govern in any modern democracy is to perpetuate a fiction, even though we may call it a 'noble lie.' If we take at the start the more realistic view that the public merely elects the rulers or policy-makers we shall not be disillusioned when we learn that a high and impossible theory drawn from the small model does not and cannot fit the facts of political life.

Since the principles listed in Chapter 4 are closely knit and everything cannot be said at once, I shall for the moment not define 'popular,' but assume a 'wide' franchise and the existence of the political freedoms, and center attention upon popular control and the other functions of elections.

Elections must be considered from several viewpoints if their full role in a democratic system is to be understood:

(a) From the point of view of the individual voter, elections are the means by which he takes his share in political power by voting for the representative of his choice.

(b) By means of elections the voters collectively bring the decision-makers under popular control, a control that is ever present in the minds of representatives because any part of their behavior in office (or in the case of aspiring candidates, out of office) may affect their chances at the next election.

(c) The election result is also an authorization of representatives to make decisions—to govern within the broad drift of a policy platform, if there is one, subject to the sanction of the next election. The election result invests representatives and decisions with legitimacy. In short, the government which is produced—almost as a by-product—and invested with legitimacy is the chief social purpose of the whole electoral process. I shall now take up these several points, beginning with the individual voter.

ELECTIONS AND THE INDIVIDUAL VOTER

Now, if this purpose of the election is to be carried out—to enable the voter to share in political power—the voter's job must not be made difficult and confusing for him. It ought, on the contrary, to be made as simple as the electoral machinery can be devised to make it. Hence the conclusive argument against 'long ballots' where, as in some United States elections, 40, 50, or even 70 choices must sometimes be made by each voter.

Only party identification (a 'ticket') enables the voter to find his way through the 'jungle ballot.' The gloom and perplexity of the voter is deepened when not only legislators, but also a host of administrative and judicial officials are to be elected at the same time: assessors, auditors, attorneys, judges, clerks, sheriffs, marshals, inspectors, coroners, school superintendents, printers, and so forth. The confusion of the voter is caused, too, by a multiplicity of jurisdictions, for instance in a metropolitan area where no one can be pinned with responsibility for the over-all government of the area. The situation is a very nightmare, and would tax the wisdom of Plato's Guardians when many constitutional decisions, and plebiscites on specific issues, must also be taken into account. (It is probably true, but impossible to prove, that the long ballots not only diminish the voter's feeling of sharing in power but also account for much voter apathy. A 60 per cent turnout in a Presidential year is considered good in the United States.)

Perhaps nowhere else in the world is the ballot—and much of the other political and governmental machinery—so bewildering and cumbersome as in the United States, a country which is a model to the world in its efficient technology and corporate organization. Let us be frank about it: much of the United States electoral machinery is a national disgrace, and the fact that it can be seriously defended compounds the disgrace and shows how far Americans are willing to tolerate abuses in what should be the simplest feature of democracy.

To be realistic, however, we must admit at once that the voter does not always think of his vote as a share in political power. Sharing in power is, so to speak, its political meaning for him, but its personal meaning or significance may appear quite different. The reasons why the voters vote as they do are difficult to interpret and post mortem guessing is a popular and inconclusive sport after every election. To the individual, voting may have any one or more of a large number of personal or private meanings. It may be part of his demonstration of 'belonging' (or citizenship) ; if he is angry, it may be his protest that he does *not* 'belong'; he may cast his vote to protect his personal interests or that of a group to which he is loyal; he may merely express his preference for the candidate; he may be taking part in a ritual because it is the thing to do, like celebrating a national holiday; he may be expressing his faith in democracy and his country; he may be passing judgment on the government's record or showing his agreement with a party's general policy; he may study the candidate and his party carefully; or he may simply flip a coin. 'All voting is an emotional experience for ditch-diggers and professors alike,' and 'The people vote *in* the same election, but not all of them vote on it.' [1]

Nor can we make the assumption that the voter is an altruistic student of politics, always casting his vote for the public good or viewing it as a 'public trust,' as Mill put it in *Representative Government* during the course of his argument against the secret ballot:

> His vote is not a thing in which he has an option; it has no more to do with his personal wishes than the verdict of a juryman. It is strictly a matter of duty; he is bound to give it according to his best and most conscientious opinion of the public good.

For one thing, the assumption of the altruistic and open-minded voter is empirically erroneous.

> There is a considerable correlation between social class, status, and political alignment, and quite generally, individuals in our society tend to support parties from which they expect definite benefits. [2]

Even independent voters, while by definition not pledged beforehand to a party or candidate, are not above private interests. Studies of voting behavior typically expect and find voting to be positively correlated with economic interest or sectarian or other private loyalty. (No doubt such results are partly due

---

1 S. Lubell, *Revolt of the Moderates*, New York, 1956, p. 90. Bernard R. Berelson, Paul F. Lazarsfeld, and William N. McPhee, *Voting—A Study of Opinion Formation in a Presidential Campaign*, Chicago, 1954, p. 316.

2 H. J. Eysenck, *The Psychology of Politics*, New York, 1954, p. 258.

to a statistical bias: voting may easily be correlated with sectional loyalty, but how is one to correlate voting with the 'public interest'?)

But the chief reason why we need not assume the altruistic voter is theoretical: it does not matter whether he is altruistic or not since all candidates and parties stand for some specific version of the public good. Yet the 'public good' is never on the ballot. What is on it are the names of a few candidates, often only two, between which the voter makes his choice. If this sounds a misleading way of putting it—after all, parties and their policies may stand behind the candidates—let us say that since a conception of the public good is behind every candidate's name, then whatever its private significance may be, objectively every vote is always cast and cannot help being cast for a conception of the public good. Where anti-democratic parties are on the ballot, then the vote is also for or against democracy.

A sense of public duty may sometimes impel some voters to vote, and presumably enlighten their choice, and voters are constantly urged to take a wider view and transcend their personal or sectional interests. Yet the impartial informed voter is one of the myths of democracy, and fortunately is not necessary, either for the validity of democratic theory or for the practical success of democracies.

There is another myth or half-truth about voting: the simple notion that the purpose of voting is to choose 'the best man,' in some quasi-Platonic sense. It is found in splendid simplicity and confusion in, for example, the works of Milton and Sidney in the 17th century. Somehow, they thought, the wise, rational, unprejudiced public would choose 'the best' representatives, preferably for life. But what the signs are by which we shall know the *politically* best, we are not told. The unspoken assumption—more understandable then but inexcusable in a democratic age—is that there is a 'naturally wise' elite who would be recognized almost on sight by the small electorate. A more naive and common form of the myth is the belief that personal virtues (as in a good husband, an honest man), or success in another occupation (a successful doctor, undertaker, merchant) is somehow a qualification for the political art of making public policy. The prescribing of Good Men as a cure for Bad Government rests upon the fallacious identification of the two spheres of private and public life, of private and public virtue. In spite of the most discouraging evidence of history, people will persist in believing that puritans necessarily make good rulers and bohemians, bad. Even more, such a belief usually blinds those who hold it to the corrupting influence of power even upon—perhaps especially upon —the righteous man filled with zeal for rebuilding men and society.

Neither is an election merely a popularity contest. The difference between a popularity contest and a political contest is that the former does not invest the winner with power. The student election of a Rector of Glasgow University, for instance, is often a popularity contest: it makes little difference who wins. If the Rector were being authorized to make important decisions, a new factor would at once be introduced into the voting. Representatives settle issues, and so issues affect the way many (perhaps a third) of the voters vote, and issues are the stock in trade of the candidates as they compete for votes.[3] But more important, even if no particular issues were in dispute, the voter knows that those elected will in fact have to make important and unforeseeable decisions as they arise, and these will affect his life in many ways. There is nothing irrational about voting on a broad preference for a person, party, or policy, or the general drift of a candidate or party. It may appear irrational in an economic sense (with its prudent and specific calculation of costs and satisfactions, or ends and means) but the rationality of economic behavior is a very narrow type which, applied to other things in life (love, friendship, arts, learning, and even political policy), is as absurd and impossible as Bentham's 'felicific calculus.'

[3] S. Lubell, op. cit. p. 94, states that usually the man and the party, not issues, is what the voter votes on. He also offers the interesting view that the Republican victory in 1952 was *not* a vote for the man (Eisenhower), but much more on the Korean War issue.

ELECTIONS AND POPULAR CONTROL OF LEGISLATORS

Whatever the private meaning of the ballot to the individual, there is very little dispute that it is the prospect of the election which keeps governments under popular control and sensitive to public opinion. Collectively, the voters bring the representatives under popular control by the ballot, the democrat's ultimate weapon. The election from this viewpoint is a kind of accounting for stewardship, and may be equated roughly—very roughly —to Assembly control of the Council and officials in the Athenian democracy. We must say roughly, because the Athenian Council was not elected or re-elected by the Assembly, which could thus not give any guidance for the future to any particular Council.

The submission of the government to the verdict of the voters is not accomplished by asking for a mere *yes* or *no* (as in Nazi Germany, for instance) but by the provision of alternatives. The only way one group can be voted out is by voting another in. Yet by a process of elimination in successive elections, or by voting for or against a government, it is possible for the electorate eventually to get to almost any destination, as in a child's game of 'hot or cold.' Whether in office or in opposition, or merely aspiring to office, all candidates have their eye on the next election, since they must be elected first if they are to make any policies later. Here the idea of responsibility comes into its own—responsibility of the individual representative where party ties are loose, and of the party where party discipline is strong. Although there is some difference of opinion on the subject, the dominant body of thought holds that the party sense of accountability is more sensitive, and consequently that electoral control is more effective and direct in a two-party system with a high degree of party unity and discipline. The united party finds it less easy to escape the punishment, easier to reap the rewards, of its stewardship; the voter in such a case finds it easier to distribute his reward or punishment.

Where the party in a two-party system is a loose alliance of individuals using the same party label, as in the United States, the representative need feel responsible only to his own district in order to get elected. The result is to strengthen the forces making the party's record a congeries of ill-assorted promises and policies. But where party unity is strong, the appeal can be to the voters as a whole (or a majority of them), and—other things being equal—the program of policy-making can be better co-ordinated, and hence more readily judged by the electorate. If this seems to pitch the tone too high, at the very least we can say that the large unified party can often afford to ignore the parochial issues and make its electoral appeal in wider terms of national policies.

It is with reference to this judgment at the polls that some writers have thought that an election is like a jury trial. The analogy is not altogether a good one, since voters are not impartial, i.e. indifferent to the outcome and judging only on factual evidence; if used at all the analogy is only appropriate to a two-party system where a verdict of *guilty* or *not guilty* can be passed on the government; it can scarcely be used in a multi-party system, because no one party in a coalition is wholly responsible for what the government has done, neither need any of the parties aim at the national majority to get a bloc of members elected. Again, although the voters may be swayed by the record (like a jury), the victorious (acquitted) candidates are not protected against double jeopardy, but must undergo another equally searching trial at the next election, and sometimes for the same offense. Likewise, the sound theoretical reason for never limiting representatives to one term of office is that they would as a result be exonerated from public trial, and so could not be held politically accountable for their decisions when in office.

ELECTIONS AND THE PRODUCTION OF A LEGITIMATE GOVERNMENT

Whatever the private motives which individuals may have for voting, or running for office, the social outcome or function of the election is to produce decision-makers, i.e. a government, and hence, indirectly, decisions or policies. A comparison may be made with economic activity, which is carried on by worker, manager, and investor alike for private purposes of a livelihood and profit. The social purpose, which gets performed incidentally so to speak, is the creation of business institutions of many kinds which in turn produce and distribute the goods and services in public demand.

Of some countries, for example those with a parliamentary system and two parties, one can perhaps say that the predictable outcome of the election will be both a government and an opposition. Yet even in such cases we cannot say that the voter casts his vote for the government-to-be, or for the opposition-to-be, because he cannot know beforehand which party will be in which role. The best he can do is vote for the party which he *hopes* will be the government. Where there are a number of parties or none, then, except by the overly optimistic, the vote clearly cannot be cast for the government-to-be since the government—inevitably a coalition of some sort—is formed later among the representatives themselves. The wider the choice of parties, the less the voter can be said to choose the government directly.

Disappointed politicians often talk of public ingratitude for past favors. But this is to confuse the personal reasons why the individual votes as he does with the fact that all election results—whether intended or not—are by their nature future-oriented. The authorization to form a government and to decide future policies is always given by the voters collectively, and taken as such by the successful representatives. To the voters who are conscious of this, it is presumably not what they think a party has done, but what it will do, that counts most on election day. Such a diagnosis helps to explain the so-called ingratitude of voters for past favors, and why indeed gratitude for the past should have only a minor part in voting, except insofar as past actions afford some clue to future actions. (The other part of the reason for seeming ingratitude is that sin makes news; and so the electorate remembers mistakes of politicians much better than the policies that were successful.)

On the question of what makes the policies of elected representatives legitimate, and hence morally binding upon citizens, there is a school of thought which, under the influence of the direct democracy tradition, tends to talk the language of 'as if.'

The decisions made by a majority of the representatives are thus said to be as legitimate 'as if' they were made by a majority of the voters directly. But since they are not in fact made directly, to sustain the argument a tenuous chain of logic must be constructed.

The first link of the chain is to identify representatives with voters. Only if this link can be constructed can the arguments for the majority principle used by the Athenian or other direct democracy then be available for service.

Now, it must be admitted at once that the link is an extremely weak one, depending in the first instance on the effectiveness of the electoral system in this respect. An electoral system based on proportional representation, if properly designed, can (within its assumptions) 'represent' accurately and make every vote count equally; but it is virtually impossible for any system of single-member constituencies with plurality counting to do so. The latter system may, however, roughly approach the ideal, if districts are of approximately equal populations (and voters) and are kept so by frequent revisions or apportionment, and if there is no gerrymandering. But even then there will normally be—to judge from experience—a congestion or waste of votes in 'safe' districts. The best one can hope for is that safe seats, on both sides, will balance out; then, if the marginal voters or districts decide (given a two-party system), the majority of seats will go to the party with the majority of votes.[4] But there is no guarantee that this will happen, and frequently, in fact, it fails to do so. Even if it does happen, it does not necessarily produce 'representation' in the sense which the 'as if' argument requires. In a multi-party system (if there is not preferential voting), one may hope that parties will secure seats roughly in proportion to their popular votes; but again there is no guarantee that they will do so.

The link which identifies voters and representatives (even in an arithmetic sense) is thus more than tenuous; it is often non-existent, and virtually every democracy turns up examples of governments supported by a minority of the voters. Hence any

[4] Cf. Dankwart A. Rustow, 'Some Observations of Proportional Representation,' in *Journal of Politics*, February 1950.

theory of democracy which depends for its validity upon the assumption that only a majority-supported government is legitimate and can make legitimate decisions is clearly at a serious disadvantage here.

The second link in the chain is to identify actual voters with all eligible voters. The link is necessary because the number of actual voters is never equal to the number of those eligible to vote. A percentage of 85 would be unusually high in a free election; more commonly, it runs between 60 and 75. At the local level of government, interest in elections is normally much less marked, and the percentage drops sometimes as low as 10.

The reasoning to support the second link usually runs along these lines: those eligible to vote could vote if they wished; the possibility that they will do so is always present—for instance, if they feel aroused about a public issue or a candidate. The potential voters are always taken into account by parties and candidates in their restless search for votes. The conclusion is that the non-voter tacitly agrees to accept the verdict of the voter as to the representation, and consequently as to the policies, on the understanding that the channels are kept open and he may change his mind and vote at the next election.

To avoid this roundabout way of identifying actual and eligible voters the alternative sometimes proposed is the institution of legally compulsory voting, which with a universal franchise could make actual and eligible voters practically identical. Compulsory voting has not, however, found favor in most democracies, being in use only in Australia, Belgium, and a few others, in some of which the law is a dead letter.[5] The overwhelming argument used against it is that it forces people to the polls who would otherwise not have voted, and since these are by hypothesis persons who have no preference for one side rather than the other, it would probably be an entirely irrational vote.

A third link in the chain—the identity of actual voters with the total population, including minors and future and past generations, does not, I think, raise any special problem. Among the many responsibilities which conceivably weigh upon the

[5] See Henry J. Abraham, *Compulsory Voting*, Washington, 1955.

voter when he comes to cast his vote is that of duty to all those not qualified to vote—to children, to posterity, and to ancestors; it is, that is, part of the question how he ought to vote. It is thus not a question of identity, but of rightful authority (as well as duty) exercised on behalf of minors and others.

The question of a government's responsibility to the past, i.e. for past policies, raises some interesting questions on a not-very-much-explored subject. On the one hand are legal obligations— contractual and financial; on the other, self-government is made a mockery if new laws and new policies cannot be introduced, and any living generation is always bound by its predecessors and is, as it were, 'governed from the grave.' As always, in politics it is a question of degree: of balancing disorder, discontinuity, uncertainty, and the damage to expectations against the antici-pated advantages from new policies. But it is the present gov-ernment (and generation) which makes the all-important de-cisions, even the decision to stand by the past decisions. There is no one else to make them.

The weakest link in this chain of reasoning constructed to account for the legitimacy of elected governments and their policies is the first one. As we have seen, it is sometimes a miss-ing link, since electoral systems being what they are, the ma-jority of the representatives are sometimes elected by the minor-ity of the voters.

Fortunately, we need spend no time seeking the missing link. To talk in terms of identity of the whole public with the voters, or of voters with representatives, is to strain language and sense, and to bog down in the riddles of representation. Legitimacy is needed because, as Rousseau put it: 'The strongest is never strong enough to be always the master until he transform strength into right and obedience into duty.' But nowhere in the world does the legitimacy of democratic government depend on representa-tives being collectively a microcosm of the voters—still less of the total electorate and of the total population past and pres-ent. In every democracy, the successful representatives are looked upon as authorized to make the political decisions on behalf of all, including the non-voters; and those who voted against the successful representatives acquiesce in the result, subject always to the next election. Children and non-citizens as well as ancestors and posterity must take their chances. The public agreement on this legitimacy is an unwritten clause of the whole democratic constitution. In the modern world no other principle of legitimacy is remotely as powerful, no other 'credenda of power' will carry intellectual conviction.

> If we ask what makes our government the legitimate government of our country, and by what right it governs, surely the answer must be that it is because it is the government which has obtained power in accordance with the constitution.[6]

I am suggesting that the constitution consists in the rules of the game, the agreement which authorizes public policies before they are enacted or even discussed. But the prospect of the next election is always an implied condition. 'Authority is a deposit which the community is capable of vesting in the holder of authority as in a trustee.' It is a 'virtual contract,' a 'deposit which the trustee is expected to return and get no thanks for it ... a contract with a time-limit.'[7] Wherever a legislature contains both elected and appointed members the authority of the former is usually regarded as superior just *because* they are elected—a truth which is underlined by much colonial experience.

The language of principal and authorized agent is often helpful here, and is perfectly understandable, as when I appoint an agent to manage my estate: he is better qualified to make wise decisions. Yet if I do not like the result, or the agent, I can change to a new agent, who in his turn will then have rightful authorization. (I do not wish to press this analogy very far—we cannot govern ourselves, but we could for instance invest our own money; all of us do not necessarily appoint the same business agent, but we all live under the same government, etc. Nor is there any necessary implication in the language of agent and principal of the maxim often unhappily used of politics: *delegata potestas non potest delegari*.)

The legitimate authority of a freely elected government is

6 J. W. Gough, *Locke's Political Philosophy*, Oxford, 1950, p. 54.
7 Eric A. Havelock, *The Liberal Temper in Greek Politics*, London, 1957, p. 149.

sometimes said to be based on consent. If we use the strict meaning of *individual* consent—that a citizen is bound only by the policies to which he specifically consents beforehand—it is obviously impossible to build a political system upon such an anarchical principle.[8] The voters who favored the opposition can scarcely be said to consent to the policies of government, though they may acquiesce and obey; while not even the voters who favor the government can be said to consent to all its decisions, since they too, often obey under protest. We can say perhaps that legislators who vote for a measure after full debate consent to it, but this is at a very far remove from voter consent. Yet the opposition in legislature and country acknowledge the government, and recognize the legitimacy of its policies, even though they may dislike both. There is no gain and much loss of clarity in putting legitimacy in terms of individual or minority consent, or in identifying the voter's personal choices with all policies of the government.

OBJECTION ONE: THAT ELECTIONS ARE TO DECIDE POLICIES

Objections may be raised to the meaning of elections and legitimacy as outlined above. One objection often heard asserts that the voters do in fact decide policies directly by their votes, and that is what elections are for. On this view, the voters are guided by issues more than anything else. All that we can say is that the empirical evidence does not support the assertion for two-thirds of the voters, though we have no way of knowing as yet that what is true of one democracy is true of all.[9] A concern with issues—even if typical of only a minority of voters—explains why in a non-party or loose party system (as in the United States

---

8 Cf. J. P. Plamenatz, *Consent, Freedom and Political Obligation,* Oxford, 1938.

9 '... about a third of the electorate builds its vote primarily out of concern for issues.' Alfred de Grazia, in *Research Frontiers in Politics and Government,* Washington, 1955, p. 126. In short, persons, not issues, count more (cf. also footnote 3). De Grazia suggests (p. 127) that 'ideological psychological' grounds will in future count more, containing both national and international issues.

Congress) the elaborate records of 'voting divisions' are publicized. The past voting record of a representative is of some guidance for the future, in spite of the fact that many issues will inevitably come up during another tenure of office, on some of which there will have been no previous stand while on others government and opposition may not differ.

Political platforms contain many issues, some of them vague (e.g. 'an enlightened farm policy'); some specific (e.g. to raise the sales tax by x per cent). They are mixed bags of goods—containing whatever is calculated to win elections. In choosing, the voter must, whether he likes it or not, take the whole package of the party he votes for. Specific policies may occasionally be decided directly by the voters—in those rare cases where one issue dominates. For instance, the voters may be said to have rejected Gladstone's Licensing Act in the election of 1872, when the Liberals were 'borne down in a torrent of gin and beer.' But usually it is the general drift of its policy, or the 'major items,' which the victorious party feels most free to enact, with the defeated party being equally free to attempt to block the enactments (or to vote for them). Moreover, in cases where one dominant issue may be said to have been settled by the voters, the corollary follows that *on other matters* the representatives have received virtually no guidance at all from the election results. On these, in fact, the wishes of the electorate are all the more concealed, and can only be guessed at.

> If they [the government] bring in very controversial measures on these points they are often attacked by their opponents on the ground that they have no 'mandate' for these measures. But there is no generally accepted principle here. The only established convention seems to be that those who object to the measures should make protests of this kind and that those in power should take no notice of them. This seems on the whole a sensible arrangement. (G. C. Field, op. cit. p. 155)

We are not to conclude that policies are not affected by election results. They are indeed affected indirectly in many far-reaching ways, even though the votes may be cast for persons, and that is the social reason why control of the policy-makers is important. But an election is not a plebiscite on a number of specific issues. In some countries it is more accurate to describe an election as a plebiscite on the 'head man'—in Britain the prime minister, in the U. S. the president.

OBJECTION TWO: THAT ELECTIONS ARE TO ASCERTAIN THE POPULAR 'WILL'

A second closely related objection to interpreting elections as a choice of decision-makers, not a settling of policies, has it that the purpose of the election is to ascertain what policies the public wants. The recognized implication is that the duty of the representatives is to enact the wishes or 'will' of the electorate as revealed by the voting. This doctrine, that the purpose of elections is to find, and of representatives to enact, the popular 'will' does not, I think, hold water, for the following logical or practical reasons.

(a) As we have said above, the policy wishes of even the majority are usually not known, since the election will have given, at most, only broad policy directions—such as a general drift to left or right—and even this may not be very clear-cut, in view of the many possible interpretations of the electoral verdict. After an election, we all wonder what the government will do—we do not assume it will carry out all its campaign promises, and we should be amazed if it did so.

(b) In any event, the legislators are forced to make decisions not only on matters where they think they know the wishes of the majority of voters, but on the many new issues that arise, and on these they can only guess what the majority wants and hope that the guess will not be held against them at election time.

(c) Majorities are fickle. A government would be foolish indeed that tried to implement every transient public mood, out of a sense of electoral obligation, and then expected gratitude at the polling booths. A majority may easily resent the particular law which expresses its former general desire.

(d) Majorities are also shifting, according to the issues involved. It is unlikely in the extreme that the same majority of persons would line up behind several public policies. A majority of votes can be counted at one moment of time, but we can never know, except in a rough way, whether there is a popular majority for this or that specific measure passed.

(e) The majority may have few specific wishes, until there has been legislative and other public debate over details of a proposed policy. To know exactly what one wants is often difficult enough for the individual in his private affairs, and it is much rarer for the voter to know his policy-wants on most political issues.

(f) A government is not passive: it can hope to 'sell' a policy to the electorate before the next election. A government thus has more freedom of action just after an election because it has more time to persuade the public to accept the decisions it has made. At this point there is plenty of room for leadership and 'statesmanship' by the few (for instance, a Cabinet), who make a decision and then persuade their legislative supporters and later the public.

(g) When we move from the 'will' of the majority, even more troublesome questions arise concerning the minority 'will' and the 'will' of the non-voters. There may—occasionally—be some sense in which we can speak of the 'will' of a majority, but what sense can there possibly be in relating elections to the common 'will' of a divided or indifferent total electorate?

> The truth appears to be that what we mean by a common will is no more than that there shall be an available peaceful means by which law may be changed when it becomes irksome to enough powerful people who can make their will effective.[10]

(h) Elections have often been historically important, and still are, without parties, and when they merely settle a series of contests for office among individuals. Such contests have little or nothing to do with expressing a popular will on party issues— let alone national ones—but they do nevertheless support political liberties and authorize a government.

[10] *The Spirit of Liberty; Papers and Addresses of Learned Hand,* ed. Irving Dillard, New York, 1952 and 1959, p. 41.

The language of popular 'will' is too nebulous to be very useful in any democratic theory. Nevertheless, a real question remains: what policies is the representative to support once he is elected? We may approach an answer by considering two historical replies: one, that he should be guided mainly by what his district wants; the other, that he should be guided by what the national majority wants. To those who like their politics more high-sounding, the debate can be couched in terms of duty to district or to nation (or even to humanity).

If the emphasis is put on the district, and what its population wants, the question arises whether the local wishes to be followed are of those who voted *for* the representative (assuming these enlightened individuals can be identified) or of those who voted against him, as well as those who did not vote at all. The same difficulties may be couched in national party terms, and then an additional question arises of reconciling the local and national claims on the party. At once we see that we are back again to the doctrine of the popular 'will.' We may, without repeating what was said earlier on this doctrine, note one of the subsidiary errors to which it has given birth.

The delegate doctrine of representation by which the representative is held to be narrowly limited or 'instructed' is an old one, perhaps the most logical if we think that the representative should be a mouthpiece or channel for doing what his district wants. The representative today, however, cannot normally be a bound delegate of those who elected him (or of his district as a whole) for very good reasons: since he has not been given specific instructions as to what he should do, and the voters who elected him may have cast their vote for many different reasons, he finds it impossible to know exactly what they want of him. He cannot therefore do other than trust his own judgment of what they want. Democratic theory does not require that he follow the results of every public opinion poll. The bound delegate doctrine has lingered long and died hard but it is very little heard today, the tenor of democratic thought having made it virtually obsolete. (One logical extension of the delegate doctrine—the practice of both instruction and recall of the representative by his principal, the district—is usually illegal and deservedly so.) [11]

The position is simplified by highly united parties, so far as local versus national interests are concerned. In earlier days, with looser parties, the English legislature was unquestionably more local and trivial in the matters it took up; one has only to compare the Commons in 1850 or 1950 with a century earlier. Where the party is loose or non-existent, the representative will be much more sensitive to the local majority. Everything depends on whether the representative owes his election to the party name and organization. Hence some of the studies show that the representative in the United States system tends to vote in the legislature as the local pressures upon him seem likely to influence his fate at the next election. The empirical finding is thus in line with the theoretical expectations. (The dilemma of serving party vs. public, or national vs. local majority, is less acute in a multi-party system where parties do not broaden their platforms in order to aim at the national majority.)

If disciplined, the national party prevents much catering to local interests—and even makes it harder to cater to special interests on a national scale. Yet district and party will always put a representative under some conflicting pressure. Although released from some local pressures, the representative in a disciplined party is not wholly free. He must always assume that the party interest is the public interest, and if the two should differ, his best chance of bringing them together is to work behind the scenes. The Gordian knot can be cut if we assume— as we must—that the first consideration of the party is to get

[11] The Weimar Constitution said that 'They [the representatives] are subject to their conscience only and not bound by any instructions.' 'Instructing' was commoner before 1832 in Britain. It was, of course, perfectly proper for state legislatures to instruct United States Senators (a formula adopted in 1793) since they appointed them: Senators are 'hereby instructed, and the Representatives requested.' Instruction by constituencies is apparently not illegal in the United States—and is, in fact, provided for in some state constitutions, but is a dead letter. The Electoral College members are also instructed. The 'recall' can be applied to single representatives, but hardly to a whole legislature, or it would be equivalent to a dissolution. The signed resignation— as an instrument of control of M.P.'s—is illegal in Canada. (Cf. Mill, *Representative Government*.)

elected, and the second, to get re-elected. (Occasionally, perhaps, a party may wish to be out of office for a term—when the problems to be faced are particularly difficult—especially if a spell in opposition is more likely to ensure a return to office in the future. Now and then, too, a party member will put his conscience before party, or for other reasons break with his team; but if he does this very often he may be defeated, and then he is out of the political arena and is not our concern.)

If these at first sight cynical conditions are not observed, then the party will doom itself to opposition and so be unable to make any public policies, and also will show itself insensitive to public opinion and votes. In a democracy, it is not so much what the majority wants which will be enacted (even if what they want could be found out) as what, in the judgment of the party, will contribute to winning the next election.

Nor are these conditions, in fact, at all cynical. Within the limits set by the goal of winning the election, party members are free to consider the 'public interest' in high or low terms, and to consider their collective conscience. Nothing is more common in legislatures and political campaigns—popular impressions to the contrary—than appeals to high moral principles. Burke put the issue falsely when he contrasted his independent 'judgment' with the mere 'opinion' of his constituents. But Burke's feeling was right—against instructed delegates and the mouthpiece theory. Just as behind the demand curve in economics there is room for a thousand good or bad desires, all brought to a common focus on purchases in the market, so in politics there is room for a thousand good or bad reasons in making political promises or decisions, all of them brought to a focus for the voter upon the ballot box on election day, and for the representative upon the division in the legislature.

Subject, then, to the ever-present limits of what is likely to alienate or attract voters, the representatives can only use their own discretion or judgment. (It is perhaps unnecessary to add the need for Parliamentary immunities, and rules about non-office-holding, interest in contracts, etc., in order to free the representatives to use their judgment.) The 'mandate' that representatives are given is like a blank check with a very high maximum amount, and so the representatives are entitled to guidance on what the public wants. But it is a matter of accepting guidance only, not of finding and following a popular 'will,' whether manifested in instructions from constituencies, public opinion polls, or the superfluity of conflicting advice from individuals and organized groups. The voters do not want everything in one program and nothing in that of the rival party; nor does it make sense for a party to determine policy for years by how the voters felt on election day, or for the government to legislate only for its majority supporters, since these may fade away and be replaced by many of the former minority who voted against them.

It is often forgotten too, that legislatures themselves develop a club spirit, a remarkable *esprit de corps,* to which all representatives can testify—whether in the House of Commons at Westminster, the Senate at Washington, or elsewhere.[12] What Lord Bryce called a 'collective self-esteem' makes any legislature much more than an aggregate of individuals and parties, and raises the whole moral tone of decision-making. Men act differently when forced to play different roles, and the roles of the representative are varied and may be harmonized in many different policy patterns. There is also, of course, more than policy decisions to be made by the representatives; there is the general supervision of the day-to-day administration, most of which deals with the accumulation of the historical functions assumed and decisions made by previous governments. For the most part, the principles of these are non-debatable, in that they have become so widely accepted by the citizens that they may be said to be 'the will of all,' or 'beyond politics,' as they have moved slowly from the political to the governmental spheres.

Again, although we have talked of the elected representatives, or the majority of them, making the decisions, the theory is not upset by the fact that much of the effective decision-making and initiative is taken by party caucus, or by a strong Cabinet or other committee behind the scenes, and the legislative stamp of approval is sometimes automatic—except in Assembly-type gov-

---

[12] See William S. White, *Citadel,* New York, 1957, for an account of the corporate life of the United States Senate.

ernments, like the French until recently, where owing to the many intransigent parties and the dependence of the executive on Assembly support, executive leadership was virtually impossible. It can be assumed, quite realistically, that caucus and Cabinet are aware of public opinion and party opinion, and take these and other factors into account in proposing policies and laws before they are ever introduced in the legislature. For that reason, what has been said above of legislature or party can easily be translated into the reality of the total political and legislative process and leave the theory untouched in all essentials. Nor should it be forgotten that on many major matters the ordinary representative—even in the opposition—can and often does rise to the occasion, in the House as well as in party conclave, and help more directly to influence the decision which is pending. The ultimate sanction of the voter has a far-reaching effect that penetrates into every corner of the political process. A simple example is how it contributes to the assessment of those criteria called, in the U. S., 'candidate availability.' Another is how, when policies are made, they are always made subject to what Carl Friedrich called the 'rule of anticipated reactions.'

Finally, to reject the classic doctrines that elections are to settle policies or to ascertain the popular 'will' is by no means all loss. It has in fact one supreme advantage: it bypasses the mountains of traditional criticism of the universal suffrage erected on the simple fact—and it is a fact—that the bulk of the voters are quite incompetent to judge complex details of public policy. Judge Learned Hand spoke for all voters when he said:

> The simplest problems which come up from day to day seem to me quite unanswerable as soon as I try to get below the surface. Each side, when I hear it, seems to me right till I hear the other. I have neither the time nor the ability to learn the facts, or to estimate their importance if I knew them; I am disposed to accept the decision of those charged with the responsibility of dealing with them.[13]

The citizen, in this more realistic theory of the purposes of elections, does not need competence; he leaves complex deci-

[13] *The Spirit of Liberty*, p. 72. A first-rate little book on elections came to my attention too late to incorporate in this essay: W. J. M. Mackenzie, *Free Elections, An Elementary Textbook*, London, 1958.

sions to his representatives. Indeed we may go further: even the latter need not be experts since they have at their disposal all the technical expertise which the country can command. The place for the technical expert is in the administration, not in politics; his role is advising, not decision-making. Only if the expert is subordinate can we have a democratic system in which elected representatives are responsible for policies.

But although the charge of voter incompetence may be repelled, that of being 'less democratic' (in a direct or Athenian sense) must remain. The only way to meet it is to say we do not in fact live in the *polis,* that a democratic system in which decisions are usually made by the electorate nowhere exists or could exist.

Why Popular Control at All?

Behind the mechanism of free elections as a means of popular control of decision-makers lurks the more fundamental question: why popular control at all? This clearly rests upon a normative or moral principle, and its validity must first be established or taken for granted if there is to be a case for a democratic system which institutionalizes the principle.

At bottom, the general principle is an old one, which has commended itself to innumerable political philosophers and been used to justify many different political systems. The principle is simply that political authority should flow from the people, in distinction to flowing from another political source— the will of a monarch or Duce, a political elite, a foreign power, or the like. Authority to make decisions binding on the citizens is located in the body of citizens and not elsewhere. In older language the principle was stated as the doctrine of popular sovereignty. At once all the historic justification in favor of this source of political authority may be summoned to our aid, to make a case which in terms of contemporary plausibility (and the deficiency of alternatives) is so powerful today that it commands almost universal assent. Accordingly, no general defense of this source of political authority will be attempted here. (But see Chapter 11.)

The general principle is not enough to justify democracy. It has been turned to justify several different types of political regime throughout history, as when the sovereignty of the Roman people, supposedly transferred to the Emperor for life, justified Roman absolutism. Today popular sovereignty is also alleged to be the basic principle of Communist systems. Democracy as we are outlining the system institutionalizes the periodic transfer of popular authority by means of a free electoral choice of legislators. The short but sufficient justification of this method is that no other can be devised to prevent the absolutism of a permanent transfer: without the institutional channels and safeguards any despot can claim that his authority is derived 'ultimately' from the people.

Given, then, the common assumption that political authority should flow from the people, and the corollary that only the procedures of free elections keep the channels open for popular control, the question next to be examined then becomes: why should the 'people' or 'popular' control be identified with a wide (universal) franchise rather than a narrow franchise? In the next chapter we turn to an examination of the nature and justification of the universal suffrage, but before doing so we take a side glance at theories of representation.

APPENDIX | A NOTE ON THE THEORY OF REPRESENTATION

INTRODUCTORY

Theories of representation are something of a morass, into which I shall take only a few cautious steps. The general subject of representation contains a number of different and complex notions. At one extreme is the view of Rousseau, who flatly denied the possibility of representation at all, since the representative would merely be substituting his will for that of the people. Those who deny or distrust representation either tend, like Rousseau if they are democrats, to favor the machinery of the primary assembly in small units of government, or else, accepting the unit of larger scale, they tend to favor 'direct legislative devices' such as the initiative or the referendum. The idea of direct democracy through the primary assembly is similar to that of 'presentation' in the House of Lords (the Lords could 'present' themselves in person). The commoners, on the other hand (knights and burgesses), were too numerous, and had to be 'represented,' whether the representatives were chosen by lot, or rote, or appointment, or election. However chosen, their title to represent—to speak for and bind the larger body—was equally good. We are reminded again by this example that it is electoral procedures which distinguish democratic from earlier forms of representation.

The idea of non-political representation is old. In drama the actor stands for, portrays, or symbolizes a virtue, vice, idea, or natural force. Representation as symbol or substitute is also common in religion. In a similar way, we set up the figure of John Bull or Uncle Sam today as representing Britain or the United States.

Although representative institutions were known in antiquity (and are not Teutonic in origin, as some have held), they 'were nearly everywhere of far less importance than the "primary assemblies" in which all citizens participated.' [1] Possibly the most important kind of political representation has traditionally been the single ruler who sums up in his person the whole realm: he *is* the realm. The Hobbesian monarch, appointed for life, was of a similar kind, the only element of popular consent lying in the initial social contract, and possibly the tacit consent implied later by giving obedience and remaining in the realm instead of emigrating. Hobbes gave plausibility to the Leviathan, and to virtually unconditional obedience, by posing the blunt choice of chaos or despotism.

The idea of single-person representation carries over easily into the Führer principle, i.e. the idea of the self-appointed ruler who represents and knows best the 'real' interests of his people. Even when they are coerced, people are 'really' represented, i.e. their 'real will' is represented: that 'will,' intuitively

[1] J. O. A. Larsen, *Representative Government in Greek and Roman History,* Berkeley, 1955, p. 228.

perceived and contrasting with and underlying the superficial fitful desires and conscious interests, that 'will' which is rational and harmonious and therefore ultimate and absolute. Philosophers of high renown have perpetrated this invidious distinction. At the low level of modern dictatorship, Lenin used to claim this god-like gift of divination of the people's 'real' interests, and Hitler used to say 'My pride is that I know no statesman in the world who with greater right than I can say that he is the representative of his people.' [2] Even when due allowance is made for the later censorship, propaganda, coercion, and all the other methods by which the 'will' of the Germans was shaped after the image of Hitler's will, it is probably quite true that the great majority of them did want many, if not most, of the same things that Hitler wanted for Germany. In this sense, he did interpret and represent his people, and his boast was substantially true. And that it was true turned out to be Germany's shame and the world's misfortune.

If we put aside all such notions of the non-democratic sort, then I think that the idea of democratic representation—by means of free election—has crystallized around a few simple ideas.

REPRESENTATION OF PERSONS, NOT 'INTERESTS'

Substantial agreement has been reached on the belief that per sons as individuals, not corporate estates or 'interests' or places are represented, although for convenience a territorial basis is usually adopted.[3] Elections by persons, not 'interests,' is implied, I think, both by the principle of *popular* control of legislators and by that of equality of voting: 'interests' cannot be measured, but votes can be counted. Modern democracies have thus in the

---

[2] Alan Bullock, *Hitler: A Study in Tyranny*, London, 1952, p. 367. The notion that people will approve a policy after it has been made, and even if they had never thought of it beforehand, is, however, common and legitimate and even essential in democratic politics. Without it we could not explain initiative in policy-making.

[3] The use of the Athenian 'tribe' and *deme* was also a convenience for elections on a territorial basis. The representation of places may be said to have lasted in England until 1885, when the principle of roughly equal population was adopted.

main agreed, though not without dispute, that the adult citizens should vote and be represented as persons, and not in their capacities as farmers, teachers, business men, landlords, and the like. In this as in so much else, democracies were anticipated by the Levellers of 17th-century England who shifted the emphasis to human beings and away from corporations, vested interests, and rights of property or status as the elements to be represented in Parliament.

The alternative theory, only occasionally heard now, but popularized by guild socialists in the 1920's, is that some form of 'interest' or functional representation should prevail, and votes be allocated accordingly. Now it is a truism that people are members of many 'groups,' and hence there has been hopeless disagreement on whether the interest to be represented should be 'estate' or class (as earlier when the vote attached to the land), or industry, occupation, religion, or race. Class or property interests have usually been the strongest opponents of the extended suffrage in most western countries, but in others, religious, and still more, racial interests have supplied most of the opposition.

Burke thought the British constitution was not, as so many of his time believed, a balance of Crown, Lords, and Commons, but a balance of the 'great vested interests' of the country—an idea similar to John C. Calhoun's 'concurrent majorities.' In fact, however, elections took place in Burke's time on a geographical or borough basis, and it was merely fortuitous if the results happened to represent the 'great vested interests.' One might say that the borough (or territorial) basis of election just 'grew' in Britain (from the medieval idea of communes such as boroughs and counties conceived as corporate bodies) with theories being later invented to justify it. In the United States, in turn, the representation of counties and towns grew from the British tradition. But in all cases the territorial basis today amounts to a rejection of the interest representation principle. Representation of interests divides the citizens, stressing their differences, while election on a territorial basis unites many diverse interests, and stresses what they have in common.

Many, before and after Burke, have defended 'interest' representation. Aristotle thought that a stable polity would be an aristocracy with democratic elements, at least for advisory purposes—a kind of class representation or 'balance'; and his strictures on democracy were based on his definition of democracy as a one-class or mob government. Montesquieu's defense of interests is also well known—his separation (or balance) of powers: *'le pouvoir arrête le pouvoir.'* Originally—at least in Norman England—the High Court of Parliament represented the 'estates of the realm' even though Lords and clergy (unlike the Commons) were not elected. Today, the theory of 'countervailing power' is as much a political as an economic concept, and is a kind of interest-pressure-equilibrium theory, by which 'interests' cut across and find expression through popular elections and representation.[4] In some respects it resembles the so-called interacting 'interest group' theory of politics, except that in Galbraith's theory government is not merely passively moved by 'original power,' but may also actively promote 'countervailing power.' Hence the theory is, or could be, a guide to policy as well as a neutral description of what does in fact occur.

Schemes for occupational representation for elected second chambers have sometimes been drafted, as in the Webb's Draft *(A Constitution for the Socialist Commonwealth of Great Britain, 1920)* and sometimes such schemes have been put into effect, as in the old Irish Senate of 1922-30. Almost invariably these proposed or actual chambers have been economic councils of some kind. They have not flourished or found favor for two reasons. One is that it is far from plain why economic, and not some other, basis should be the 'interest' so represented. The second is their unhappy flavor of the 'Corporate State' associated with Fascist Italy and with quasi-Fascist Portugal.

It is of course true that where representation is on a popular, territorial basis, some interests do often secure representation owing to the fortuitous circumstances of geography, as when one area is predominantly agricultural and another manufacturing; or one is predominantly of one religion, another of another; or even of one sex, as in the northern districts of Yukon or Mackenzie in Canada, where the population is overwhelmingly male.

---

4 J. K. Galbraith, *American Capitalism: The Concept of Countervailing Power,* Boston, 1952.

But all of these are regarded as accidental, and the dominant theory is couched in personal terms.

Although interest representation is generally rejected as the principle of legislative composition, alternative methods to ensure some political representation of interests and minorities are worked out in virtually every democracy. Some common examples are the representation of interests in the Cabinets of Canada, the United States, and Britain; in the appointment of judges, civil servants, and so forth. The tendency is especially marked in federal states, where the regions or states are generally also represented in upper houses, so that in a sense federalism may be regarded as a modified form of functional though not primarily economic representation.

Perhaps the most systematic theoretical defense of 'interest' representation and power was that of John C. Calhoun: a doctrine of 'concurrent majorities,' i.e. that the majority of every substantial interest (or minority) should concur in all substantial legislation which affected that interest.[5] The scheme was in fact a justification for a minority veto of the decisions of the numerical majority, and was not always reconcilable with his doctrine of states' rights or with federalism, and still less with the democratic principle of decision-making by a majority of the popularly elected representatives.

Today the only substantial theory of interest representation (apart from federalism) is connected with 'communal' representation, and separate electoral rolls. The theory has been devised chiefly for ex-colonial territories, newly entered upon the stage of self-government, where divisions among the population (usually of race and religion, either singly or together) have made it appear unlikely that the common electoral roll, and the principle of equal voting, would be at all workable, that is, accepted peaceably by the powerful minority sections or interests of the society who would be outnumbered by the majority belonging to other sections. It has thus been a method devised for 'plural societies,' sharply divided and without enough basic unity to trust themselves on the full flood of equal voting and

[5] John C. Calhoun, *A Disquisition of Government and Selections From the Discourse*, ed. C. Gordon Post, New York, 1953.

the majority principle of decision-making.[6] Where the separate electoral roll has not been adopted by some new democracies, an alternative has sometimes been the achievement of the same end by maintaining the principle of the common electoral roll but restricting the franchise by class, and thus avoiding, for instance, a racial conflict; or by the judicious use of a certain amount of 'honest' gerrymandering, as in Ceylon. These devices are a second-best to the full principle of political equality of voting and throw considerable light upon the social and other conditions necessary for working a democratic system.

In summary: interest or functional representation has been rejected as the electoral basis. Instead, all democracies vote on a territorial basis, and the representatives are conceived of as representing persons.

REPRESENTATIVES NOT 'MICROCOSM'

The second idea which virtually every democracy has rejected in practice (if not in theory) is that the representatives should collectively be a kind of mirror-image or, better, a 'map to scale' of interests or opinions in the country as a whole. Yet the tenacious doctrine that representatives should be a microcosm of the population at large is still widely held, again largely, I think, because of our tendency—whether conscious or not—to imitate the Athenian or New England town model, to try to approach as closely as possible the direct or 'face to face' democracy. The tendency is also linked, psychologically, with ideas of a popular 'will' that should be reflected as accurately as possible. Thomas Paine could say, after the French Revolution, that he grafted representation upon democracy, but in this he was not in the radical tradition of Rousseau which distrusted representation as distorting the popular 'will.' Bentham, however, thought that by identifying legislature and country, the interests and hence 'will' of the two would be identical: the general, not the particular, interest.

[6] W. J. Mackenzie, 'Representation in Plural Societies,' in *Political Studies*, February 1954. It should not be necessary to point out that 'communal' representation has not always had the motives of the South African ruling class.

Now it is a familiar fact that all classes and groups in a state are not represented in the legislature in proportion to their numbers in the country. The representatives are not an occupational cross-section of the voters: lawyers and farmers, for example, are often over-represented (certainly so in the United States), housewives are invariably under-represented. Consequently, extensions in the suffrage have not always been matched by corresponding changes in the composition of legislatures, a fact which may help to explain a certain amount of disillusion with franchise reform. Yet—to repeat—it must be said that the microcosm view of legislatures is not a part of generally accepted democratic theory. The troublesome questions are: what is a cross-section for political purposes? A person can be 'represented' in many capacities—as a resident of a locality, as tenant or landlord, as consumer (and different types of consumer); by occupation, by industry, by race, religion, and sex. Why should occupation, as some suggest, be chosen as the criterion from among innumerable other bases? Why indeed should any economic basis be chosen? (Let no one imagine that a sampling theory, such as that used in Dr. Gallup's polls, solves these normative problems.)

Three further points are, I think, conclusive against the 'microcosm' view. It is wrong to suppose that most people want to be represented by persons like themselves. Secondly, since politicians are quasi-professional, or should be, does it matter what the (former) occupation of our representative may have been—whether tinker, tailor, soldier, or lawyer? The politician has other roles to play than that of merely reflecting his class interests or social (or other) background. Finally, the political parties as informal systems of representation supplement the formal structure of government. As H. G. Nicholas puts it (*The British General Election of 1950,* London, 1951, p. 64):

> ... each major party, in varying degrees and, of course, with its own variations of emphasis, presents itself to the electorate as offering a cross section of the population. None can claim a monopoly of representativeness; none apparently wishes to pose as the exclusive vehicle of one group.

In view of the obscurities and misleading notions of representation theory, I am inclined to think that politics would gain if we gradually dropped the word 'representative' altogether and coined a new one to replace it, or came to confine popular usage to Senator, Congressman, M.P., legislator, and the like. Democratic theory has little to gain from talking the language of representation, since everything necessary to the theory may be put in terms of (a) legislators (or decision-makers) who are (b) legitimated or authorized to enact public policies, and who are (c) subject or responsible to popular control at free elections. The difficulties of policy-makers are practical and there is no need to confuse democratic politics by a theory that makes the difficulties appear to be metaphysical or logical within the concept of representation.[7]

TENURE OF LEGISLATORS

We turn now to glance briefly at more practical questions concerning representatives (since we must use the term) as policymakers, questions that lead away from the morass of representation theory.

Consider first the question: how often should elections be held? It is hard to see how theory can give clear-cut answers to such practical problems as the term of office of legislators. On the one side is the argument that to ensure the utmost popular control, the tenure of office should be short, that is, elections frequent. The Chartists in England, for example, had annual elections among their demands, and the one-year term has often been used in local government. On the other side are practical arguments, such as that public business is too complicated to be learned in one year, or that a legislator can give less than wholehearted attention to his policy duties if he has always to keep one eye on an election in the near future; while in addition elections are expensive and if held frequently are a confounded nuisance to all concerned. The result is a compromise between popular control and legislative efficiency, with the result

[7] Cf. R. Wollheim, 'Democracy,' *Journal of the History of Ideas*, April 1958, pp. 235ff.

that in most democracies a term of office from two to five years is the common rule, with current opinion tending, as a rule, to favor the longer rather than the shorter term.

SIZE OF LEGISLATURES

Again, how many legislators should there be? In the extreme case, it is possible to have only one, as in the 'plebiscitary democracy' of France in the 19th century, and in the 'popular dictatorship' (during emergencies) of ancient Rome. Much the same idea of one man representing the whole is familiar to us in the United States Presidency, though his role of representation, and of policy-making is shared with Congress.

The case at the opposite extreme, expounded mainly by proponents of Proportional Representation, is that every body of opinion or interest in the country ought to have a representative who will at least be its spokesman in the legislature. But at once we run into the same difficult questions which faced us when we considered whether the legislature collectively should be a microcosm of the country: What interest is to be our basis? What is a 'body of opinion'? And how far short of *tot homines quot sententiae* shall we stop? These questions are usually avoided by advocates of P.R., and the argument instead is given that every *party* should be represented according to the votes cast for it, with presumably an implied assumption that bodies of opinion or interests which feel strongly will in fact form their own party, and the further implication that they *should* do so. Still further in the background may be the absurd assumption that 'if legislatures can be made "truly representative," differences will be easily and peacefully resolved.'[8]

Again, somewhere along the continuum, practice must give an answer to the question of numbers, and it has been arrived at in history by a process of trial and error (if that is not too rational a description) and by modifying the institutions of the past. The usual answer—on the national level—is a number of representatives up to 1,000, but seldom, if ever, more. An upper limit might appear to be set by the number which can be seated and heard

---

[8] David Truman, *The Governmental Process*, New York, 1951, p. 525.

in one room, but this is a very high upward limit indeed nowadays, with an increased knowledge of acoustics and the invention of mechanical public address systems. Such a large number has everywhere been avoided.[9] A more practicable and smaller limit is the number which can meet and take part in debate, in friendly or easy fashion, while avoiding the atmosphere of a public meeting. The English deliberately designed their House of Commons, in the rebuilding after the war, so as *not* to provide seating accommodation for all the M.P.'s (neither are desks provided), on the realistic assumption that not all M.P.'s will be in attendance at all times, but that when momentous debates occur there will be a crowding, with some members standing, which will in turn enhance the importance and solemnity of the occasion.

Clearly this British view of the size of the Commons rests upon one of several possible views of the proper function of the legislature, whether, for instance, it is to decide policies or to control the policy-makers. Mill thought that Parliament should not be for decision-making, which should be done by the executive, but that instead it should be for debate and redress. Debating, to serve the dual purpose of leading and sounding public opinion is, like redress and ventilation of grievances, a function on which all agree. The further question is, why should public opinion be educated and sounded by debate? And here the only possible answer can be that it may be given its chance to affect (a) election results directly and (b) the political decisions indirectly, even if the latter are initiated by the executive and merely ratified or implemented by the legislature.

The number of legislators may also be a function of the amount and detail of business to be transacted and how the work of the legislature is organized—the committee system, length of session, etc. I do not see how these questions can be settled in advance, since within the democratic framework of decision-

---

[9] The problem of size will have to be faced, however, if a world government should ever be devised on a 'representation by population' basis. A method of indirect election (or appointment)—as now for representatives at the UN—could be adopted, but in that case, if 'representation by population' is to be the rule, the solution might be for each representative to have votes in proportion to his country's population.

making by representatives there is obviously room for great variation: one legislature may take on many functions, another fewer; one state may be large, another small; one may have the Parliamentary, another the Presidential executive, and so forth.

Another interesting minor question is whether the shape and seating arrangements in a legislature have any effect on its nature. These differ widely: the Norwegian seating arrangement is alphabetical, the Swedish by constituency; the rectangular shape is used in the United Kingdom, the semicircular in the United States and some European countries. The British rectangular model, with government and opposition divided and facing each other, is generally thought to emphasize and dramatize the basic party conflict and the continuing scrutiny of government by opposition.[10]

[10] Many other differences between legislatures are found, e.g. in voting methods, in the Cabinet system (in some countries Ministers are M.P.'s, in others not), in choice of Cabinet (by the Prime Minister or by the House), whether Cabinets are strong (as in Holland), or unstable (as in France until recently). Should legislatures meet annually? (Only ten United States state legislatures do so.) Has the increased practice of consultation with interested parties reduced the importance of legislative meetings? Are decisions becoming more influenced or made by executive departments, and less by legislatures or Cabinets?

SIX | *Political Equality and the Franchise*

INTRODUCTORY

In this chapter we examine the second of the principles characteristic of a democratic system. Who are the 'people' who exercise popular control by means of elections and what does it mean to say they are politically equal?

The legal equality of citizens in politics was, in the original Athenian democracy, confined to a proportion of adult males. How can we say then that the universal adult suffrage is essential to democracy? We must say that, in the past, it was not so regarded; we must equally conclude that in the contemporary world there is no logical stopping place short of the universal adult suffrage. Popular control means that all adults share the political power; to say people are in law politically equal means at least that each adult has the vote. The suffrage is thus one criterion of democracy: to the extent that the suffrage is less than universal, to that extent the system is less democratic, less under popular control. The suffrage is of course only one criterion, necessary but not sufficient, and since there are several criteria, it is possible for one country to rate well on some scales but not on others.

There is, then, little serious questioning of the principle that the franchise should be co-extensive with all adults, regardless of such differences as those of sex, race, religion, or wealth, all of which are regarded as politically irrelevant. Moreover, all democracies rate rather well in putting the principle into practice. In view of the wide acceptance of both the practice and belief, it might be thought to raise no problems of justification, and to need none. Why bother to prove what everyone knows and does? Nonetheless, an examination and justification of the principle is worth noting, as we shall see in due course.

'FITNESS' TESTS FOR VOTING

As a preliminary, it may be noted that the right to vote has not always been thought to be attached, as now, to persons. That is, it was not thought to be based upon personal, political equality. Formerly, in Britain for example, it was looked upon as a right adhering to property (the freehold). Harrington in the 17th century noted that power follows property, and also that it should do so. A trace of the same belief can occasionally be found in local government even today—for instance, in voting on money by-laws—and was much in evidence in the disputes over the broadening of the franchise in the 19th century, when most of the steps in the process still linked the vote with a property qualification. A common 19th-century attitude was that expressed by Sir Robert Peel:

> ... it was surely absurd to say, that a man with ten thousand pounds a year should not have more influence over the legislature of the country than a man of ten pounds a year ... How could the government end but in a democracy if the influence was merely according to numbers? [1]

More recently in Britain, widows with property were granted the vote before it was granted to all women on the same terms as men.[2]

In the course of time, the argument for linking property and

[1] B. Keith-Lucas, *The English Local Government Franchise*, Oxford, 1952, p. 143.

[2] The view of senior governments has sometimes been (and still is) that local governments are primarily trustees of public funds—a view which, as in 19th-century Britain, tended to limit the local vote to rate-payers, and to limit also the purposes on which local authorities could spend money. Is it far-fetched to regard this view—i.e. that elected representatives are primarily trustees of public funds—as tacitly accepted constitutional doctrine in the days when Parliament was called only to approve taxes? Or is it rather that the granting of money by Parliament was merely a convenient device to control the executive (monarchy)?

the vote altered its emphasis, as the accepted theory of representation altered. The possession of property was no longer looked upon as conferring a right to vote, but came to be regarded as somehow a test of 'fitness' to vote, as somehow measuring or guaranteeing the responsibility of voting. By contrast, until 1936, the Soviet Union deliberately disfranchised all those who lived from property, ownership of productive property being *ipso facto* a test of unfitness to vote, since the capitalist was by definition an 'exploiter.' Democracies, virtually the world over, have abandoned the idea of the vote as a property right, and also of the possession of property as any test of fitness to vote.

Fitness tests of other kinds are still used in some places today, being sometimes, perhaps always, put forward to exclude some classes from voting. They are often disguised as literacy tests. Illiterates would in any case be penalized by a form of balloting that required a reading knowledge (to read the ballot), although it is perfectly easy to design a method of balloting (with symbols, as in India; with colored balls as in Burma) even for a population most of which cannot read or write. Occasionally, high-minded persons like Mill have advocated literacy tests—'to read, write, and I will add, perform the common operations of arithmetic.' [3] Such simple tests may not in theory be discriminatory provided that elementary education is within reach of all, a corollary which Mill was careful to add. Why, then, are literacy tests not more widely adopted? (They are adopted in some 20 states of the United States, New York having the most stringent; and they are used in Australia as a device to exclude certain classes of immigrants.)

The trouble with all literacy tests is that knowledge of the three R's is not much of a guarantee of anything else. Certainly it is not a sign of a sense of political responsibility or political wisdom, or as some put it, 'intelligent voting'—and it is pre-

[3] *Representative Government*, McCallum edition, Oxford, 1947, p. 212. Mill also wanted all voters not only to pay indirect taxes, but also to pay a direct per capita tax. Hence his argument for exclusion of paupers from voting (op. cit. p. 214). Poll taxes are still in use in a few southern states in the United States, but not, I venture to say, for the reason Mill gave, i.e. 'that so everyone might feel that the money which he assisted in voting was partly his own, and that he was interested in keeping down its amount' (loc. cit.).

sumably something like this which a fitness test is designed to guarantee. Since we cannot in fact test for these qualities, and since voters are never impartial, then to start by excluding the uninformed, the prejudiced, the interested, would not only lead us into a hopeless maze of distinctions, but would, if the process of testing is taken further, end by wiping out the franchise altogether.

Underlying the idea of fitness tests of any kind for voting is a particular view of politics and the purposes of elections. The view of politics involved is that:

(a) Some political decisions are wiser than others.
(b) Some people know which decisions are wiser.
(c) These people can be found by fitness tests of some kind.
(d) All adults can be persuaded to accept the first three propositions, and hence to accept the legitimacy of restricted voting.

The view of elections is related, namely that their purpose is to enable the electorate to decide the issues or make political decisions directly.

Several ways are available of dealing with these assumptions. The shortest is to say briefly that they mistake the purpose of elections, which is not and should not be to decide the many complex issues, but to give everyone an equal vote in choosing decision-makers (representatives). Once this is granted, fitness tests of political wisdom related to issues become quite irrelevant to popular voting (and if used at all—which of course they cannot be—such tests should presumably be given to politicians).

There is, however, a little more to it than that. Even if we grant the truth of the first assumption above—and it is a truism which can hardly be denied—it is of very little help, since in the specific case there is no impartial jury to which it may be shown *beforehand* whose decisions would be 'wiser.' It is the absence of such agreement beforehand which accounts for politics. We are, in fact, by the notion of fitness tests and political wisdom, taken back to a kind of quasi-Platonic view of politics. Democratic theory, on the other hand, does not start from that premise, but with a method of choosing and controlling decision-makers. Fitness to make the political decisions is assumed to reside in those who are elected, and in their advisers, though the kind of decisions to be made play some part in the election campaign, in the guise of platform promises and a party's record. It is absurd to suppose that a democratic system can cross its principles with the institutionalizing of the quite different assumptions about politics given above, neither is it plausible or feasible that a democratic public today can be brought to accept restricted voting, or the 'fancy franchise.'

Since an election is not an exercise in direct legislation, the ordinary textbook views on the suffrage are often questionable. To take one example from a good recent text: it is commonly assumed that 'a literate person is better equipped to exercise the function of voting in an intelligent manner than is his non-literate brother'; and that the suffrage problem is one of 'insuring that those granted the franchise will have the knowledge and the interest necessary to guarantee its intelligent use.' [4]

The same sentiments used to be put much more plainly in the last century by those who feared, like Bagehot, the 'supremacy of ignorance over instruction and of numbers over knowledge':

> Take two persons, one from the lower and another from the higher classes, and propose to them any political question: which will be likely to give you a right answer—the man who has had some kind of education or the man who has not passed beyond a moderate acquaintance with reading and writing, probably somewhat the worse for wear? Stripped of the attributes of number and power, can any one doubt as to the answer? [5]

Often today the demand for fitness tests is a relic of earlier days, and is fundamentally a desire to limit the suffrage, with a test for competence as the ostensible reason. When the demand for fitness tests is more respectable (as in the textbook cited), it wrongly conceives the voters' task to be that of deciding difficult questions of policy for which detailed knowledge is needed. Once we have made democracy rest on voters' competence of that kind how-

---

[4] John M. Swarthout and Ernest R. Bartley, *Principles and Problems of American National Government*, New York, 1955, pp. 200, 205.

[5] *Nineteenth Century Opinion*, ed. Michael Goodwin, Harmondsworth, Middlesex, 1951, p. 225.

ever, we have, I think, given away the case for democracy entirely to its critics. Nor is this to disparage universal education—the carrying out of Robert Lowe's exhortation to Parliamentary advocates of suffrage extension in 1868: 'Educate your masters.'

What knowledge does the voter after all require? If he knows the general reputation of the candidate and party he has enough: '... and if he knows the big thing about the parties he does not need to know all the little things.' [6] The democratic voter, like the ultimate consumer in economics, insists on judging by the results without knowing everything about or getting caught up in the complexities of the means. He can, in any case, usually vote for only one of a few parties, each of which has its share of brains and knowledge. Literate, even educated, voters with vast knowledge of political questions also differ in their voting and often indeed divide in the same way as the unlearned.

> Degrees in geology, physics, chemistry, mathematics, botany, etc., contribute in themselves nothing to political education. The university franchise [in Britain] disclosed no greater wisdom or judgment on the part of university graduates than that shown by any other constituency.[7]

It comes to much the same to say that the classical theory (still taught in our colleges) pre-supposed the alert and impartial citizen, always thirsting for knowledge and ready to discuss political questions, always moved to vote on principle for the 'public good' as distinguished from sectional interest, and always carefully calculating ends and means like economic man. All of this approach appears to be empirically quite false, and it can scarcely be wise for us to conduct our political affairs upon a false orthodoxy. Fortunately, therefore, democracy does not require these assumptions in order to work and even to work well.

> No worse nonsense is talked than what we are told as to the requisites for the elective franchise. To listen to some people, it is

[6] Bernard R. Berelson, Paul F. Lazarsfeld, and William N. McPhee, *Voting— A Study of Opinion Formation in a Presidential Campaign*, Chicago, 1954, p. 321.

[7] William A. Robson, 'Education and Democracy,' in *Political Quarterly*, Jan.-March 1959, p. 76.

almost as solemn a function as to be a trustee of the British Museum. What you want in a body of electors is a rough, shrewd eye for men of character, honesty, and purpose. Very plain men know who wish them well, and the sort of thing which will bring them good. Electors have not got to govern the country; they have only to find a set of men who will see that the Government is just and active.... All things go best by comparison, and a body of men may be as good voters as their neighbors without being the type of the Christian hero.[8]

THE BROADENING OF THE FRANCHISE

The history of the franchise in recent times has been one of widening the classes of persons entitled to vote, a process which everywhere was regarded as a nearer approach to democracy. Any country that introduced voting at all was under heavy pressure to go the limit. In ancient Athens, the class of citizens made up —with their families—perhaps a third of the population, a proportion which was much larger than the narrow class of property-owning voters of whom Locke wrote in the England of the 17th century, and very much larger than in England before the first Reform Bill of 1832. The Founding Fathers of the United States (or most of them) favored excluding slaves and certain other adults, while religious restrictions on the suffrage also existed in some states at that time.

The modern widening of the suffrage came, for men, in the 19th century; by 1850 in the United States substantially all males were enfranchised, except for Negroes and a few foreigners. For women, the period of enfranchisement was chiefly that between the two world wars, starting in some countries with single women and widows with property. This kind of start was made in Britain, for example, when married women—known to the common law, aptly enough, as *femes coverts*—had no political rights. In France, however, women were not enfranchised until 1945, in Belgium not until 1949, and to this day in Switzerland (often thought to be a model democracy), women are only partially

---

8 Frederic Harrison, cited in John Morley, *Oracles on Man and Government*, London, 1923, pp. 97-8.

enfranchised. As a general rule, Roman Catholic countries have been slower to give women the vote, notably those in Latin America. As late as 1941, when women were enfranchised in the province of Quebec, some of the highest clergy protested against it. (Women could, of course, vote before then in Canadian federal elections.) The history of the 'votes for women' movement, and of the feminist movement in general in the modern world, is so grotesque, undignified, fatuous, and tragic-comic (the adjectives are deserved rather more by male arguments and resistance against the suffragette movement) that it must forever make us doubtful of the value of rational arguments alone to persuade a vested interest to grant political and social concessions.

It is, then, only recently that the democratic logic has been thought to imply universal adult suffrage—that all adults should, in Gladstone's fine phrase, be brought within 'the pale of the constitution.' This late development is a reminder of how slow the process has been of getting agreement on even a simple principle of democracy. While the principle is recognized in every democracy today, there are some localities where discrimination is practiced, by exclusion from the electoral roll, or by discouraging voting. These are, however, generally recognized as abuses, as departures from the right principle, and where they exist are regarded as legitimate objects of reform. (A limited franchise may perhaps be reasonably defended, on expedient grounds, for a short transitional period, during which democracy is being introduced from the top down in a former colony or autocratic regime.)

A few uncontroversial exclusions from the suffrage are made everywhere, such as incarcerated criminals and the insane, but they do not affect the principle. There are a few borderline cases, however, which cause perplexity, and the rulings upon them seem to vary from one jurisdiction to another. The clergy have sometimes been excluded from voting, and from legislatures. There is something of an empirical case for keeping sectarian and religious controversy out of the campaigns, if feelings run high, but not much for a general exclusion of clergy from voting. There may be a case, however, for the exclusion of those who have deliberately withdrawn from the world—e.g. anchorites and some classes of monks and nuns. Should released felons, having served their term, be excluded? or judges? or dishonorable dischargees from the armed forces? or are such exclusions merely anachronisms today? [9] Should aliens be allowed to vote if they satisfy the normal residence requirements? At what low I.Q. level, if any, should a person be debarred from voting? I do not see how the general principle of the adult suffrage can give much guidance on these matters, any more than it can tell us whether the voting age should be 21 (as it commonly is) or some figure slightly higher or lower; or than it can tell us what the residence requirement should be within a particular jurisdiction. The residence required varies greatly, from six months in the United Kingdom to two years in some American states, with usually a 'locality' waiting period required as well. The locality period unquestionably works against the enfranchisement of mobile elements in the population—a group discriminated against nearly everywhere —and is not easy to justify.[10] Nor will acceptance of the general principle answer the many detailed questions which arise from its practical operation—e.g. how the electoral roll should be compiled, the arrangement for printing ballots, the mechanics of voting, and all the rest of it. It is not my purpose, however, to discuss these subsidiary questions.

JUSTIFICATION OF THE ADULT FRANCHISE

We may now ask the question: how does one justify the normative belief that all adult citizens should be entitled to vote? The

[9] Occasionally, when public feeling runs high against some classes of citizens, legislators will be found to try to deprive them of the vote. Thus in 1918 the United Kingdom Parliament—reflecting or sharing the popular feeling against conscientious objectors—enacted a law (Representation of the People Act, 1918) depriving these people of their right to vote for a period of five years. A bill was introduced in the United States Congress a few years ago to deprive convicted Communists of their right to vote, but it did not pass. The question of withdrawal of voting rights as a form of legal punishment for electoral and other offences is an interesting one that needs further examination.

[10] The American position is further complicated by two kinds of citizenship status, that of the United States, and that of the separate states. The District of Columbia has been disfranchised since 1874, a situation certainly in conflict with the democratic principle of political equality.

main arguments or reasons that have been put forward from time to time are these:

The *first* reason uses the language of 'rights': the entitlement to vote is said to be an individual, universal right. From being a radical and Jacobin doctrine, this human right has now become a tame, almost self-evident truth, easily taught to every school child. Sometimes it has been held to be a 'natural right'— as in some of the 17th-century versions of natural law. As Ireton said in the Putney Debates: '... if you make this the rule [i.e. adult male suffrage] I think you must fly for refuge to an absolute natural Right ... ,' and Colonel Rainborough replied: 'Every man born in England cannot, ought not neither by the law of God nor the law of nature, to be exempted from the choice of those who are to make laws, for him to live under, and for him, for aught I know, to lose his life under.' Curiously enough, it was held to be a natural right of men only, while at other times it was not a right of all men, but only of property owners. I shall not pursue the argument in terms of abstract or natural rights. If one believes in this particular right to vote, no further justification is necessary: it is an ultimate. If one does not believe in it, I do not see how a convincing case can be made in terms of natural rights. Fortunately there are other arguments in the armory.

The *second* argument is closely related and is also moral, and is often said to be derived from the postulate of the ethical value of individual personality. Now, it is rare to find any political (or moral) theory which does not purport to put a high value on human personality. Indeed, since morals and politics both treat of the relations of human beings with one another (rarely of their relations with gods or beasts) moral and political theory cannot but deal with men, i.e. with human personality. We may also admit that democratic theory puts human beings at the center of its moral and political theory. If it is agreed that moral action involves choice, a case can be made for wide freedom of choice in general. But choice-in-general hardly justifies the particular instance of voting choice, and it seems to me that we cannot logically deduce the adult suffrage from an emphasis on human beings and moral choice. The argument for the adult suffrage from human 'dignity' is of the same kind, with the chain of reasoning from 'dignity' to the franchise a simple deduction only if the ultimate of 'dignity' is of a particular political kind—in which case the conclusion is smuggled into the premise.

If the deduction from human personality to the vote is invalid then we must fall back again upon the ultimate: that adults *should* be free to choose their governors. If we accept this, well and good; if we do not, then the case for it must be built along other lines.

The *third* argument uses the language of justice. As well as a general obligation to obey the laws, a government imposes many specific duties, such as that of paying taxes; and on grounds of justice or 'fairness' or 'equity' the individual should be entitled to vote, and thus help to decide what taxes and laws he should be subject to. Insofar as it refers to taxes only, it is the old argument enshrined in the slogan: 'no taxation without representation,' which someone has called 'that immortal dogma of our national greatness.'

If the argument is couched in the historic American form— that the payment of taxes creates the entitlement to vote—then the implication is that *only* taxpayers should vote. On this premise too is it not logical to give votes in proportion to the amount of taxes paid? Can these implications really be a part, let alone a cause, of 'our national greatness'?

But we have abandoned the implication of this tax argument in such cases as paupers, while *per contra,* taxpaying resident aliens are not usually allowed to vote; nor do we usually take away the vote because of a conviction for tax evasion. The argument of relating taxes and voting is slightly old fashioned; we realize today that no distinction can be made between those who pay taxes and those who do not. All are taxpayers (just as all are recipients of public funds) to some amount, directly or indirectly. Putting aside the tax argument, shall we then grant the wider argument that since all adults are affected by government policies, therefore all ought, in fairness, to be able to help choose their governors by voting? It is an argument of considerable force in today's climate of opinion, but if we adhere to it, then resident aliens must be explained away on other grounds, which is not at all easy to do with any consistency.

The *fourth* is an argument of a related kind, namely that of self-protection. Any section of society is likely to have its opinions and interests overlooked and perhaps trampled upon unless it has the vote to ensure its share of the control of government and hence of policy. At the very least any section can make its voice heard through its representatives, or its influence felt upon the attitudes of representatives even though it may have no direct spokesman, or may not be large enough to elect one—for example, if it is a small minority in every constituency.

The force of the argument lies in historical experience, and in the contemporary struggles that always take place in a legislature (or behind the scenes) over policy, both of which tend to confirm its validity. Mill had this in mind as well as women's suffrage—and he was profounder than he knew—when he said: 'Men as well as women, do not need political rights in order that they may govern, but in order that they may not be misgoverned.' The argument could also be derived from an *a priori*, pessimistic view of the nature of politicians, for instance the assumption that they will always try to maximize votes, and thus only voters will be attended to. The argument is, however, one that tends to emphasize individuals less, and group or sectional interests more, and so it may easily lead in the direction of functional representation of some kind.

In any society with the full range of political liberties postulated by democracy, any group, even if its members cannot vote or have only a few votes, has other ways of making its opinions and influence felt—this must be admitted in view of the abundant empirical evidence; but it is also true that the ultimate peaceful sanction is the vote—a sanction whose strength depends upon many contingent factors, such as the number of votes the group can muster, their distribution, whether the group votes as a bloc, etc. In short, self-protection is a strong argument for the vote, and is far more realistic than the assumption of enlightened voters, judging altruistically of the public good.

The *fifth* argument relates to the idea of the 'common good.' It goes back to the Athenian argument for political equality, used by Aristotle as well as by the Greek 'liberals': each contributes to the polity, and each should share in political power. The life of any society is in some sense a whole, made up of the contribution of every section, indeed every person, in it; the political life should follow suit—a condition fulfilled only if every adult has voting power. If any section plays an important role (and all do so) in other ways—economic, educational, etc.,—it would be depriving the political life, as well as being inconsistent, to withhold the voting role as well. The argument unquestionably has great persuasiveness, but based as it is on the idea of 'contributions' (which are unequal) it does not logically lead to *equal* voting.

The *sixth* argument is that the right to vote should be a proper attribute of adult citizenship, as it was for males in the Greek *polis*. One important aspect of citizenship activity is stifled without this right.

Although this is a powerful argument, adult citizenship and the suffrage are usually legally separable. In 1875, for instance, the United States Supreme Court decided that the suffrage was not a necessary incident to adult citizenship, and this decision still stands, so the vote is regarded legally as a privilege conferred by the several states, and not as a right, a very odd situation indeed in a country so permeated by a belief in natural individual rights.[11] In broader terms, however, I do not think the ordinary citizen regards the vote as a privilege to be conferred or withdrawn by government, nor should he so regard it in a democracy. The right or entitlement to be a voter must obviously be widely distributed, or popular control of government is impossible. Accepting this, it is quite reasonable to conclude that the best way to ensure popular control is to make adult citizenship ordinarily carry the implication of the right to vote. As was said long ago, the virtue of democracy is equality; the vote gives it substance.

Now, all of the arguments listed above may be held at once to fortify the case for the adult suffrage, since they need not be in conflict. They all unite in rejecting the idea that, in any democ-

---

11 *Minor v. Happersett*, 21 Wallace 162 (1875). The U. S. Constitution forbids the *abridgement* of the vote on specific grounds of race and sex.

racy, the right to vote is merely a question of expediency, as some jurists (putting the state above all else) have contended. The latter view is rightly held to verge upon a Führer or even totalitarian principle, by which the rulers (many or few) know and express best the 'real' will of the public, so that voting need only be a convenient device to enable the public to endorse the 'real' will, or a ritual to raise morale or to demonstrate solidarity to skeptics. It should be noted, however, that some of the reasons given come very close to a theory of the representation of interests instead of persons.

The particular reasons given do not necessarily explain why the franchise has broadened in any specific historical case. Sometimes concessions have been wrung from a reluctant government by demonstrations and threats—as with the militant suffragettes, and the stormy public agitation for the first Reform Bill in England. At others, the suffrage has been extended for crafty reasons of party calculation, as when the enfranchisement of Negroes was undertaken in Dixie in the Reconstruction period, largely because the new Republican Party hoped this might ensure its election. These and other instances which could be multiplied indefinitely show that groups holding political power have normally resisted extensions of the franchise, and few groups (though there have been some) have ever obtained the vote without a struggle, often severe.

The direct exclusion of minorities from the suffrage is frequent. It can be said that in general a dominant group which has a bare majority or is numerically in the minority will never favor an extension of the suffrage which would put in jeopardy its control of the government.[12]

In summary, I am inclined to think that today the universal adult suffrage is merely an inseparable part of the wider argument for democracy, i.e. for a political system marked by popular control of government, as distinguished from alternative systems; that once popular control is assented to, it leads logically to no stopping place short of the adult franchise for all sane adults. In

[12] Jean La Ponce, 'The Protection of Minorities by the Electoral System,' in *Western Political Quarterly*, June 1957, p. 319.

accepting popular control—free election of decision-makers—one may take it as an ultimate, part of the very definition of democracy; yet some of the arguments in favor of the universal suffrage make out a strong independent case for any wide franchise, and hence for popular control itself.

IS THERE A DUTY TO VOTE?

There is another question connected with voting which is sometimes raised but seldom examined. Apart from the right to vote, is there a corresponding duty to vote? Or, conversely, is there a right of the eligible voter not to vote sometimes?

The usual argument that voting is a universal duty runs something like this: A successful democracy depends upon widespread interest and participation in politics, among which voting is an essential part. Deliberately to refrain from taking such an interest, and from voting, is a kind of implied anarchy; it is to refuse one's political responsibility while enjoying the benefits of a free political society. The right of non-voting, if widely exercised, would hasten the end of a democratic government; non-voting is a mode of action impossible to universalize in a democracy, and so fails to meet Kant's test for the categorical imperative. In Rousseau's words, 'As soon as any man says of the state: what does it matter to me? that state may be given up for lost.' [13] Further, in the earliest democracy, that of Athens, it was entirely taken for granted that a citizen would perform all the rituals which attached to citizenship.

Those who take this common view—and it must be admitted that it has considerable force—deplore political apathy among the public, and in particular are disturbed whenever a small proportion of the eligible voters turn out at election time. The lack of vitality of local government, where the proportion voting is typically low, is usually blamed upon apathy, although why there

[13] Mill put it thus: 'Again representative institutions are of little value, and may be a mere instrument of tyranny or intrigue, when the generality of electors are not sufficiently interested in their own government to give their vote...' *Representative Government*, p. 113. Note he says *generality*, not the *all* which Rousseau implied: a typical instance of the difference between the two minds.

should be more apathy at the local than at the national level is not clear. The frenetic campaigns by public-spirited organizations to 'get out the vote' and the enactment of compulsory voting laws in some countries are based on the assumption that apathy is bad and voting is a duty.[14] Plato, too, provided for some compulsory voting in the elections for the Council which he envisioned in the *Laws*.

It does not follow, however, that because 'substantial' voting is necessary, or is felt by some people to be a moral obligation, all voting should also be made a legal obligation, since many social duties are left, and may properly be left, to the individual conscience—among them the duty to subscribe to charities, to work, to run for office, to enlist in volunteer armies, or to rescue people from drowning. Again, a compulsory voting law may be unenforceable (like the laws of some American states against adultery), or the enforcement may be attended by consequences that are highly undesirable or even wrong, and outweigh the advantages (if any) of 100 per cent voting. An argument on the moral duty to vote, even if accepted, does not necessarily lead to a conclusion for legal compulsion to vote.

Against those who take the ostensibly patriotic line of the moral duty of all to vote at all elections (which is what we are discussing), there are several considerations which, taken together, have great cogency. In the *first* place, the duty to vote is one frequently not recognized, which should perhaps give us pause; but on the contrary, the right *not* to vote is often admitted to be legitimate and is sometimes used as a recognized political tactic in the instances where certain parties or groups boycott the polls, as in Ireland and in Malta in recent years. A *prima facie* distrust of the universal duty to vote is also engendered by the example of totalitarian states, where voting is regarded as a duty and non-voting as disloyalty.

Secondly, it is hardly disputed that a good case may sometimes be made for individual abstention, even by persons with an in-

[14] Citizen apathy is not the only reason why compulsory voting has been instituted. Less admirable reasons have often been prominent, e.g. the expectation that the non-voters, if driven to the polls, would favor a particular party; that is, it was desired that voters should vote the 'right' ticket and not for the opposition.

terest in politics. Some studies have shown that where a group is under conflicting pressures, the voting turn-out will be low. And who can deny that such a voter abstinence is reasonable? Again, the eligible voter may believe that all the candidates are equally bad and stand for policies which he abhors, or he may think it does not make much difference who wins. It would seem to be a very odd duty that requires an undecided person to vote by the toss of a coin, or for a party to which he is indifferent, or for a person or party which he believes will ruin the country.

Thirdly and more important, it is (perhaps fortunately) true that not everyone is actively interested in politics. There are many ways in which a person may make a contribution, even a political contribution, to the society in which he lives other than by taking part in its voting. What is regarded as a purely private life—the smooth currents of domestic joy—may have a social value. From Epicurus onward there has been a strain of thought which has counseled withdrawal from active civic life. The politically conscious, especially the zealots, need constantly to be reminded of limits to politics and zeal, of Dr. Johnson's words:

> How small, of all that human hearts endure,
> That part which laws or kings can cause or cure!

Instead, therefore, of preaching the duty to act as a political animal to those who have no inclination that way, and would do it badly if compelled, it may well be wiser to leave them to cultivate their private gardens, and to rely merely upon the experience of democracies that there is always in fact a wide enough interest in politics and voting to work the political machinery. It is not an established truth that democracy suffers from voting apathy, or that any democracy has fallen because of it. It should not be very difficult to prove this one way or another. My own impression is that the evidence points overwhelmingly the other way, that there has always been wide, almost feverish public interest in politics and voting in countries where democracy has collapsed, e.g. in the Weimar Republic; and that democracy has not been lost through voter apathy, but because it has been overthrown by non-democratic parties, e.g. by the Nazis in

Germany, the Communists in Czechoslovakia, and the Fascists in Italy. To say that there must be a 'substantial' public interest and voting is quite true; but to say that 'substantial' requires 100 per cent voting or any figure approaching it is obviously false, as the experience of nearly every democracy confirms.[15]

Rousseau once said, 'A people constantly assembled to dispatch public business is impossible to imagine.' We do not need to press a case in *favor* of apathy, but we may say that a large public which is not constantly excited and interested in political questions is probably healthy in any democracy for this reason: interest (and voting) go with partisanship and it is virtually impossible to increase one without the other. The heavier the vote, therefore, the less likely are the voters to be the rational citizens of classical theory contemplating the public good. The apparently private vice of disinterest in politics may therefore be a public virtue and a sign of social and political stability. We must remember, too, that the potential as well as the actual voter is a strong control over a free political government. (I do not wish to overstate. Political apathy and non-voting may also be unhealthy if, for instance, it results from wide disillusion and a feeling of hopelessness.)

A notion closely related to the alleged duty to vote for public reasons is that one has a duty to oneself to vote; that by doing so one is 'expressing one's personality.' But while this may be true of some, other personalities may be warped by being forced into a direction for which they have no talent or inclination. It is begging the question to assume that voting is a method of expressing everyone's personality or is a desirable personality trait of all. (Athenians seem, however, to have made something very like the assumption that political activity was expressing a citizen's personality, and certainly the notion of a right of non-voting would be very un-Greek; but then, any individual right in any modern sense would be un-Greek.)

[15] The 'politically active' in the United States make up some 2 to 3 per cent of the adult population, or about two and a half million—about as many as there are active criminals. 'Politics, in what may be the most free political system in the world, is the work of a few people.' Alfred de Grazia, in *Research Frontiers in Politics and Government*, Washington, 1955, pp. 130ff. The 'politically active' is not, of course, the same as the number voting.

It was noted earlier that part of the defence of the universal suffrage was based historically upon the need for protection of the particular group or section to which voting was extended, such as landlords, lodgers, paupers, or women. The duty to vote is correspondingly sometimes put in terms of loyalty to the lesser group to which one belongs. But to say that this is a universal duty is to say that a lesser group loyalty must always be put first, above, for instance, that of the country as a whole, and is also to avoid the question: which group shall we vote for if different group loyalties lead us in different directions? If there is no duty always to vote for the country, it is far from clear that there is always a duty to vote on behalf of any smaller group.

Thus it is quite reasonable to conclude that while there may be some universal duties of all adults (or all citizens) in a democracy—such as paying taxes and obeying the laws—there is also a class of specific political duties, which do not and ought not to press upon all adults all the time, such as the duty to run for office, and that the duty to vote is sometimes one of the latter. If this case is sound, it follows, I think, that we should cast a skeptical eye on the popular appeals to 'vote as you please, but vote.' By emphasizing the duty of everyone to vote we risk creating inner conflict in many good non-political people, while at the same time we salve the conscience of the less sensitive who feel they are good citizens just because they have gone through the motions of marking a ballot or pulling a lever.

No Plural Voting

We return now to the principle of political equality, to examine its second implication: that it involves *only* one vote per person.

Again, it is not debatable in modern democracies that equality of voting means also that one person should not have more than one vote. That is, the logic of political equality rules out any type of plural voting, which for the most part is found nowadays only as a relic in local elections where occasionally an extra vote may be cast by virtue of property ownership.

One of the more persistent anachronisms, abolished in 1948,

was the plural voting in the United Kingdom where, in addition to the personal vote, each owner of business premises had a second vote in the district in which the property lay; and each university graduate had a second vote in the election of M.P.'s from the universities. In spite of Churchill's firm campaign promise that the Conservatives would restore the university representation, the Conservatives did not do so, nor attempt to do so. Plural voting for university graduates, however it may be defended on other grounds, is clearly at odds with the democratic logic of equal voting, and hence plural voting has been advocated mostly by hostile critics such as Ruskin, who thought the masses could be more easily managed if votes were given in proportion to education, age, and wealth; but how to sum these three incommensurables he did not say. Mill was one of the last democrats to argue for plural voting, but the best he could do was to suggest that 'the nature of a person's occupation is some test.'

EACH VOTE COUNTS EQUALLY— THE QUESTION OF ELECTORAL SYSTEMS

The third component of the meaning (and formal condition) of equality of voting is that each vote counts equally, i.e. shares equally in electing representatives. While the general principle is scarcely debatable, there are some sizeable departures from it in practice, and it will be profitable to notice these and the justification proffered on their behalf.

We are inevitably faced here with the question of electoral systems. Although interest or functional representation has been generally rejected in democracies—as pointed out in Chapter 5— the problem still remains for elections in which persons are represented: how best to secure that each vote counts equally in electing representatives. The problem hardly presented itself in earlier days when the emphasis was territorial and it was the constituencies that were represented. With the shift of emphasis to representation of persons, and the territorial division merely a convenience, then equality of voting took on this third aspect or meaning.

Given a party system (the simplest case), the desired result could theoretically be obtained in several ways, but a number of acute practical difficulties arise, apart from objections to the theory. Arithmetically, the best way perhaps is for the whole political unit (say the country) for which the election is held to form a single large constituency. Then with two or more parties, a list system, and a quota, each party could secure seats strictly in proportion to its popular votes. The large political unit has many drawbacks, however, among them the impersonality of the election, and it is nowhere adopted. Perhaps the electoral system of Weimar Germany came closest to the arithmetical ideal, and there the country was divided into a few large electoral districts, with a quota and list system of voting, a method similar to that in use in post-World War II France. Even if there is no party system (as in many local elections), something very close to the ideal can be obtained by eliminating the low candidates and holding successive ballotings to the point of a 'run-off' in order to obtain an absolute majority. But this is, on the whole, quite impracticable, at any rate on a national scale and for more than a second ballot. France used to have the second ballot (not more), and so do some ten southern states of the United States today in their primaries for state legislators and officials.

Apart from the list and quota system (and occasionally the second ballot or 'run-off'), advocates of proportional representation have put forward many ingenious schemes. The most common—to which the initials P.R. are usually applied—is the multi-member district with some form of preferential or transferable voting, by which second and third and lower choices are also indicated on the ballot by ordinal numbers, and counted by transferring either from the surplus of those reaching the quota, or from the eliminated lowest candidate, in successive steps until the number of seats is filled. This system, sometimes with slight variations, has been adopted in a number of countries—for instance Ireland and parts of continental Europe—and for some elections in the British Commonwealth. It is not used in Britain, and in the United States is used by only a few cities. (The original P.R. system put forward by Thomas Hare in 1857 envisaged the whole country as one large constituency, with transferable votes and a quota necessary for election. This was the system popularized by Mill in his *Representative Government*. The list system, however, is common in northern Europe.)

An elaborate discussion of proportional representation would be a digression here, but some comment is called for. It can be safely said, I think, that most of the proportional representation schemes on the market do permit and count the expression of a wider range of preferences by the voter. The question is the significance and consequences of the wider preference. Whether the counting of all choices equally, by a transfer of votes, makes sense psychologically, is perhaps doubtful. In what sense other than the arithmetical can my first preference be added to and equated with your second, our neighbor's third, and so on? In view of the 'plumping' that always takes place with the transferable ballot, there may even be doubt about the significance of second and third order preferences to a single voter.

Waiving these objections, what is the purpose of providing a wider range of voting preferences? It goes back, as suggested in Chapter 5, Appendix, to the view that the representatives should be a scale model or microcosm of the voters and hence of the population at large, or (as usually expressed) that every body of opinion and every minority should be represented in proportion to its members. (The microcosm theory also assumes, I think, a definite 'will' on the part of the represented, and thus tends also to justify the logic of the recall, and direct legislative devices.)

Once this ambiguous scale-model view is rejected, as it should properly be in any realistic political theory, then the nicely calculated advantages of any form of proportional representation need not concern us; nor for that matter need we dwell on its disadvantages—for instance that of encouraging and perpetuating divisions among representatives with all the consequences this entails. A wider choice at the polls and hence a more divided legislature almost certainly gives less popular control over government and inhibits positive policy-making. It apportions the frustrations of weak government more equitably (a dubious good), though to some extent it may enable the voter to 'let off steam' by providing a candidate and party of his first choice to vote for. On the other hand, there is undeniably much frustration in the single-member plurality system also—for instance in being able to vote only for one of two parties, and occasionally in voting with the majority only to find that the government is one elected by the minority of voters.[16]

It is a moot question which system is more frustrating to the voters, but there is no doubt which frustrates government and policy-making more. The point is that the proportional representation theory is built almost entirely around one purpose of elections—that of 'accurate' representation—and this it pushes to the logical extreme regardless of the other purposes and consequences of elections. Even if we grant that it solves difficulties of representation, it increases the difficulties of policy-making, and a political system exists to make policies, not merely to give psychological release to voters. The theory is strong and insistent on the very letter of the third aspect of political equality—making every vote count equally—but weak on the spirit of other democratic principles.

The original impetus to schemes of proportional representation came from those who feared the universal franchise. The danger from the enfranchised masses might be less, it was thought, if the enlightened minority could be sure of some representation, and were not completely swamped by the less enlightened voters. This was the reason for Mill's advocacy, and also for his suggestion on plural voting according to occupation. His failure to do more than suggest occupation shows how difficult it is to agree on the minority characteristics which should be given extra votes. Proportional representation has generally been popular with smaller parties e.g. the early Labor Party and the present Liberal Party in the United Kingdom, and with cultural and other 'permanent' minorities who can scarcely hope to be a popular majority. Conversely, where a two-party system is

---

[16] Some people argue that voting by principle, or party, is less 'mature' than voting for a person and trusting him. P.R. is then condemned as immature and anti-democratic 'because it interferes with the free expressing of feelings...' For this curious argument see D. W. Winnicott, 'Some Thoughts on the Meaning of the Word Democracy,' *Human Relations*, vol. III, June 1950, p. 176.

working successfully, proportional representation is usually repudiated on the grounds that it would give 'undue' influence to minorities (i.e. represent them by separate legislative parties) and so make stable and effective government difficult.

It appears to be true that proportional representation is a system which can give stable government only if the many parties are willing to unite and compromise in order to govern. Where there is not this willingness (some would say 'maturity'), the government is unstable and indecisive, and the policy decisions get made by people behind the scenes—e.g. permanent officials—or go by default. France, with many parties and unstable coalitions until recently, was often contrasted on this point with Sweden and stable coalitions. Where there are two parties— with or without proportional representation—the compromises can be made beforehand *within* each party if it is united, instead of later, after the elections, by party blocs. Where the two parties lack close unity and discipline, as in the United States, the representatives do not automatically divide on party lines in their voting. Each party is, so to speak, a loose coalition of blocs, comparable in many ways to the variety of party groupings formerly existing in France; the difference being that the Presidential type of government and leadership saves the United States from the worst of the French stalemates, though not from the bickering. (Without the Presidential type of executive, would the United States also have many parties and unstable government? It is not true I think that French *policies* are more unstable than American policies.)

The conclusions are as follows: it must be admitted that proportional representation can *represent* or reflect voter preference more accurately, despite psychological questions arising from summing the voting preferences; but often where it has been adopted (as in France, though the French system was that of 'true' P.R. only from 1945-51) it has inspired no confidence in the results, in terms of either good government or stable government. Yet the examples of where it has given better results, as in Sweden, have been less remarked on, largely I think because in such cases stability has in fact been achieved. Where the political divisions are many and deep among the population it is doubtful whether any kind of electoral system could produce stable government. On this, the French example has, I think, often been misinterpreted by observers, especially by political scientists with an Anglo-Saxon bias, who have too often tended to blame French political instability and many parties upon the electoral system instead of the other way around.

> First, the case against France misinterprets the nature and causes of the systems of two parties (or two blocs of parties) prevailing in Anglo-Saxon states...
>
> Second, the electoral systems which France has used have been used elsewhere and have not been accompanied by a multiplicity of undisciplined factions...
>
> A country's party system is determined far more by its political institutions and traditions in general and by the social factors affecting its politics than by the electoral system. The case against France involves a third error in that it neglects the age and depth of the divisions among Frenchmen.[17]

The other type of electoral system is based upon single-member districts and plurality counting (the plurality or first-past-the-post system for short), a method which has 'just growed,' but has in the course of time developed its rationale. The chief reasons for not altering it to multi-member districts and transferable voting are, I think, partly inertia and partly objections to the theoretical premises of proportional representation and to the practical consequences which—*ceteris paribus*—always flow from proportional representation. The plurality system produces many, often gross, deviations from the principle of 'each vote counts equally,' some of them inherent in the system, others a product of deliberate policy to make some votes count more than others. Those which are inherent obviously cannot be altered without adopting a different electoral system; the others are perhaps more feasible reforms.

An obvious and common violation of the principle that each

---

[17] Peter Campbell, *French Electoral Systems and Elections, 1789-1957,* London, 1958, pp. 30-32. Cf. also Maurice Duverger, *The French Political System,* Chicago, 1958, p. 186: 'In reality, the fundamental defect of French politics is exactly the opposite of what superficial observers diagnose. France suffers not from excessive instability but from excessive stability, from what has been called since 1953-54 "immobility." '

vote should count equally is found in the grossly unequal populations, and hence numbers of voters, in constituencies. Where rural districts are immense in area, the population dispersed, and roads and communication facilities sparse, there is something to be said on purely practical grounds for departing of necessity from the principle of equal weight to each vote. This sort of defense of a practice recognizes the principle, and justifies departure from it as highly exceptional and dictated by practical considerations. This less-than-full application of a principle is common enough in all of life. In science too, the abstraction of the frictionless machine, or the perfectly pure chemical, is the ideal, but is only approached, not reached. But few of the inequalities between voting districts can be justified on this exceptional ground. Many of the worst inequalities exist within urban areas, with no difficulties of communications or of sparse populations. Examples are abundant nearly everywhere.

One type of unequal voting, resulting from districts of unequal populations, is common in nearly every country and is sometimes defended by a primitive type of theory. I refer to the rural-urban division, and the fact that so many countries grossly overweight the rural vote at the expense of the urban by creating less populous rural districts. The theory behind it, such as it is, is a form of 'interest' representation: that somehow the rural population (alternatively, the farmers or the stout yeomen) are the backbone of the country, superior in some relevant way to urban dwellers; or that farming is a more 'basic' industry, again in some relevant political way, and thus ought to be more than proportionately represented; or one occasionally hears an argument for the 'equilibrium' or 'balance' of town and country—a phrase with as many misleading ambiguities as the 'balance of nature.'

All these arguments are extremely weak and specious, and the inequalities between rural and urban districts for the most part must be regarded as anachronisms. They have grown as the product of historical accident and group pressures. Some of the over-represented areas—for instance, American rural counties in Georgia or Florida—may fairly enough be regarded as the 'rotten boroughs' of the 20th century. The political remedy is naturally difficult, for the electoral laws themselves are usually in the hands of legislatures in which the rural elements are over-repre-sented, and what they have they hold in defiance of the demo-cratic logic, but in the solid historical tradition of all entrenched groups.

These inequalities or 'tacit gerrymanders,' generally admitted to be wrong in principle, exist because the legislatures have either not enacted laws to ensure regular revision of boundaries, or else have themselves violated the laws of revision. In short, individuals and parties, hoping to gain or perpetuate electoral advantage by the inequalities, often tolerate gross deviations from a principle to which they give lip service. Electoral reform of these large inequalities is a cause to which public and politicians alike ought to devote themselves. If it is not undertaken, two dangers to a democracy arise. One is the disregard for apportion-ment law, where it exists, and the hypocrisy always engendered by preaching one thing and practicing another; the other is that minority interests will get their way, at the expense of the majority interests.

Two methods of periodic revision (known also as re-distribu-tion or re-apportionment) are possible: the *first,* by a revision of boundaries—say after each census—which may be performed either by a legislative, and hence political, committee, or by an independent tribunal which is usually non-partisan.[18] The latter is less common, but there would seem little rational argument for refusing to adopt it in any country which fully admits the prin-ciple of equality of voting, that is to say, if the principle itself is regarded as beyond political dispute and is thus a part of the underlying consensus.

The *alternative* method is to maintain existing boundaries, but to increase or decrease the number of representatives which the district is allotted. This method may also be by legislative committee or independent tribunal. For the most part the prac-tical difficulties in this method—resentment at reduced repre-sentation, the fact that the total number of representatives must

[18] Occasionally in the United States it is done by the executive, e.g. for the national House of Representatives it is done by the Census Bureau and the President, within a total of 435 seats set by the Act of 1929; or in some states it may even require approval by the electorate itself. Some state govern-ments have ignored their constitutions, providing for regular apportionment for many years.

continually increase with increase of total population, and the fact that the method is not feasible in a country with only single-member districts—makes its sole use generally quite out of the question. In fact, most democracies rely upon the first method, sometimes modified by use of the second. So long as the end result, of constituencies with approximately equal population (and hence of eligible voters), is obtained, then the principle of equal voting is more nearly approached.

It is approached, but voting districts of equal populations are by themselves not enough. Their shape and boundary lines must also be taken into account. And it is here, also, in the practice of gerrymandering, that abuses of the electoral machinery have crept into many democracies. The purpose and effect of deliberate gerrymandering are to enhance the advantage of this or that party or politician, and hence in some degree to violate the principle of equal voting. Gerrymandering is one of those abuses almost universally condemned in principle, but often tolerated in practice. Its existence is an argument for an independent tribunal to set boundaries, but also a difficulty in the way of adopting the tribunal method. A two-party and simple plurality electoral system can in general work well only if the parties do not divide on 'communal' lines—Canada is a very good example; but if parties do so divide, then a multi-party system and P.R. may well prevent majority domination of cultural minorities. What the cost may be in terms of frustration of the majority, political instability, and social discontent is another matter.

The point must be emphasized, however, that even when districts are of approximately equal populations, and there is no gerrymandering, and there are only two parties, it is impossible to make every vote count equally in a plurality system. It is not merely that minorities may be under-represented; they may equally well be over-represented. In short there is, except by accident, nearly always a greater or smaller lack of proportion between the votes cast and the number of seats obtained. And so we have the familiar phenomenon of presidents and governing parties being elected by a minority of the voters, a situation which can be much worse in a multi-party system.

What justification may be given for the plurality electoral system (as distinct from its abuses), within the bounds of the other conditions of the democratic principle of equal voting? The defense must, I think, be along these lines:

First, it may be quite reasonable to put up with less than 100 per cent application of one principle when to do so would promote fuller application of other principles. It is quite reasonable, for instance, to maintain that popular control of government (and the production of a government by elections) may be hindered by an electoral system that aims first and foremost at 'accurate' representation, and subordinates everything to that aim.

Second, there may be practical inconveniences or disadvantages from pressing one principle to its logical end, and these may offset the gain. There are, other things being equal, certainly several inconvenient results from P.R. wherever it has been adopted.

Third, experience may convince us that in a working democracy this particular deviation from equal voting does not matter greatly because we can in fact rely on minority-supported governments not to 'exploit' the majority (and vice versa), or because there are other channels, apart from voting, by which the majority (or under-represented minorities) can make their political influence felt, or because there are other means of representing majorities and minorities.[19] This point may be carried even further. One can fall back upon a kind of 'virtual representation' theory, i.e. a certain disproportion of seats and votes may not be regarded as important so long as the representatives take into account what the majority (or minority) of voters are believed to want, as candidates will always do in bidding for electoral support. The total of representatives will still feel responsible to the total of voters. To play down the importance of a disproportion, however, is a dangerous form of argument if carried very far; neither is it always valid, since there is no point in bidding for the majority of the votes if a party can count on being elected by minority support. (The old doctrine of 'virtual'

---

[19] The influence of minorities is generally conceded to be favored by the American electoral system, especially in the Senate and Presidency, yet the electoral system is such that many minorities are not given any significant representation in Congress, though perhaps few are without a spokesman.

as opposed to actual representation was used in England in 1776 with regard to the colonies in America. Burke condemned it then, but later made use of it, in opposing the movement to make Parliament a body representative of the people. The answer is this, as Macaulay pointed out: if virtual representation yields the same results as actual representation, why not grant the latter if there is demand for it, and stop the argument?)

These arguments are not meant to justify the gross deviations which often exist with unequal districts and gerrymandering. They are only meant at best to offer some justification of the plurality system, by suggesting that if the system is well arranged—with periodic revision and approximately equal populations—it can keep to the spirit if not the letter of equal voting.

In summary, then, of equality of voting in all its aspects, we may say: whereas the universal adult suffrage is generally followed in democracies, being comparatively easy to put into effect, and whereas plural voting is generally extinct, yet to ensure the third condition of political equality of voting—that each vote counts equally at elections—is extraordinarily difficult. And on this latter point, all democracies with a plurality system are short of the ideal. It is not only that practical abuses spring up as population shifts and voting districts become unequal, but also that it is inherently difficult to make a simple plurality electoral system equitable even when its obvious abuses are eliminated; while it is just as difficult to justify, to say nothing of installing, a more representative system. Proportional representation systems can represent public opinion more accurately, but this gain, if a gain it be, is—*ceteris paribus*—attended by resulting disadvantages and is open to some theoretical objection. Either system is compatible with democracy, and which is used depends more on historical and other factors than on the single principle of political equality. The mechanism of electoral systems no doubt affects the voter and the election result in many ways, but the spirit is unquestionably more important than the letter, and a rough approximation to equality is usually enough to satisfy the principle in combination with other principles and demands of democracy. 'Measurement is for things measurable.'

SEVEN | *Effective Choice and Political Freedoms*

In the preceding two chapters two principles of a democratic political system have been examined: popular control of policy makers, as expressed by means of elections; and political equality, as expressed in the franchise. Throughout those two chapters the existence of political liberties and the other conditions of effective choice at the election polls was assumed. I turn now to the third principle or feature of a democratic system, which we may call the effectiveness of the vote, without which elections are a farce and popular control of policy-makers impossible.

THE SECRET BALLOT

The first, the minimum component, is that the voting should be free and uncoerced, within the range of candidates or parties offered. This involves in the first place the secret ballot, formerly called the Australian ballot. Its origin is said to go as far back as Sumeria; it was also used for the voting of the Athenian juries; but although it was later used in some places, for instance in municipal elections, its general, almost universal adoption is recent. The justification for it is as follows.

If choice is to be free, then the voter must neither be directly coerced to vote in a certain way nor go in fear that any particular choice may have unpleasant consequences visited upon his head by the rich, by employer, priest, neighbors, or others. (All choice may be free in one sense, e.g. even at the point of a gun we can still choose between death or dishonor. But this is not what anyone means by political freedom.) Because the secrecy of the ballot was not insured in Nazi Germany—'storm troopers at the ballot boxes'—everyone outside that unhappy country rightly suspected the freedom of the voting. (It may be proper to note, however, that voting under the Nazis did not pretend to be the final step in a process of free elections.) The intimidation by Federal troops at the ballot boxes in the South after the American Civil War, and by the Ku Klux Klan later, were also violations of free voting and hence of effective choice.

The secret ballot was adopted in modern democracies not for theoretical reasons, but as the historical remedy for the abuses of open voting—chiefly bribery and intimidation of voters.[1] One can never be sure, with the secret ballot, that the bribed or threatened voter will vote as he says he will. Again we are reminded that democracy, like any political system—except possibly anarchism or the classless society—is constructed for sinful men, not for saints.

There is, however, a small persistent school of thought—of which Mill was an exponent—which advocates open voting on the principle that the suffrage is not a right of the citizen, is not 'given to him for himself; for his particular use and benefit, [but] as a trust for the public,' and since it is a trust, the public are entitled to know how he voted. The victory of the secret ballot is an interesting example of the defeat of a principle, not by another principle or by theoretical argument, but by practical abuses.

FREEDOM TO RUN FOR OFFICE

The secret ballot is not enough to make effective choice possible. It is only a beginning. Choice at the polls further depends upon whether there is a meaningful choice or live option among candi-

---

[1] With a limited franchise and open voting, bribery was so widespread in Britain in the early 19th century 'as to be practically a part of the Constitution.' The Ballot Act of 1872 (secret ballot) probably did more than anything else to eliminate bribery; while electoral corruption was finally wiped out by the Corrupt Practices Act of 1883. 'From now on, the game is simply not worth the candle and honesty becomes not the best but the only policy.' H. G. Nicholas, *To The Hustings*, London, 1956, p. xiii. Even so, some bribery still went on in municipal elections at the end of the century. B. Keith-Lucas, *The English Local Government Franchise*, Oxford, 1952.

dates, and this in turn depends on whether candidates are free to offer themselves for election. Now, it is possible for more candidates than offices to be presented to the voters—thus apparently giving a live option—but the choice is Hobson's if all candidates are of the same party, committed to the same policies, and carefully chosen beforehand by the ruling group.

Candidates, then, must be free to present themselves if they wish to do so, a condition which is not appreciably violated by such minor restrictions as the securing of the signatures of a few friends on a nomination paper, or the requiring of a small deposit fee to prevent frivolous candidatures. Thus it is possible to specify the ease and freedom with which candidates may put themselves forward as another criterion by which to classify governments as more or less democratic. (This formally equal chance at public office cannot be equated to the Athenian equality of the lot, and is another instance of the differences between Athenian and modern democracy.)

There are two broad types of obstacles to freedom of candidature, present to some degree in nearly every democracy. These are legal and financial.

Legal restrictions and difficulties are of various kinds, such as cumbersome nominations procedures (where these are subject to law), the notorious legal barriers which many American states erect in the way of third parties, and the like. They raise no theoretical problems, being everywhere recognized for what they are: discrimination by entrenched groups against threats from the outside.

Financial obstacles arise from the unequal incomes and wealth of candidates and groups. A democracy—or any other system—is always subject to the risk, indeed the certainty, that legal freedoms or rights may not be practically realizable on account of differences of wealth and income. On the other hand, we cannot jump to the opposite extreme, and maintain that personal equality of income and wealth is a *sine qua non* for democracy.

As long as political campaigns are costly of time and money, as they all are, freedom of candidature and hence effective voting choice can be realized only if there is freedom of organization, so that contributions of time and money may be received on behalf of the poorer candidates. The financial obstacle can, in short, be circumvented by the well-known freedom to solicit, receive, and spend funds for political purposes and to form political associations and parties. Already we begin here to encroach upon the topic of political freedoms, and we need note only (a) that financial or other extra-legal barriers to freedom of candidature are by no means insurmountable—as the existence of working-class parties in many democracies abundantly shows; and (b) that such barriers do nevertheless bias public policies in every democracy in the direction of wealth. This is one of the reasons why democracies often receive more 'conservative' government than the majority would probably prefer, other things being equal. (There are also biases in the other direction. Moreover, to equate a bias toward 'conservatism' with a bias toward wealth is not always to equate the same things. There is probably no greater force making for social change than business initiative.)

One financial obstacle to freedom of candidature is worth at least passing mention, namely, how can the successful candidate, if poor, act as a legislator? And if he cannot afford to sit, is not this a deterrent to running for office? Aristotle thought it was characteristic of Athenian democracy—as it properly was—to pay for attending to public duties. In the past, as poor candidates came forward and were elected, they were often supported afterwards by contributions from party and friends, as in the early days of the Labor Party in Britain. Occasionally, the community or local district paid its representative. But these were cumbersome and inequitable methods, another bias of the machinery of government in favor of the well-to-do. The remedy was found in the payment of representatives, although representatives are seldom, even yet, paid adequately for their duties despite popular opinion to the contrary.

The anti-democrats of the 19th century had a sure instinct on this point when they objected to the payment of members of Parliament. The objections have, however, been drowned in almost universal reform, the chief exceptions being found now at the local level, where to serve as a councilor is still not a practicable choice for many people of medium and low incomes. As a result, municipal government even today is often monopolized by the leisured and/or the well-to-do, although the remedy is in the hands of the public if they feel strongly about it: to form political organizations and to press for the adequate payment of councilors. But since elected local councilors are largely part-time people, especially in smaller places, the remedy is not a panacea; and hence local government will for a long time be the preserve of people who can afford to serve without great personal sacrifice. That is why so many retired people serve.

The question of candidature is often intimately connected with that of representation. Two of these connections may be noted, one practical, one theoretical.

It is well known that representatives are by no means drawn from all classes and groups in any society in proportion to their members and voting strength. In this special sense, the broadening suffrage has not led to proportionate representation of members of the enfranchised groups. No doubt the full reasons are complex; partly, as hinted above, this is owing to legal-financial barriers, so that a quite disproportionate outlay of effort and money is required on the part of some groups; and partly it is a question of leadership. The social and financial barriers against candidates may be responsible for the fact that extensions of the suffrage have not always brought to the newly-enfranchised groups the benefits they expected, which in turn has led, time after time, to widespread disillusion and even cynicism. But this is not the last word on the subject, since there is abundant evidence to show that over the long run, the extended franchise does tend to bias government policies towards the more numerous voters; and this is one of the meanings to be given to the phrase 'government *for* the people.'

Apart from these practical considerations, the 'representativeness' of candidates takes us back again to the theory which requires that the legislature should be a microcosm of voters or population. As we have seen—in Chapters 5 and 6—the theory raises troublesome questions about the principles of selection. Somewhere, politics reduces the innumerable forms of possible representation to a few—to two in a two-party system (though the possibility of more always exists) and to a few in a multi-party system. But even a multi-party system is not the same as cross-sectional representation. Nor is it necessary, on grounds of protection of a group or class, that its representatives be wholly or even partially drawn from that section. The candidates, whatever their background or occupation, so long as they are anxious to be elected (as they are by definition) may be trusted to bid for votes by offering what a group wants. It is this deference to the voters which ensures popular control of government. And it is on these lines that democratic theory meets the 'scale-model' view of candidates and representatives.

THE RANGE OF POLITICAL FREEDOMS

Why do we say the political freedoms are characteristic of a democracy? The case may be made in several ways. A sufficient reply would be that we build them into the generally accepted definition of democracy. Another reply is to say that political liberties follow logically from the principle of popular control of government. A third is that they are entailed as part of the empirical conditions of effective choice for the voters: if rival candidates are to present themselves and their claims publicly, if there are to be alternatives to the government in power, then a number of political freedoms are in fact necessary.

By common consent, effective choice at election times implies a range of political liberties in which candidates and their supporters may campaign, in which information and criticism may be circulated, and in which at all times political influence may be openly asserted. No exhaustive or exclusive list of these political liberties has even been agreed upon, but there is virtually unanimous agreement on the minimum freedoms essential to legitimate politicking. These are the traditional freedoms of (a) speech—orally and in print and perhaps today by radio and television; (b) assembly and meetings; and (c) organization and joint action. What Tocqueville said of the press is true of all these freedoms: 'I think that men living in aristocracies may do without the liberty of the press; but such is not the case with those who live in democratic countries.' Freedom of speech, a genus of which a free press is one species, is rightly called the 'first freedom' for political purposes, and in the discussion of public policy it comes as near to being an absolute as it is possible to get in human society. In a democracy:

> This is true liberty, when free-born men,
> Having to advise the public, may speak free.

The case for political liberties is sometimes made on other grounds: that democratic voting presupposes a rational man who can judge rationally only if he has access to information and knowledge and can share in public debate. So far as this goes, well and good; but we must not fall back into the error of assuming that impartial informed voters decide the intricate questions of public policy. (See Chapter 5.)

It is absurd to take the view that because none of these freedoms is or can be 'absolute' (i.e. completely free of legal restraint) in any country, they are thus mere pretence. It is equally absurd to assert that because the rich have easier access to the costly media by which to spread their views, therefore the political freedoms are a 'sham,' or meaningless to the poor. The thriving social democratic parties in many countries are evidence enough to the contrary. In fact, it is a typical Marxist or Nazi way of arguing, that because there is not complete economic equality, or a complete absence of legal restraint, then these political freedoms mean nothing at all. Once more, we come to the all-important difference in degree which, as nearly always, is what distinguishes a democratic from a totalitarian regime, or a free society from a tyranny.

FREEDOMS — PROCEDURAL AND SUBSTANTIVE

In stressing the procedural freedoms of democracy, I do not mean to imply that they are valued only as a means to free elections and control of policy-makers. It will be recalled that Mill's famous defense of liberty of opinion was couched for the most part in instrumental though not exclusively political terms: liberty of opinion is conducive to the discovery of new truth, and enables us to see and understand more clearly those old truths which we hold. At the same time, with a grand illogic, he could fall back upon the language of rights:

> If all mankind minus one were of one opinion, and only one person were of the contrary opinion, mankind would be no more justified in silencing that one person, than he, if he had the power, would be justified in silencing mankind.

It is possible to say of modern democracies, as of the Athenian, that these political liberties—like the corresponding free participation in civic life which they make possible—are valued for themselves: that is, they are valuable as part of the 'way of life' highly regarded (though not necessarily by everyone) in a democracy, and so are among the democratic 'values.'

These essential political freedoms have other uses or aspects as well; they may, for instance, have religious or aesthetic or economic importance, as with freedom of assembly or printing. In a similar way, the usual civil (non-political) liberties such as freedom from arbitrary arrest, freedom of religion, and the like, may all at one time or another have their political aspect or uses. Habeas corpus, for example, has mostly been connected with justice and was first valued on that account, yet in its guarantee of freedom from arbitrary arrest and confinement, it is also clearly of great importance as a procedural liberty to protect freedom of political action.

To many people in a democracy, it is almost impossible to praise these essential political liberties too highly, apart altogether from their political utility. That is why the line cannot be sharply drawn between political liberties and other liberties (and civil 'rights') of the citizen, or between the procedural and other liberties in a democracy. Like the line between policy and administration, or goal and method, or civil and criminal law, so there is a blurring on matters of substance and of procedure in the political liberties. The difficulty of separating procedure and substance is also well illustrated by the U. S. Supreme Court's shifting interpretation of the 'due process' clauses in the Constitution—interpretation which gave rise to the curious phrase 'substantive due process.'

Liberties (and still less, rights) of the governed did not come into being for the first time with 19th- or 20th-century democracy, but some of them were traditionally enjoyed in aristocratic or monarchical states. Among these rights and liberties were habeas corpus, trial by jury, property rights of many kinds, freedom of worship, and so forth. Indeed, it seems plain that in western history—and perhaps all history—concern with substantive rights of this sort came upon the scene long before the use of liberties for political purposes.[2] Some historians have thought that religious freedom was the parent of political freedom.[3] Burke desired many rights and liberties for Englishmen—some substantive, some procedural; they were, he said, the product of 'prescription,' of the slow growth of the British constitution, yet he was far from believing that adult suffrage or legal political equality was among them. By 1870 in England, John Morley took 'the right to think freely and to act independently' as a principle definitely established once and for all in England; yet England was then obviously less democratic than now, in the sense of the adult franchise. In the same way, French women, although not allowed to vote until 1945, were regarded as having more political influence because of their other substantive rights and liberties than German women who did have the vote. Similarly, Negroes

[2] Freedom of the press from prior censorship by licensing came in England in 1695, not so much for reasons of political liberty as to break down the Stationer's monopoly of printing, i.e. '... all but incidentally to the elimination of a commercial monopoly.... Unlike Milton, who called for liberty in the name of liberty, Locke was content to ask for liberty in the name of trade; and unlike Milton, he achieved his end.' Maurice Cranston, *John Locke, A Biography*, London, 1957, p. 387.

[3] A. N. Hattersley, *A Short History of Democracy*, Cambridge, 1930, p. 109. On this also Sir Thomas Murray Taylor: '... in the battle for religious freedom. It is there that we have to look for the foundation of all our civil liberties... The freedom won in spiritual matters was later transferred by analogy to the realms of politics.' *The Discipline of Virtue*, Oxford, 1954, pp. 51-2. But this is a dubious—at least ambiguous—interpretation of history. Religious freedom and toleration appear to have been adopted or enforced for political reasons—expediency, a quiet life, *raison d'état*. Property rights long ante-date religious rights and liberties in Europe. Lord Acton thought that 'The revival of democracy was due neither to the Christian Church nor to the Teutonic State, but to the quarrel between them.' *Essays on Freedom and Power*, Boston, 1949, p. 146.

in the United States enjoy many freedoms and substantive rights, even if here and there their voting is still restricted.

All of this is to say also that procedural and substantive freedoms are sometimes enjoyed by groups which are not enfranchised. On the other side, it is also possible to vote without being politically free, as in the Soviet Union. But for a democracy both the vote and the political freedoms are necessary, and to the extent that these are restricted, the political system is less democratic. One might even say that a democracy becomes effectively less democratic when, although political liberties are permitted by law, their exercise is narrowly circumscribed by the social climate of opinion, or what Mill thought of as social tyranny.

The great movement known historically as 'liberalism' (a word almost as ambiguous but not quite so 'honorific' as 'democracy') is by no means identical with what is called democracy, but at least this connection between the two remains: the common interest in procedural freedoms. (In other ways a democratic state of today may be far removed from the traditional liberalism which emphasized chiefly those freedoms connected with the market economy.)

Yet if we are to keep close to the usual meanings of liberties, it is possible to draw the distinction, in discussion if not in life, between political freedoms which are procedural (or both procedural and substantive) and those other substantive freedoms like freedom of religion which may be found in most or all democracies, but which may (and occasionally do) also exist in other types of political systems. The procedural liberties are part of the very definition, or at least of the necessary political conditions, of democracy; whereas some of the other substantive liberties and rights may or may not be found in a democracy, depending on the temper of the public and on whether the democracy is governed well or badly.

Although these political freedoms, as part of the very definition or the conditions of a democratic system, are almost beyond debate, one of the consequences of a political process conducted within the framework of these freedoms is widely misunderstood by the layman. I refer to political parties.

POLITICAL PARTIES

It is scarcely necessary to document at any length the early feelings against political parties, or the modern expression of the same sentiment. One instance will suffice—Macaulay's account of his idealized ancient Rome:

> Then none was for a party;
> Then all were for the state;
> Then the great man helped the poor;
> And the poor man loved the great:
> Then lands were fairly portioned;
> Then spoils were fairly sold:
> The Romans were like brothers
> In the brave days of old.

(One of the troubles with attractive words, whether in verse or prose, is that they lure us into accepting beliefs which are not true.)

Organized parties have grown slowly, with the broadening of the franchise, and one may make the historical generalization that political parties have been 'perfected' in steady correlation with the extension of the franchise and political freedoms. Now, it is possible to have government without political parties—they do not always appear, for instance, at the local levels of government, and parties may not be logically entailed by a definition of democracy—but experience gives no ground for believing that we can have political democracy at the national level without at least two political parties.

The existence of political opposition—by individuals and groups, by the press, and above all, by organized parties—is the litmus-paper test of democracy. It requires no subtle definitions, nothing that a child could not apply. One can fake the trimmings of democracy, especially the voting and popular support, but the opposition, of party, press, etc., cannot be faked.[4]

Parties are the almost inevitable response to the divided opinion and interests in a large electorate, as 'factions' were with a narrow franchise. Organizationally, they became more necessary

---

4 Cf. Suzanne Labin, *The Secret of Democracy*, New York, 1955, p. 19.

with the larger electorate: a better organization was needed to garner the votes. Parties are, in Max Weber's phrase, 'the children of democracy, of mass franchise, of the necessity to woo and organize the masses...' In the course of their growth, parties have promoted democracy in several ways, but in particular by enabling the voters to make an effective choice between practicable alternatives. They help to make a popular 'will' as well as express it; lead as well as follow; are independent as well as dependent variables in helping to determine the outcome of policy-making.

This is not the place for a full discussion of parties, but in general we may say that parties carry out a number of almost indispensable functions in a large electorate: in choosing and presenting candidates, in bearing election costs, in initiating policies, in channelling discussion of public policies, in 'educating' the public politically, in unifying or reconciling the many divided interests and opinions, in mediating between the government and the citizen, and (in opposition parties) in criticizing and presenting an alternative government for the electorate. Finally, when in office the legislative branch of the party makes policies and supervises the administration of policies. Democratic government is party government, and parties help to keep the government democratic.

Only under a deadly threat, for instance during a major war, is party opposition ever suspended and a virtual one-party or crisis system instituted. But even in wartime no democracy has ever approached the monolithic one-party peacetime system of the totalitarians. Much as we may criticize a system of parties, it is much preferable to the one-party system, the only practicable alternative. But in noting the indispensability of parties, one need not take the party system of any particular democracy as the norm or ideal: there are democracies that seem to work well with a multi-party system—e.g. Switzerland, Scandinavia—and others where the two-party system prevails. One suspects that on this, as on other matters, our knowledge of the cause and effects of different party systems is too meager to substantiate any solid generalizations.

Hume, ordinarily so astute, regarded parties with mixed feelings, among which disapproval predominated when he spoke of parties of principle as 'known only to modern times' and 'the most extraordinary and unaccountable phaenomenon that has yet appeared in human affairs.' Burke, in closer touch with politics, was yet not able to keep a note of disapproval from his view of parties: 'party divisions, whether on the whole operating for good or evil, are things inseparable from free government.' [5] But if they are inseparable from free government, as they are, there is no question of giving them conditional approval: they are a necessary feature of modern democracy, and it is only a lack of sophistication, or a fanaticism, or else a pining for non-democratic forms of government that leads people to withhold their full approval. The freedom to criticize and oppose the government and to organize against it in a party in order to make the voting and opposition effective has no substitute. It is, in a very real sense, the unwillingness to recognize the legitimacy and loyalty of opposition parties and critics which marks the fundamental misunderstanding of democratic politics.

The essential feature of Western democracy and the feature which alone gives any reality to the choice at an election is the existence within the country of an organized opposition recognized as an element in the country's political life, and left so free to develop its programme, its organization and its resources that it can take over the government at a moment's notice.[6]

By contrast, there is the official view of the Soviet Union, where elections are always 'a race with one horse':

Is not the existence of several parties in society the sign of true, genuine democracy? We Soviet people give a clear and unequivocal

[5] Yet Burke defined party in terms of principles as 'a body of men united for promoting by their joint endeavours the national interests, upon some particular principle on which they are all agreed'; a definition which makes it harder to see why he should say for 'good or evil' (unless he thought some parties had 'bad' or 'evil' principles). Cf. C. S. Emden, *The People and the Constitution*, Oxford, 1956, p. 121. It is rare nowadays to find a political scientist who is 'anti-party,' but there is something of that spirit in E. S. Griffith, *Congress: Its Contemporary Role*, New York, 1956, chapter 13.

[6] J. D. Mabbott, *The State and the Citizen*, London, 1952, p. 176. A disloyal or illegitimate party is, of course, possible, e.g. a secessionist or Communist or other party whose object is to destroy the democratic system.

answer: no, it is not. The democratic or anti-democratic nature of public life, of a state, of a government's policy, is determined not by the number of parties but by the substance of the policy of this state, of these parties—by whether this or that policy is carried out in the interests of its overwhelming majority, or in the interests of its minority. That is how matters stand with regard to the first question—whether democracy coincides with the existence of one or several parties in society.[7]

The origin and historical growth of parties is not our concern here. It is possible to say, however, that by the 1830's in England, parties had come into being from the former loose groupings such as Court and Country, corporate ministerial responsibility to the legislature had become established, and party affiliation took the place of 'division' lists, to enlighten the electors on the record of their representatives. A system of loosely-knit blocs or groups without much unity provides the electors with much less guidance on policy, and makes it harder to hold a party accountable. The tighter the party discipline in a two-party system, the more easily it can carry out its pledges and platforms, and be identified as responsible for policies by the voters. Party discipline in the United States today is not much tighter than in England under Queen Anne—and it is not surprising that many Americans have all the aversion of Queen Anne to parties, and that voter apathy is so widespread. The American voter must rely on detailed 'division' lists to inform himself on the stand taken by his representatives—a cumbersome procedure, which makes it more difficult to hold the representatives accountable; while it also makes it as difficult to say who won the election as in Queen Anne's day. The fact, however, that there are nominally only two large parties, and that one of them secures the Presidency, makes the United States system quite different in other respects from

7 *The Soviet Crucible; Soviet Government in Theory and Practice,* ed. Samuel Hendel, New York, 1958, pp. 335-6. It is just barely conceivable that a state with a strict one-party system could be partially democratic (and in time more fully democratic) if the party were open to all, and were itself democratically run, to permit internal liberties and opposition. It is this sort of condition—perhaps found in Mexico and Turkey—that we call a 'virtual' one-party system. Needless to say, this is far from being the case today in the Soviet Union.

the earlier groupings in the United Kingdom Parliament or in the French legislature.

It has been rightly stated that only the party system which usually provides the country with a president and a Congressional majority of the same party, has saved the American constitutional system from either collapsing itself or leading to the collapse of the state.[8]

When a party is only a loose aggregation, lacking unity for whatever reason—because it has no distinctive political philosophy or program, or because the national party with its funds and organization has not been the means of electing the representatives, or because the leader cannot dissolve the House—then the party leaders and organization lack a powerful means of control over the legislative members, and the party, we say, is undisciplined. To say with Disraeli that 'England does not love coalitions' is to say that England does not love a loose party system, but loves strong cabinet government and a disciplined party.

Whatever view we take of parties—the high-principled associations of Burke's famous definition (which is perhaps the most misleading view we could normally take, in a two-party system), the permanent organization to compete for office and its patronage, or merely the team and its leader playing a political game for votes like the Guelfs and Ghibellines—in all cases parties carry on the struggle for the power to make public policy; the political conflict 'always turns upon who should hold the chief power in the state.' [9]

The chief charge against parties is that they stand for sectional and private interests, as against the public or national interest. But who knows the public interest—*das Ding an sich*—and how it should be promoted? The public interest is an end or goal which every party conceives in its own way, and tries to promote. Even the most sectional party is irresistibly driven to clothe its ambitions in the moral claims of the public interest. Parties and

[8] John H. Hertz, *Political Realism and Political Idealism,* Chicago, 1951, p. 183.

[9] There is, however, another type of party system, that of the old Germany, where, having no real power because of the constitution, the parties were doctrinaire and based upon special classes and other sectional support.

politics exist because there is controversy, because there are conflicting private interests and many particular views on what constitutes the public interest and how it may be promoted. The anti-party attitude rests to some extent on a mistaken view of democratic politics, and even more on a kind of incipient dogmatism in nearly all of us: we almost invariably think that what we favor is *really* the public interest, and those who oppose our view of the public interest are by definition merely factional or partisan. (Compare Chapter 1 for the tendency to 'depoliticize' politics.) It is an attitude which, taken a little further, leads to the destruction of political opponents rather than meeting them with arguments or in the free political contest for office. For a short time, perhaps, as in war, the crisis may breed unanimity and a party truce, but crisis living always invokes desperate remedies which would be fatal if continued.

If parties are of opposing ideologies, their struggles may of course be inimical to democracy, for instance if they divide deeply on class or religious lines, or if they paralyze government by an unwillingness to compromise. There is a limit, then, beyond which fundamental party disagreement should not go if democracy is to endure, and how to keep within this limit is a difficult empirical problem. (See also Chapter 11.) It is thus fortunately true that in seeking to attain power, parties commonly look around for policies that will have wide voter appeal, instead of the other way round, adopting a policy of principle and then trying to sell it to the public. Ideological rigidity (purity) is often a handicap to a party, dooming it to perpetual opposition, as with the Communist party in Britain or the United States.

Parties which start with an ideology or a coherent set of proposed policies to distinguish them from other parties, by the time they become major parties, usually end up with a program that is at most a matter of differing emphasis from that of other parties. This is true, for instance, of the career of the Labor Party in Britain. Principles and a distinctive philosophy are rather less characteristic of the Conservative Party (perhaps of all conservative parties), and of the major parties in Canada and the United States.

Our political parties are built not on the rock of faith but rather on the broad mud flats of popular desires and individual ambitions.[10]

We need not quarrel, however, if loyal supporters of these great parties wish to call their party attitudes on particular issues a matter of high principle. In any case, contemporary issues keep breaking in and stands must be taken, even by the most eclectic of parties. Third and fourth and fifth parties—typically found in multi-party systems—with little hope of office are pre-eminently the parties of ideology: intransigent, uncompromising, and of course not responsible because not in office or likely to be. These parties are constantly being plagiarized by the larger parties, and in this lies, perhaps, their chief contribution.

It is not surprising that the two parties which make up the 'ins' and 'outs' should come to resemble each other markedly. Each, in striving for electoral support, tries to antagonize as few voters as possible and to win the support of as many as possible, and hence is driven to become moderate, giving way entirely to no single group pressure. This is the case in the United States, in Britain, and in several other democracies. Where several parties of uncompromising principle exist—as in France and other countries with several ideological parties—none tries to bid for mass support by toning down its program.

Apart from the distinction between 'loose' and 'tight,' a two-party system may be of two kinds: (a) where, as in the United States or Britain, the parties tend to become alike, as they bid for the majority votes; and (b) where they are parties of principle or class, or parties supported by a 'cultural' minority and majority respectively.

The latter type of system is much harder to work—the party divisions encouraging both majority domination unsoftened by the need to attract floating votes, and minority intransigence untempered by any realistic hope of office. The system also tends to be unstable since it tends towards a multi-party system, which

10 Pendleton Herring, *The Politics of Democracy: American Parties in Action,* New York, 1940, p. 226.

may in fact be an improvement in such cases (if it avoids civil disturbance), though it may generally be preferable for minorities to spread their support to both parties. When they do so spread their support, the parties become 'informally representative' of the total public, and this party 'representativeness' serves tolerably as a substitute for cross-sectional representation in legislatures.

DEVIATIONS FROM THE PRINCIPLE THAT DECISIONS ARE MADE BY ELECTED REPRESENTATIVES

According to the theory which is being outlined, policy decisions are made by the elected representatives. The outcome of an election is a government authorized to make the legitimate decisions and receive the obedience. The question then arises: what if decisions are made or partly made elsewhere—that is, neither made nor subject to full control by the elected representatives? Such deviations from the principle of democratic policy-making do occur, as the following examples demonstrate.

(a) SECOND CHAMBERS

Hardly anyone would dispute the prima facie contradiction between an hereditary upper house that can make or substantially alter decisions and the principle of democracy by which decisions are made by the elected representatives. A quite different and non-democratic theory must be called in to justify such an institution. Since the two theories conflict, there is always much friction while the democratic principle is becoming dominant. Morley speaks of

... the attested fact that the principle of a hereditary chamber supervising an elective chamber has worked, is working, and will go on working, inconveniently, stupidly, and dangerously.[11]

The democratic logic has prevailed and hereditary upper houses now exist nowhere except in the United Kingdom. The extension

[11] John Morley, *Oracles on Man and Government,* London, 1923, p. 101.

of democracy in Britain has been accompanied by a process of denuding the House of Lords of its ancient political powers, until all that is left since 1948 is the 'suspensive veto'—the power to delay a non-money bill for two (instead of three) successive sessions of Parliament (roughly about a year's delay). Even this delaying power is unlikely to be exercised in cases where the Commons has a strong majority determined to put its legislation through. In Goldwin Smith's words: 'to suppose that power will allow itself on important matters to be controlled by impotence is vain.'

> The government in power, whatever its complexion, will have its way in the long run. This is indeed one of the fundamental principles of the operation of the whole of contemporary British politics; it shapes the relations between the Government and the Opposition in both Houses of Parliament.[12]

It cannot be seriously maintained that the Lords is a rival policy-making body—even now that it contains distinguished peeresses for life—and in any case, in the last analysis it is always within the power of the Commons to alter the Lords, even to re-forming it out of existence. The Lords, one may say, keep a certain amount of theoretical power providing they do not exercise it on a matter about which the Commons is strong and persistent. Such restraint (and efficiency) as the upper House does display is due to 'the permanent absenteeism of most of the peers' —those 'intrepid rearguards of conservatism.'

Another type of upper house is the nominated or appointed, of which the Canadian Senate will serve as an example. Senators are appointed for life on a regional basis by the Prime Minister, as vacancies arise. The appointees are almost invariably of the same party as that led by the Prime Minister, and hence con-

---

12 P. A. Bromhead, *The House of Lords in Contemporary Politics*, London, 1958, p. 143. Other functions of the Lords—the debating (which very occasionally ensures publicity for important controversial measures), the legislative (which includes the proposal of often useful amendments and the minor revision of bills), the committee work on private bills, the judicial (the Lords is the final court of appeal, acting through a few specially qualified lawyers who are generally peers for life only)—cannot be said to interfere with the policy-making power of the elected Commons.

flicts of upper and lower house are possible should a different party come to power in the Commons and find the Senate overwhelmingly composed of Senators of the other party. (This contingency did in fact occur with the Conservative Party victory of 1958—the Senate being overwhelmingly Liberal, as a result of over twenty years of Liberal rule.) The Senate, by the British North American Act, 1867—that is, by the letter of the constitution but not by usage—is equal in power to the Commons, except for initiating money bills. But in practice the Senate seldom exercises its legal powers, and normally does little more than endorse, with brief debate or none, the measures sent up to it by the Commons, a natural course when both Houses are of the same party. Nevertheless, certain potentialities do exist, much more than with the House of Lords, and it is possible that a serious clash between the two houses could occur, with resulting constitutional strain. For our purposes, however, we need only say that a Senate nominated for life (or a long term), if it has a real power, is plainly in contradiction to the democratic principle of the making of political decisions by elected representatives. But there are not many examples to be found of the phenomenon of a powerful nominated Senate.

The more common and more difficult case is where the upper house is elected, and particularly if the election is not on a population basis. Policy-making is then shared between a chamber elected on a democratic basis and one elected (directly or indirectly) on some other basis. There is certainly a conflict of principle here, as we may see for instance in a unitary state such as France. Under the Third Republic, the Senate was indirectly elected by means of electoral colleges (with 9 year terms, one-third being renewed every three years). The Council of the Republic (equivalent of the former Senate) in the Fourth Republic was also indirectly elected, on a territorial basis, but was renewable in halves. The Council had substantial powers, though not equal to those of the lower house or National Assembly, and it could be overruled on amendments to bills by a two-thirds majority of the Assembly. If it is admitted, which I think it must be, that direct election is more democratic than the indirect process, then it must also be admitted that the Council was less democratic in its composition than the Assembly. Further, it was much more difficult for the electorate to hold the Senate accountable, i.e. to exercise popular control—a serious objection from the viewpoint of democratic theory.

A similar conflict of principles, this time of election on a population basis for the Assembly or lower house, and on an equal county (geographical) basis for the Senate, may be seen in most of the constituent states of the United States, which in this respect have tended to copy on a state scale the federal elements of the national constitution, in spite of the fact that a state is not a federation, but within its jurisdiction is unitary.

The usual argument for upper houses has been that of putting a brake upon popular enthusiasm and temporary majorities: the famous 'sober second thought' argument. But it has seldom been made plain that to thwart the elected majority is in conflict with the usual theory of democracy (unless voluntarily assented to by the popular house), and never shown what qualification or means the upper house (admittedly less representative) has of gauging the probable course of public opinion more accurately than the lower house. In some cases, it has been suggested that the Upper House will be more impartial, but it is puzzling to know how it can be maintained that one party to the dispute, the less democratic upper house, can be both partisan and impartial referee.[13]

Elected upper houses in a federal state are open to the same objection of violating the democratic principle of equal voting, in favor of another principle: the equal representation of regions (or states, or provinces as the case may be). The reasons for such upper houses are of course found in the history of the different federations, the non-popular regional representation in the Senates being normally the price paid for federation. The preexisting states have been unwilling to combine without special protection of their interests, i.e. they have not been willing to put themselves at the mercy of popular representation and hence

[13] Other cases where the charge of being less democratic may be leveled: where one house is elected for a short term and another for a much longer term, or where the age qualification for candidates to the upper house is substantially higher.

of the national majority. (The point is often forgotten that they are always at the mercy of the special majority which can amend the Constitution.) The less democratic nature of these upper houses is easy to understand not only by reference to history, but also by trying to imagine the rule of equal voting applied today in the United Nations. No great power is willing to trust itself to the weight of numbers in the rest of the world.

Unitary states have similarly been unwilling in the past to trust the popular representatives, and by implication the majority of the voters, but in some states the democratic logic has inexorably prevailed—in the United Kingdom by reducing the power of the Lords, in New Zealand and a number of other countries by abolition of the upper house, and in Nebraska, the only state in the Union with a unicameral legislature, and in nearly all the provincial legislatures of Canada.

In federal states, however—of which the United States is the outstanding example—the same process has not gone on, with the result that the American Senate, probably the most powerful upper house in the world, is much less democratic in its composition (on the criterion of equal voting), so that the United States presents us with the example of a political system which partly follows the democratic principle and partly another principle, that of equal state representation. The two Senators from sparsely populated states have equal power with the two from populous states. The result is a representative system which makes it very difficult indeed for the national majority to prevail, if the national minority concerned can command a number of Senate seats, as it often can, or a majority of Senate seats, as it sometimes can. The party system could perhaps overcome this if the parties were highly unified and disciplined. But they are not. One might say that the American parties are also 'federalized.'

For the moment it is enough to make the point that upper houses, even if elected, as long as they are not elected on a strict population basis, do violate the democratic principle of equal voting. And the further point that they violate also the principle that in a democracy the policy decisions are made by a majority of the representatives elected by equality of voting.

Now it is certainly a mistake to devise a definition of democracy which puts a federation like the United States among the non-democracies. Indeed, it cannot be done legitimately, because democracy is defined by reference to several principles, not to one alone—and one on which federal systems may rate low. Because there are a number of characteristic democratic principles or criteria, then it is perfectly reasonable to say that on some of the criteria a federal system is, by the very elements of federalism, less than fully democratic. As we have also seen, even in elections for lower houses, few democracies fully practice the principle that each vote counts equally, while many unitary states are like France and Italy in having upper houses with substantial powers but only a partially democratic base.

Yet some deviation from equal voting, which may be unavoidable even under 'rep. by pop.' with a first-past-the-post electoral system, is clearly not of the same order as constitutional guarantees which reject the whole principle of equal voting for a powerful upper house. We are thus compelled to say that federal states mix two types of political beliefs or principles: one type, that of equal voting, and decision-making by the majority of representatives so elected—which is characteristic of democracy; and another, that of equal state's representation or state's rights—a kind of geographical-interest representation, or a principle of personifying the separate states, as in the United Nations; and this latter principle is at a considerable distance from democratic principles.

If we take this position, then we can freely admit the undemocratic, because unrepresentative, character of the American Senate. We explain it by reference to the historical circumstances, and by the existence in the country today of the same sort of forces and opinions which led originally to the establishment of a federal, and in that respect undemocratic, state, rather than a unitary and more democratic one. The Senate has become to some extent more democratic, in that senators are now directly elected, instead of being chosen by state legislatures as formerly. On the other hand, its filibuster rule makes the Senate a less democratic body than the House of Representatives. The Senate, as William S. White says in *Citadel* (pp. 2, 24, 221):

... believes in a kind of democracy (though the precise kind is a tale in itself) but it is in some things majestically undemocratic... the Doctrine of the Concurrent Majority is as much a part of the Senate as is the daily journal that is so rarely read... As an Institution it has not yet, in fact, gladly confirmed the concept even of national sovereignty over the States.

In a similar way, we shall have to explain the other complica tions of the United States political system—that the representatives in the lower house (the more democratic element) share the power of decision-making not only with the less democratic Senate but also with a President, who is elected on something close to the democratic principle of equal voting. To say that decisions are made by a group of representatives freely elected on the principle of equal voting is clearly not a sufficient explanation of how they are made in the United States. There are three classes of representatives: the President, the Senators, the Representatives, all of them powerful in law and policy-making. The democratic principles in the constitution are crossed with other strains, as it is in those unitary states with a powerful upper house.

The alternative position one could take would be to redefine democracy: to refuse to admit that political equality of persons is a principle of democracy. We could then call democratic a type of system with deliberately weighted voting, e.g. with upper houses elected on a different principle from that of equal voting. To do so is surely to abuse language and confuse theory, after the style of re-definition of democracy typical of the Soviet Union, where 'true genuine democracy' is defined not by procedural principles but by whether the policies are 'in the interests of the people'—with the single-party leaders making the fearsome decision that their rule is in the 'real' interests of the people.

Re-definition of democracy is not normally the method used in political discussion in the United States; instead there is often the frank recognition of the conflict of democratic principles with other principles, and an admission that the United States is only partially democratic. But so strong is the prestige of democracy, that we often hear contemporary arguments that the administration—mostly the permanent civil service—is more representative of the public than the Senate, and this offsets the non-democratic element in the legislature. In the sense that the civil service may be more like an occupational cross-section of the public than is Congress, no doubt the point is well taken (it is also probably true of some other countries); whether it is true that the civil service is more sensitive to public opinion (popular influence), because it is a 'representative' bureaucracy, may or may not be true. Even if it should happen to be true, does it carry the curious implication either that policy-making is a function of the civil servants instead of elected representatives, or that the civil service should not be under the control of elected representatives?

(b) THE CHARGE THAT POLITICAL POLICIES ARE
    MADE BEHIND THE SCENES

One charge of being 'undemocratic' is commonly made against all the western democracies, and is based on quite different grounds. It consists in arguing that political decisions are not made by legislators at all, but are made behind the scenes by powerful and sinister interests of various kinds, so that legislatures are a facade and representative democracy a sham. The best known of these charges is the Marxist, which asserts that the decisions are made by capitalists and merely ratified by politicians, and that the voters are manipulated and misled.

Others have brought forward similar charges, while differing from Marxists in the identity of the 'real rulers.' Mussolini used to say:

> The democratic regime may be defined as from time to time giving the people the illusion of sovereignty, while the real effective sovereignty lies in the hands of other concealed and irresponsible forces.[14]

In the 1930's many such conspiracy theories of political power flourished. Bankers, for instance, were alleged to manipulate the affairs of mankind through their stranglehold on finance; or the Jews were the hidden hand; or the Communists. With one grand

[14] *The Political and Social Doctrine of Fascism*, London, 1933.

burst of illogic, Major Douglas and his Social Crediters—so much like the Nazis—wrapped up the conspirators in one bundle: 'Bolshevik—Jewish—international-financiers.' (Possibly only the fact that so many bankers are Scotsmen prevented this sort of nonsense from sweeping the English-speaking world.)

If we leave the Marxist, Fascist, and quasi-Fascist charges aside, a more moderate charge emerges: that there are classes or groups in any society which dominate politics even if they do not actually rule. Max Weber noted the impotence of legislators in Germany in face of a nobility and an entrenched bureaucracy:

> ... the interests of the prince were joined with those of officialdom *against* parliament and its claims for power ... Considering all this, what then became of the professional politicians in Germany? They have had no power, no responsibility, and could play only a rather subordinate role as notables.[15]

In Britain the loosely-knit ruling class is known collectively as the Establishment (in Cobbett's phrase, THE THING):

> So I believe that England is still ruled by a hereditary but an absorbent upper class, and I believe that this agile social unit exercises the greater part of its power through Parliament and Government ... Political power may be temporarily withdrawn during periods of Labor Government, but social power will inevitably draw it back again.[16]

C. Wright Mills has found a 'power elite' in the United States, made up of a closely interlocking military-corporate-political group of leaders.[17] Others regard the Supreme Court judges as modern 'grey eminences.' Innumerable studies of 'decision-making' and ruling elites are now going on, many of them trying to locate, usually off-stage, the effective decision-makers in local and national government.

---

15 *From Max Weber*, eds. H. H. Gerth and C. W. Mills, New York, 1946, pp. 89, 112. Many observers find disquieting signs of an 'emasculated parliamentarianism' and 'managed democracy' in the Bonn regime today. The resemblance is to an elected council in a colony, where despite an elected assembly, final control is still in the hands of the executive appointed by the imperial power.

16 Philip Toynbee, in *Twentieth Century*, Oct. 1957, pp. 301-302.

17 C. Wright Mills, *The Power Elite*, New York, 1956.

Whatever the truth in the old charges and from the newer studies, it is clear that policy-making in any political system is highly complex, far more complex than the simple model of democracy tends to imply, namely that policy is made solely by the elected representatives. A short excursion into political realities will help to show both the usefulness and limits of the model.

POLICY-MAKING IN EXISTING DEMOCRACIES

In the theoretical model, the elected representatives are conceived as the final decision-makers, with responsibility also for implementation. As it may be put:

> The *point of final decision* is that stage in the sequence at which decision-makers having the authority choose a specific course of action to be implemented and assume or are assigned responsibility for it.[18]

Yet it is well known that in any actual system the contributions to policy-making come from a great variety of sources and at all stages of the process. The word 'decision' is too precise and sharp, and tends to give the impression that policies are made at a moment of time by rationally calculating individuals. All theories of decision-making—e.g. those of game theory—are almost certainly too rational, and underplay the improvisations, the historical, accidental, and emotional elements in politics.

> In a small unit like a university it is extremely difficult to get a policy formulated, accepted, and consistently applied. It is even more difficult in a democratic state, and indeed the attempt is never made.[19]

We must often therefore speak of policies being developed or growing, and sometimes of just drifting into policies, while we must always take note of their administration or enforcement—which gives them their substance—in order to judge the effectiveness of the representatives in making policies.

[18] *Political Behaviour, A Reader in Theory and Research,* eds. Heinz Eulau, et al., Glencoe, Ill., 1956, p. 353.

[19] Sir Ivor Jennings, *Problems of the New Commonwealth,* Durham, N. C., 1958, p. 40.

Not all policies are made in the same way, although formally the configuration of forces may be the same in each case—for instance public opinion, interest groups, mass media; or Cabinet, legislators, and lobby, but the influence of the various factors varies from one case to another. When public interest is weak, as in the peace treaty with Japan, the government is much freer to act as it sees fit.[20] Policy-making is thus unique from case to case, but a formal theory cannot excavate the details which only case-studies can provide. We cannot expect our model to supply us with empirical information: a theory model is an abstract version, to enlighten and guide but not to photograph reality in all its rich detail.

It is easy enough, however, to make allowance for political realities; the theory of democracy does not presuppose policy-making in a void, or assume that all representatives are equal in the influence they bring to bear on policy, or that we can ignore executive initiative, the influence of civil servants, of party caucus and bosses, of interest groups and their innumerable ways of putting pressure on both policy and its administration, of opinion polls and all the rest. Even the mere existence of an 'interest,' without organization, is of an immediate political influence, since a government is influenced nonetheless even if it merely refrains from action that might stir up the 'sleeping dogs.'

What is more remarkable is not that any one interest or lobby gets its way, but how many groups get enough of what they want to keep them loyal to the democratic system, with the result that contradictory policies are frequently, perhaps always, enacted by governments. Anyone who expects democratic government, or any other kind, to follow a policy program which is always consistent, and to carry policies through 'efficiently'—like a business firm with its standard of profit and loss—is asking the impossible. (The influence of the civil servant may perhaps be a factor making for rationality, efficiency, and consistency in government.)

So long as the political liberties exist, many methods of bringing influence to bear on representatives will also properly exist. Leadership and influence, reciprocal play between Cabinet and

---

[20] See a case study—Bernard C. Cohen, *The Political Process and Foreign Policy: The Making of the Japanese Peace Settlement*, Princeton, 1957.

electorate, legislature and executive, legislature and public, and many more are always going on. Where else could initiative come from, if not from a few?

> When we realize these institutional facts conditioning the politicians in a democracy, we should not wonder that so many of them render only a thoughtless reflex of the ripples on the surface of the wide sea of public opinion ...
>
> The thing to be explained is rather that so many politicians do exert real leadership, that they succeed continuously in taking the longer view without losing power, and that they can strive, not only to give the electorate an articulate voice, but gradually to educate it.[21]

It is the elected leaders' response to pressures—subject to the sanction of elections—not the mere existence of pressures, which is characteristic of political policy-making in a democracy. It is individuals who vote, and their votes can be courted, often over the heads of their group leaders. It is parties and legislatures, not interest groups, which resolve the group conflicts. No matter how many intermediates there are between electorate and politicians, the politicians are exposed directly to the judgment of the individual voter.

Political activity and pressuring may look enormously powerful, but activity is not the same thing as getting one's way in politics. So long as it is the politicians who finally decide and reconcile, policy-making is not handed over to the pressure groups, and the democratic principle is preserved—at least as much as it can be in real life. The great forces of movement in politics, however they originate, must finally act through representatives, and this is all that our democratic model presupposes in policy-making. It does not exclude influence, whether by bribery or briefing or in any other way. The principle of policy-making by the elected representatives thus stands, even when allowance is made for the fact—as Bagehot put it—that 'to illustrate a principle you must exaggerate much and you must omit much.'

21 Gunnar Myrdal, *Value in Social Theory*, London, 1958, p. 21.

EIGHT | *The Majority Principle and Its Limits*

The preceding chapters set up and examined three of the four tightly knit principles characteristic of democracy as a political system: the popular control of policy makers—by means of periodic elections; the political equality—of adult voting; and effective choice—exercised through the procedural political freedoms.

It was taken for granted that the representatives so chosen and controlled are collectively the political policy-makers in a democracy, a point touched upon briefly in the latter part of Chapter 7. But representatives are divided, reflecting, however roughly, the divisions among the electorate, so there must then be a principle for decision-making among the representatives themselves. The democratic principle is that when there is a conflict the decision goes to the majority of the representatives for the time being. I now turn to the consideration and justification of this principle of decision-making—which we may call the fourth principle of a democratic system—and to the question of what limits, if any, can be set upon it.

In the Assembly and large juries of the Athenian democracy—as we noted in Chapter 3—the majority principle was also followed, but the decisions were in such cases made by a comparatively large sample of the citizens directly, and not by representatives elected for a period of years. When this method of decision-making is translated into modern representative democracy, it bears only a distant family resemblance to the Athenian model.

MAJORITIES—LEGISLATIVE AND POPULAR

As we have seen in Chapter 5, the decisions made by the majority of the representatives cannot always be identified with the 'will' or wishes of the popular majority. For one thing, the two majorities—legislative and popular—may differ, as when a government is elected by a minority of the voters. And for another, we cannot assume that the popular majority which put a majority party government into office approves all its policies, either *ex post* or *ex ante,* although they may obey the law. In spite of this, the normative defense of the majority principle—indeed sometimes the definition of democracy itself—is frequently couched in terms of the popular majority, which seems a curious position if we are not able to test conclusively whether a popular majority is actually in favor of many specific government policies.[1] Unfortunately, perhaps, politics is one of those fields where the matters on which scientific or verifiable generalizations can be made

are seldom of great moment. On the really important questions, there is not and there cannot be any final answer. The search for scientific statements about political behaviour can easily bog down in a methodological morass.[2]

The kind of numerical public majority which the general theory deals with is a shifting one, different on different issues, so that we all rank with the majority or minority, depending on what issue is used as the touchstone; a majority that concentrates around leaders and parties, that crystallizes in public and legislative debate when all views and pressures have been brought to bear, including that of opponents, interest groups, and others.

Policies emerge from the interaction between legislators, executive, interest groups, and public, with one influencing all others but none determining the outcome; so that frequently the public approval is given only after the policy has been enacted or has

---

1 James Bryce, for example, could say: 'In this book I use the word [democracy] in its old and strict sense, as denoting a government in which the will of the majority of qualified citizens rules...' *Modern Democracies,* New York, 1921, vol. II, p. 22.

2 D. E. Butler, *The Study of Political Behaviour,* London, 1958, p. 86.

been in operation for some time. 'The majority is not a determinate body who lord it over a minority. In a democratic context the majority must always be discovered.' [3] In saying that the popular majority is shifting, we are in effect assuming that it is not a definable, specific, self-conscious social group or association, for instance a permanent racial majority, marked off and united by like (or common) interests. It is much more like a statistical grouping.[4]

The test of public approval by the majority is generally very rough and ready. True, there are cases on which little doubt exists that the majority favors a government's policy, as in some declarations of war, and there are also cases where it cannot be doubted that the majority is against a policy, e.g. the Leninist *coup d'état* and dissolution of the Assembly in Russia in early 1918. While distrusting the masses, Lenin was forced to argue that his party action was in their 'real' interest, or represented their 'real' will, no matter how harsh the government's repression. The democratic system is not, however, a series of devices for finding a pre-existing, conscious common will—whether of majority or of all—and then translating it into policies and law. Neither, for that matter, does it contain a set of devices for ascertaining whether the majority approves most policies after their formation. Democratic politics is instead a means of evolving—by struggle, discussion, compromise, and the rest of it—policies which may be regarded as the 'common will' *after* they have been formulated, and on the prosaic ground that they are accepted or obeyed by virtually all, after running the gauntlet of the political liberties and opposition. The decisions are made by the representatives, as they defer to voters, but any extreme form of the statement of the popular majority version—e.g. that 50 per cent plus one of the electorate gets and is always entitled to get its way—is very far removed from the actual rough-and-tumble of policy-making in representative democracies.[5] Such a statement

[3] R. M. MacIver, *The Ramparts We Guard,* New York, 1950, p. 23.

[4] Cf. Robert Bierstedt, 'The Sociology of Majorities,' in *American Sociological Review,* vol. 13, 1948, pp. 700ff.

[5] E.g. 'The term "majority rule" is most usefully reserved to denote that principle in a total governing system by which all political decisions are ultimately subject to control by at least 50 per cent plus one of the en-

is only now and then operationally testable, and as a normative principle must be qualified by the effect of strong feelings over policies. Representatives are concerned not only with differences of opinion which might conceivably be measured. At a deeper level, any government adjudicates the multitudinous conflicts of interests in society, and the policies may often be regarded as the adjustments worked out for the time being among several conflicting interests; there may be no exact coincidence between numbers and influence.

The doctrine of special majorities of representatives (or occasionally voters) for 'important' changes—for instance in the constitution—is sometimes defended as a practical device to ensure that there is in fact a reasoned and determined majority of representatives and public behind the policy at issue. The theory of the electoral mandate for substantial policy changes by the United Kingdom Parliament is of the same kind, and for the same reason, too, a case can be made for an upper house, even though hereditary or appointed, which can exercise only a delaying power over legislation. The effect is to introduce a short time lag, in which the majority support of representatives and public can crystallize while being put on the defensive. On the one hand, to admit this is not to introduce a minority veto— denying the right of the legislative majority to make the decisions —but neither, on the other side, does the majority principle necessarily require (as it is sometimes thought to) that every majority wish, even if it could be known, should be enacted in face of intense opposition. Rigid adherence to the letter of any one of its principles may wreck any system.

JUSTIFICATION OF THE MAJORITY PRINCIPLE: PRELIMINARIES

The first question to be clear on is: what are we examining? If we approximate modern democracy to a town meeting or the Athenian Assembly or a voluntary association, then the doctrine may be put thus: that the 'will' (or wishes or reasoned judgment)

---

franchised citizens.' Austin Ranney and Willmoore Kendall, *Democracy and the American Party System,* New York, 1956, p. 38.

of the majority (50 per cent plus one) of voters should prevail, on all matters when there is a division of votes. But this model cannot be used in a representative system, since we cannot always be sure that policies have the support of the popular majority.

We are concerned instead with the principle that the decisions should be made by a majority of freely-elected representatives—if they wish to press a decision—and that when so made they are binding upon all, because policies so made are rightful. This proposition seems to many almost self-evident, and any alternative almost inconceivable, to say nothing of non-democratic. It has not always, however, been self-evident that decisions should go by the majority in a legislature or other decision-making body. What sort of justification, then, can be given for it? Let us lead into the inquiry by considering two preliminaries.

The first point concerns the drawbacks of unanimity as a principle for policy-making. Perhaps because of the anarchist in us all, there is a wide reluctance to admit that the making and enforcing of political decisions inevitably result in some coercion; a tendency to believe that decisions can be avoided, until unanimity is reached. Unanimity as the requirement for all decisions was incorporated in the Polish Constitution during the 17th century. It is also the requirement usually, though not always, found in the jury system today, and in many international organizations. We have become accustomed to it for instance, in the United Nations Security Council, where all the great powers are firmly attached to their right of veto, which is merely another way of stating the unanimity principle. Although in domestic politics unanimity is regarded as an absurd requirement, in international politics it is the inevitable corollary of the highly regarded doctrine of national sovereignty. The corollary is not applied to small powers, who could be coerced by the permanent Council Members; and so we see that while all states are equal, some are more equal than others.

One thing may be said for the unanimity requirement. It does solve one of the oldest problems in political theory, that concerned with the nature of political obligation: why should I obey? Rousseau was much agitated by this question, which he put in the form: how can I obey and at the same time remain free? The conundrum of the relation of authority to the individual is solved—for the representatives—if there is unanimity in the legislature, but it is not touched so far as the voters are concerned, and it was this aspect which agitated Rousseau and led him to favor direct against representative democracy. The conundrum is solved for legislators since unanimity presupposes that any decision is my decision; and so I am merely following my own will as in every other voluntary action in life. The political problem may then be turned over to the philosophers for an analysis of 'will.'

Although unanimity solves one problem of theory, it is at an impossible cost. If there is not unanimity, then what follows? The practical objection is that so long as there is one dissenter, nothing gets done. Unanimity as a method biases policy firmly— sometimes disastrously as in the experience of the Polish Diet— toward the state of affairs that happens to exist at any one time. The continuance of the status quo, or doing nothing, is after all as much a policy choice among alternatives as any other. It is impossible to believe that in anything short of the perfect and perfectly governed state of Plato's ideal republic such rigidity or such a rule could be desirable or feasible. Unanimity is so remote a contingency in any modern legislature (on major policies) that to recommend it as a normal principle for political government is quite fantastic.

The unanimity requirement may also be looked upon as the doctrine that when opinions and interests conflict, then the dissenter should get his way. It is in effect a doctrine of veto by a minority of one, a doctrine which in one form or another has not been rare in history, and which is met today in the practice of veto by blackballing in some voluntary organizations as well as in the United Nations Security Council. (A comparatively weak version is found in the filibuster rule of the U. S. Senate.) In politics the *liberum veto* may be regarded as individualism run wild, lacking even the idealism of anarchism to justify it.

Secondly, it is worth glancing briefly at the history of the majority principle. The majority principle for decision-makers is of ancient origin, even if we go no further back than the Athenian democracy. It fell into disuse after the democracy fell, although, no doubt, traces of its use among small groups may be found in Roman institutions and Roman law. Although the doctrine of popular sovereignty—that all authority was ultimately derived from the people—was prominent during both the Republic and the Empire, this was not taken to mean that a majority of the citizens should make the decisions as in Athens, nor that a majority of elected representatives should do so, as in modern democracies. Representation was delegation of authority, often for life, however the representative was appointed, and cannot be equated with democratic popular control by means of periodic elections. There was, of course, a popular element which was potentially democratic in these Roman conceptions, but it was more easily turned to a justification of dictatorship than to anything approaching a representative democracy.

The practical device of taking a majority vote for council decisions was sometimes used in the middle ages. They were decisions among equals, with seldom if ever any implication that this directly involved the 'people.' To go by the majority vote is one of the most common methods of making group decisions. Any ruling group, in fact, may adopt this method. Since the 11th century the Pope has been elected by a majority, in this case two-thirds, of the College of Cardinals, a method replacing the former more complex methods of election. Perhaps majority voting goes on now in the Central Committee or Presidium of the Communist Party of the Soviet Union—but lacking the machinery of popular control through free elections and political liberties, it falls outside our theory of democracy.

Under Teutonic influence in the middle ages, a quite different justification was sometimes given for abiding by the majority will, of either a primary assembly or council. The problem was: how much is the minority obligated by the decisions of the majority? The answer given, however, has a somewhat strange ring in modern ears: when it was seen that a minority would be outvoted, it would withdraw its objections, after full discussion, and *adopt the majority will as its own,* as a more accurate expression of the 'will of all.' The decision would then be made unanimous and would coerce no one.

In some instances, the Teutonic conception of making majority decisions unanimous by adoption is familiar enough today. Commonly, in political conventions and other meetings (for instance, the election of the head of an Oxford college), dissenters withdraw their objections and so make the formal choice by acclamation. Again, ordinarily laws once passed are obeyed by all and felt to obligate all, so that most laws are not repealed when the minority which opposed their passage later grows into a majority and becomes the government (or elects the government). To this, we have added the notion that the minority, legislative or popular, while obliged to obey a law of which it disapproves, may continue to work freely for the repeal of such a law by persuading a majority to its point of view. The notion of provisional obedience under protest has two advantages: one, the great civilizing result that although actions may be coerced, the will and thought and speech of dissenters are not coerced; and two, we do not keep the fiction of unanimity where there is none, but are ready to admit the fact of coercion of behavior as well as obligation to obey.

In political usage, in the course of history, it was often not careful vote-counting but the 'common will' declared by acclamation which was typical of early assemblies, as in the 'sense of the meeting,' which was used in early days for election of Knights of the Shire to sit in Parliament. Much the same procedure was followed at public polls in the elections as late as the 17th century in England. Today, too, a voice vote is often taken in legislatures, and a division or roll call is taken only if the Speaker's ruling is challenged. The Quaker idea too, of 'sense of the meeting' is like a unanimity rule, and may be compared with the virtual unanimity occasionally found in legislatures and among the public, especially during national emergencies.

The belief that a majority—whether of people or representatives—could bind dissenters, even on taxes, has often been flatly rejected. As late as the 13th century in Britain, the *individual* had to give his consent to some decisions, failing which he was under no obligation; and there is something of such a doctrine of individual consent in political philosophers of a much later day. The problem of individual consent is usually evaded or ignored in doctrines of individual rights, such as Rainborough's; or else it is treated ambiguously, as in Locke. (Individual consent is not quite the same thing as the *liberum veto* in a council.)

The device of abiding by the majority decision (without the formality of 'adoptive unanimity') was used, it appears, as a convenience, or alternative to unanimity, among groups of equals, and as its usefulness became recognized it was used more and more by the governments of national states. In the 16th century it was used thus, but only on 'indifferent matters,' i.e. not on matters of high principle (or deep feelings). For a long time it continued thus, and settled into a routine, long before any moral or other substantial justification for it was evolved. The justification, when it was given, went back to the Athenians for arguments. The majority principle, as a belief, tended always to go with representative government and political equality as the franchise broadened in 19th-century British history, though usually the two majorities—of voters and representatives—were not clearly distinguished, or it was assumed that the two were identical. There was (and is) often some confusion caused by mixing the classic premises of Athens—the primary assembly—with the quite different circumstances of a representative system.[6]

JUSTIFICATION OF THE MAJORITY PRINCIPLE: THE ARGUMENTS

(1) The oldest argument is that of Aristotle: the majority is more likely to be right (with the implied premise or 'ultimate' that the right rather than the wrong should be done). As we know, the argument was devised for the Athenian democracy and its popular majorities, where there was no question of any discrepancy between representatives and voters.

Machiavelli, surprisingly enough to those who know only his

---

[6] John G. Heinberg, 'History of the Majority Principle,' *American Political Science Review,* vol. XX, Feb. 1926; and 'Theories of Majority Rule,' op. cit. Vol. XXVI, June 1932. The best examination of the majority principle in politics is that of George Cornewall Lewis, *An Essay on the Influence of Authority in Matters of Opinion,* London, 1849, Chapter VII.

bad repute, put the case (also in terms of the popular majority) as strongly as anyone in his *Discourses:*

> But as regards prudence and stability, I say that the people are more prudent and stable, and have better judgment than a prince; and it is not without good reason that it is said, 'The voice of the people is the voice of God'...And as to the people's capacity of judging of things, it is exceedingly rare that, when they hear two orators of equal talents advocate different measures, they do not decide in favour of the better of the two; which proves their ability to discern the truth of what they hear.

Burke once expressed the same faith in the people: 'in all disputes between them and their rulers, the presumption is at least upon a par in favor of the people.' Or again, in modern times, and also referring to the popular majority, the same view: 'Democracy is the recurrent suspicion that more than half of the people are right more than half of the time.' To catalogue further expressions of the same sentiment would only be tedious.

Now there is undoubtedly some persuasive force to this argument in terms of both popular and legislative majorities—particularly if two corollaries are kept in mind. The first is the free elections and the range of political freedoms. 'Many heads are better than one' is a homely truth on many matters, especially in politics, where no policy is entirely a matter of general principle. All opinions are liable to errors of judgment, since it is impossible to predict accurately the consequences of specific policies, or to present proofs that this or that measure will promote an agreed end and none other. Here, too, we can enlist most of Mill's eloquent arguments in defense of liberty of opinion, while a plausible case could also be made by an appeal to the experience of the democracies.

The second corollary is that elections and all political disputes never show the 'mob' on one side and the wise minority on the other. In every democracy all parties usually have their share of honest, intelligent, and enlightened leadership. Democratic politics allows plenty of room for leadership and many sorts of influence, and mixed motives are found behind every policy. It is only a shabby debating trick to make democracy, by definition, rule of the 'mob' or masses—in contrast with some other type of rule by carefully defined 'wise' men.

When all due allowance has been made, it must be conceded that the argument given above may easily go too far, in its own terms of popular majorities, while too much can easily be claimed for it even in terms of representative majorities. The majority of representatives, as well as voters, will sometimes be silly or unjust—as we must all admit. There is and can be no guarantee that either the legislative or popular majority speaks *vox dei*. The majority may be brought to agree to any absurdity, as in Kipling's story of *The Village That Voted The Earth Was Flat*. To say that a policy is democratic because it expresses the wishes of the legislature and reflects those of the public is not to say that it is always wise or good.

Because of the vulnerability of this first argument, the chief tactic of the critic of democracy is to convert the argument over policy-making into one of right or truth, ascertained by counting heads, and then to reject democracy because it cannot always guarantee to be right. Sir Henry Maine may stand for all the critics who take this position:

The more the difficulties of multitudinous government are probed, the stronger grows the doubt of the infallibility of popularly elected legislatures.[7]

The proper kind of answer to this misleading criticism has been given by Morley:

But we are not acquainted with any [English] writer or politician of the very slightest consideration or responsibility who has committed himself to the astounding proposition that popularly elected legislatures are infallible.[8]

If we seek to find in a political system some infallible way of making right decisions, we should try to build a theocracy. No political system can guarantee that decisions will always be right, and the argument of Aristotle claimed only 'more likely' to be right, a claim which can only be assessed when comparisons are

[7] Sir Henry Maine, *Popular Government,* New York, 1886, p. 180.
[8] John Morley, *Oracles on Man and Government,* London, 1923, p. 93.

made with the policy-making methods of alternative political systems. But it is very hard to see how we can tabulate and compare and test such probabilities of error, with any reliability (although Condorcet is said to have done so), even assuming—which is most improbable—we could agree on which decision was 'right' in all cases.

Lacking such exactitude, either for democracy or its rivals, the argument in terms of being right must, I think, be left inconclusive. But this at the very least leaves democracy and its majority principle as well off as alternative systems; while some weighting in favor of democracy is provided by the safeguards of the political freedoms which ensure that all views will be brought to the attention of the representatives.

(2) The argument for the majority principle is on stronger ground when it moves away from discourse in terms of right or truth. The case may rest more solidly upon a particular view of the nature of politics. Politics deals with decisions and adjustments arrived at from a variety of conflicting opinions and interests which exist everywhere, but which find spokesmen and legitimacy only in a free society. There are no impartial jurors, no political experts to make wise decisions, and most decisions cannot wait, even if the infallible answer could in time be obtainable.

Nor is this view opportunism or relativism. Many (probably most) political decisions do of course have moral principles as ingredients, but, like patriotism, these are seldom 'enough.' How simple the governing of men would be if all decisions were between good and evil, between right and wrong principles. How agonizing the actual decisions usually are when the choice is between several goods, or evils, one of which must be chosen. No political, perhaps no social, act is without some taint of injustice, some compromise of principle, some mixture of the ideal and the expedient. Democracy with its liberties is at least as well off as other systems in permitting and encouraging the use of moral principles in policies.

The problem of political systems is to find a method of decision-making which can deal with the particulars and the contingencies as well as the moral principles involved in every policy and adjustment; and the problem remains even when there is full agreement on the moral principles or goals involved. The majority principle may be defended on the grounds that the decisions so made are (presumably) acceptable to a larger number, that all can contribute to them, and that they have the virtue of being not final, but may be revised or reversed after the next election, as public and representatives shift their support and a new majority is formed. (This is not to say that *all* decisions are revocable—an innocent man executed cannot be restored to life.)

(3) The majority principle could be said to follow logically from the principle of political equality involved in equality of voting (unless we ignore reality and adopt an impossible doctrine of individual consent). If every person is to count equally, it follows that a numerical majority should count more: to follow the minority would be to flout the equality. The majority should prevail just because it is the majority of political equals, not because it is right or wrong. The doctrine of political equality is here an 'ultimate.' A very similar argument is that of Bentham: everyone pursues his own happiness, and all that matters is quantity of happiness, so that government ought to promote the happiness of the greatest number. (We may note parenthetically that the argument in both cases presupposes no gross disproportion of voters and representatives. Needless to say, Bentham's views on happiness are not being endorsed here.)

It is often objected at this point that to count each person (and hence each representative) equally is absurd: some people feel more strongly about certain issues or decisions than others. Would it not fly in the face of common sense and elemental fair play to argue that 50 per cent plus one of the lukewarm should overrule 50 per cent minus one consisting of passionate dissenters? In such artificial terms the answer is yes. The counter argument is that the dilemma is an imaginary one, without political relevance. Intensity of feeling—often an acute political phenomenon—has abundant opportunity to make itself felt in the many political processes which are open. It does not take much to convince the lukewarm and wavering and so reduce the majority to a minority. The place for intensity of feeling is in the give and take of politics—in campaigning, lobbying, etc.; the principle does not require that every 50 per cent plus one of the representatives should immediately enact its lukewarm wishes against a strongly emotional opposition. No party or politician gets caught in such a ludicrous trap. The real problem which arises here is that of the alienated or permanent minority (on which see the Appendix to this Chapter).

(4) There is the argument by default: alternatives are worse, since no minority or its leaders is better equipped to judge rightly or make wise decisions. In Lincoln's much quoted remark:

> Unanimity is impossible; the rule of a minority, as a permanent arrangement, is wholly inadmissible; so that, rejecting the majority principle, anarchy or despotism in some form is all that is left.

Lincoln was quite right. If the majority principle is rejected, then the credentials of some sort of minority principle must be justified—and this, to modern ears, is almost impossible, or as Lincoln put it 'wholly inadmissible,' although it was plausible enough in an earlier age. After allowance for the looseness of language we may agree:

> In the democratic tendency of the day, the theories of government by the people and by the absolute majority have superseded the theory that government is to be conducted by the enlightened and capable—the aristocracy in the strict sense of the word—for the benefit of the masses.[9]

(5) One of the oldest arguments is that from convenience and expediency. Some method must be devised, and this is a convenient one, which will by definition always displease the smaller number. Historically, as we have noted, the majority principle was adopted for convenience among equals and often only for things 'indifferent.'

Locke, who was the first of the moderns to discuss the majority principle at length, spoke occasionally of the principle as having been adopted for convenience or utility, and perhaps 'the main reason why he did so was that majority-decision had so long been established in English parliamentary practice that it seemed 'natural' and could be taken for granted.'[10] Of itself, it carries

---

[9] *Nineteenth Century Opinion*, ed. Michael Goodwin, Harmondsworth, Middlesex, 1951, p. 104.

[10] J. W. Gough, *Locke's Political Philosophy*, Oxford, 1950, p. 63.

no ethical weight and, if one may say so, carries less the nearer the majority and minority are in size. Locke reinforced the convenience argument by posing unanimity and the majority principle as the only alternatives to disintegration of the community, forgetting the alternative the most common and obvious of all—the despotism which Lincoln mentioned, whether this took the form of Hobbes' absolute monarch or some kind of minority rule.

(6) Locke also used the analogy with Newtonian physics: 'it is necessary the body should move that way whither the greater force carries it, which is the consent of the majority.' Bryce spoke the same language, 'so that [in a democracy] the physical force of the citizens coincides (roughly speaking) with their voting power.' [11]

Several objections arise: one, political 'force' or power, whether as coercion or as moral influence or any other form, may not always be on the side of the majority; all that is for certain on the side of the majority is numbers. If force is taken to mean force of arms, then there are plenty of examples of revolutions and counter-revolutions where the minority party in government and country has been successful. (Hume thought, like Locke, that power as well as numbers was always on the side of the ruled, and so he was surprised at the ease with which the many are governed by the few.) Two, the need for consent of the minority—a problem which sometimes agitated Locke—is played down by emphasizing force. Three, even if somehow force and numbers should coincide, what kind of claim to obedience does force make? Since Locke was not saying that might is right, I cannot see that the analogy with physics, even if plausible, adds anything to the moral claim to obedience based upon the political equality of persons.

(7) A social contract case may be made from Locke and—though doubtfully—from Rousseau. It was supposedly agreed by the original contract—whether made unanimously or not—to abide by the majority principle in the future. There is some ambiguity in Locke on the proportion agreeing to the original contract, as in his advocacy of the use of the majority principle afterward. For instance, he wrote:

[11] Locke, *Of Civil Government,* Gough edition, p. 48; Bryce, loc. cit.

When any number of men have so consented to make one community or government, they are thereby presently incorporated and make one body politic, wherein the majority have a right to act and conclude the rest.[12]

Rousseau's position is obscured by the obscurity of his conception of the social contract, by his dislike of representation, and by his doctrine of 'freedom' and the General Will. Of Rousseau it is possible to prove quite contradictory propositions by selected quotations; one sees it done all the time.

In any case, the social contract is a fiction; and where it does contain an element of historical truth, as in the United States federation, the majority principle is seldom specified without serious qualifications. The Virginia Constitution of 1776 spoke of 'a majority of the community' having 'an indubitable, inalienable and indefeasible right to reform, alter or abolish,' any government violating the Bill of Rights; but Jefferson's Declaration of Independence was more canny and spoke more vaguely of the 'right of the people.' If we ignore historicity, a more awkward point is: how much are we bound by a contract of our remote forefathers? Surely it does not strengthen political obligation (i.e. that we should be loyal and obey the laws) to base it upon another obligation (that we should always honor our forefathers' promises). Any constitution, however rigid, can be and always is amended from time to time, which is to say the original contract or promise is altered.

(8) Occasionally a defense of the majority principle is couched in terms of natural 'law' and natural rights. Locke, for instance, wrote that 'the majority have a right to act and conclude the rest' . . . 'as having by a law of nature and reason the power of the whole.' Grotius, too, thought that 'the majority would *naturally* have the right and authority of the whole.' It is hard to see, however, how this could have much cogency, except by way of our third argument—from political equality—in which case the two arguments are substantially identical.

Many have thought the opposite (the fanatical Thoreau, for

---

[12] For an interpretation of this—a disputable one, I think—see Maurice Cranston, *John Locke, A Biography*, London, 1957, p. 211.

example): that a majority has no right whatever to rule a minority against its consent. Rousseau wrote: 'It is contrary to the natural order that the majority should govern and the minority should be governed.' Sir Robert Filmer, Bodin, and others have also agreed that the majority principle is quite contrary to 'nature' (though they have, I think, seldom subscribed to political equality). A modern summary may be cited:

> As far as nature goes, if it goes anywhere, the only binding decision is a unanimous one, where a minority—where even a single objector—has a liberum veto, as in the Polish diet. Burke pointed out that the majority-principle was 'one of the most violent fictions of positive law,' to which men could only be brought to submit 'by long habits of obedience, by a sort of discipline in society.' [13]

CONCLUSIONS ON THE JUSTIFICATION OF THE MAJORITY PRINCIPLE

What, then, are we to make of these arguments which purport to justify the majority principle? It must, I think, be confessed that some of them are weak, when judged by canons of strict logic. The morally strongest, or at any rate the most plausible in today's climate of opinion, is perhaps that derived from political equality. Once the principles of popular control of government and political equality are accepted—and it is these that often kindle the fire of enthusiasm for democracy—it is difficult to stop short of the majority principle for decision-making.

As for the first argument which treats of political policies in terms of right or truth, it can only rest upon an ultimate act of faith—one which is generous and optimistic—in the potential rationality, integrity, and altruism of the common man. But it is not an act of faith which everyone can or will make, although acts of faith in alternative sources of political wisdom are also not easy. Lesser arguments in terms of convenience, or of the wider public acceptance (*ceteris paribus*) of decisions made by this principle, or of the defects of alternative principles, while not negligible, are not conclusive. At the most, the arguments are persuasive and cumulatively cogent.

[13] J. W. Gough, op. cit. p. 62.

The majority principle cannot, however, be judged wholly in isolation, but only as part of a tightly-knit set of principles making up a democratic political system. The theory of the system attempts, among other things, to give an answer to the traditional question of political obligation: why should we obey laws when we do not want to? No general answer or formula can be found, in any political system, which will fit every specific dilemma. Every government has some laws or policies which may cause the individual to make the dreadful decision whether to obey or resist. Hardly any law or policy meets the nice moral or other criteria of every citizen. There is, however, a prima facie obligation to obey all laws—even those we consider bad—when they are part of a total political system to which we have given our allegiance. Accordingly, the justification of the whole system, of which the majority principle is only a part, affords also a further justification of this principle itself. (On justification of the democratic system, see Chapters 9 and 10.)

It will not have escaped notice that only one of the arguments above—the first—attempts to justify the majority principle by reference to the results, or to the kind of policies which emerge from its use. This lack is logical enough, following from the outline of democracy already given, which has been in terms of a political system as a method of policy-making. Nor, in examining the justification for the majority principle, was any of the meaning 'good government' smuggled into the premises; nor was any argument based on an appeal to the experience of existing or past democracies, although this may be persuasive to many. Before coming to the question of the content of policies, however (in Chapter 10), I wish to turn to consider the important question whether it is feasible to put legal limits upon the majority principle.

THE QUESTION OF LEGAL LIMITS ON A MAJORITY

(a) THE FEAR OF MAJORITY 'TYRANNY'

In the democratic system which has been outlined, it is plain that everything is or could be at the mercy of the majority of the representatives and of the voters; that the only limits to what the majority may do lie in the political liberties and the sanction of the next election. Many people are nervous of this, today as formerly, and there have been many attempts to put legal constitutional limits upon the majority of the representatives and (by implication) of the voters. The connection between democracy and constitutionalism is admittedly close; all are agreed 'that there are certain laws or regulations that ought not to be passed even if the greater part or indeed the whole of the people favour them.' The question under debate is whether the Constitution is to be regarded as 'a systematic statement of the liberties recognized in society,' or 'as a method of guaranteeing them.' [14] Granted that the state can protect us against abuses of private power, can we not also ensure that the state will protect us against itself?

The fear of majority tyranny is extraordinarily widespread in the literature of political philosophy, in spite of the fact that so few historical examples can be found where a democracy using the majority principle could be characterized as a tyranny. Even the incomparable Plato, although he had perfectly good philosophical arguments to show that only highly trained philosophers were capable of discerning the True and the Good, was also driven by an intense fear that the majority (identified by definition as the poor), if given the power, would at once proceed to divide and squander the property of the rich. From later times, one extreme example of lively fear of the majority will suffice:

Things have grown up, under the cover of the dogmas of popular freedom, until the result is a despotism centered in the House of Commons, more absolute and absorbing than that of any Tsar or Sultan.[15]

---

[14] R. Wollheim, 'Democracy,' *Journal of the History of Ideas*, April 1958, p. 240.

[15] Frederic Harrison, in *Ninteenth Century Opinion*, p. 250. Much of this sort of discussion is vitiated by the lack of any agreement on what constitutes 'tyranny.' On the difficulties of defining tyranny in terms which enable us to recognize it in practice, see Robert Dahl, *A Preface to Democratic Theory*, Chicago, 1956, and the Debate between Morgan and Dahl, *American Political Science Review*, December 1957, pp. 1040-61.

Imaginary devils are always more frightening than real ones. By contrast, history is chock-full of tyranny by absolute rulers and oligarchies.

Much of the fear of the majority tyranny is, I think, based upon two misunderstandings, or tricks of definition. Firstly, no democratic theory (except the Marxist) advocates the majority principle without the other principles of democracy, in particular the political liberties; yet it is precisely this kind of rule, lacking the freedoms, which is sometimes re-defined as 'democracy' and—perhaps naturally enough—equated with tyranny. Where the political liberties are gone and the government cannot be turned out at the next election, democracy as I have defined it and as I think most people understand it simply ceases to operate and we have a system that is not democracy, whether the majority gets its way or not.

While admirable in other respects, Professor J. L. Talmon's book has compounded our confusion by talking at length about something called 'totalitarian democracy,' by which he seems to mean the rule of a fanatical and messianic minority, allegedly on behalf of the majority, but tolerating no dissent, and 'engineering' popular approval.[16] But it is debasing the coinage of scholarly discussion to call such a system democracy, merely because it has the ingredient of popular approval, engineered and coerced by a dictatorship, even a benevolent dictatorship. The same confusion is wrought by the term 'plebiscitary democracy': a more or less free vote is obtained to put a dictator into power, who then proceeds, on the strength of the 'mandate,' to rule as a popular dictator or—as with Huey Long—as a reasonable facsimile of one. It is common enough for people to confuse us with tendentious meanings of democracy and the majority principle, which they equate with majority tyranny, whim, incompetence, or wickedness.[17]

To identify democracy with popularly supported dictatorship

[16] J. L. Talmon, *The Origins of Totalitarian Democracy*, London, 1952.

[17] E.g. Lord Percy of Newcastle, *The Heresy of Democracy*, London, 1955; Walter Lippmann, *Essays in the Public Philosophy*, Boston, 1955. For a list of present-day critics of the majority principle see H. S. Commager, *Majority Rule and Minority Rights*, New York, 1944.

removes all possibility of distinguishing democracy from any other political systems and democratic theory from other theory. There is all the difference in the world between giving the population what the majority of the representatives will approve in the give and take of a free political process, and compelling and conditioning them to approve what is given to them by a few at the top in a state without free elections and political liberties. The making of distinctions is the beginning of wisdom, and only by noting these differences can we distinguish between a democracy and a benevolent despotism.

Secondly, it will not do, in any discussion conducted in good faith, to assume that the majority, just because it is the majority, is in fact always wrong or foolish. In any working democracy, good and able men are found on both sides of political disputes, and consequently majority parties also have their share of leaders and wisdom. It is even worse to perpetrate the trick of defining the majority as *ipso facto* wrong or immoral, and the minorities as *ipso facto* right or virtuous, or to assume that all do not stand on much common ground. All government, as Hume noted, rests on opinion, and the majority principle permits, in those countries which use it, all sorts of opinions about *what* the majority should decide, and this indeed is the very stuff of political dispute.

A good deal of the fear of the majority principle, as of democracy in general, is, of course, genuine enough. Partly, it springs from the well-grounded suspicion that 'government *by* the people' will also be 'government *for* the people'; and naturally enough, this result is a consummation devoutly *not* to be wished by those who are fearful of their special privileges. The fear that the majority (the mob, the 'great beast') might seize the property of the well-to-do seems to be the most constant historical source of the hostility to the majority principle. It may even be, as someone has suggested, at the root of the 'vast neurotic fear of what the majority might do' which exists in the United States today—a quite irrational fear, because virtually all Americans are united on the sanctity of property and have always been so. (By contrast, Marxists such as Lenin have nothing but contempt for democratic majorities, who are said to be merely subject to 'deception' by the bourgeoisie.)

But part of the fear is not so ungenerous, and is based on the realistic insight that a majority (like a minority) may sometimes be foolish or unjust. Tocqueville fed this fear of 'the absolute sovereignty of the majority,' which he took to be the essence of American democracy. Mill was among those most sensitive to the 'tyranny of the majority,' and he noted (in *On Liberty*) two possible methods which had been tried historically to prevent government from abusing its power:

> First, by obtaining a recognition of certain immunities, called political liberties or rights, which it was to be regarded as a breach of duty in the ruler to infringe, and which if he did infringe, specific resistance, or general rebellion, was held to be justifiable. A second, and generally a later expedient, was the establishment of constitutional checks, by which the consent of the community, or of a body of some sort, supposed to represent its interests, was made a necessary condition to some of the more important acts of the governing power.

The thesis which I suggest is that the first of these checks—restraint and forbearance as they operate in the free political process—is the only protection a democracy can offer against tyranny. To seek for more is to seek for the unattainable: a government legally powerful enough to do right but powerless to do wrong.[18]

(b) THE MAJORITY PRINCIPLE AND THE
'NO TRESPASSING' PRINCIPLE

What is the alternative to the majority principle, to trusting the majority of the representatives and using our influence upon them? The simple alternative, for some kind of minority rule, is not usually put forward today plainly and unashamedly. Its doctrine of political inequality is rather strong meat for the modern stomach. Its problems are insoluble: which minority? By what marks shall we know the right one? How may we remove it if we later find we were mistaken? No, the way the majority principle is indirectly rejected is to say that the dilemma of the majority principle or the minority principle can be avoided and that gov-

18 On majority 'tyranny' see also Ferdinand A. Hermens, *The Representative Republic*, Notre Dame, 1958, Chapter IX.

ernment can rest upon the majority principle, qualified by legal checks. The majority should decide, it is freely admitted, but only upon 'indifferent' matters. A 'No Trespassing' sign should be put up, and a fence erected around an area from which the majority would be excluded by constitutional law. The contents of the fenced area may differ from country to country, but it generally includes substantive rights as well as those procedural freedoms and free elections which were noted earlier as part of the principles or conditions of democracy.

As we all know, there are two or three troublesome points about incorporating this 'No Trespassing' principle by law into the Constitution. One is the lack of agreement as to what things should be fenced off. If every minority had its way, public policy and discussion would be stripped of politics, like an army mess. Another is the odd idea that 'rights' of all kinds can always be best secured if they are left alone by the legislature, instead of being actively promoted by it as many of them must be. This 'negative rights' attitude is especially troublesome if one has any sense of community, and of the realities of social and economic life. And the trouble is becoming more acute, because every day new positive 'rights' to be promoted are proliferating all over the place. The Universal Declaration of Human Rights of 1948 contains a very large number (it is hard to be certain how many, since some of the Articles are subdivided and may be counted in different ways); and any of us could think of a dozen more at a moment's notice. But the really difficult question—and this is our concern now—is how, in any reasonably free society, the majority can be stopped from trespassing upon the fenced area. How, short of unanimity, can any question be 'depoliticized' if a majority wishes to make it a matter of public policy? In brief, how can the majority be kept by law from knocking down the fence another majority put up in the first place? (I am not dealing with the logical inconsistency involved between the principle of political equality and that of limits on a majority, the latter of which by weighting the minority votes counts some persons as more equal than others.)

The first way of looking at the majority principle—by relying on moral restraint and political safeguards—may be seen in

Locke; not clearly perhaps, because Locke was not a very consistent philosopher. Locke said that the majority should 'conclude every Individual,' i.e. he asserted the majority principle; yet he also set up his well-known barrier of inalienable rights. How could he reconcile the two? He did it by assuming, quite unconsciously, I think, that the two would never conflict. That is, he believed it would never occur to the majority to violate those inalienable rights; the danger lay only from a naughty minority (such as the Stuarts). It was the assumption that the majority clearly recognized and would always respect those agreed rights.[19] He could make this realistic assumption because he was thinking of a narrow franchise, confined to a small number of property-owning males, mostly Protestant and all tending to think alike on the important political issues. Hence Locke freely recognized the supremacy of the legislature, and while he set moral limits to an abuse of its power, he prescribed no limits in positive law. Even his 'right of revolution' was apparently vested in the majority.

The attempt to put certain things—mostly individual rights—beyond Parliament was, however, made by the Levellers, and later during the Protectorate in 17th-century England. But it was abandoned after 1660 and never tried again. Halifax was skeptical of unchanging principles of government, including fundamental laws which were 'untouchable,' and thought of them as attempts to bind future generations, which, like Jefferson, he regarded as impossible. The British political and constitutional system has in fact gone along the lines Halifax suggested:

'In the British Constitution though sometimes the phrase "unconstitutional" is used to describe a statute, which though within the legal powers of the legislature to enact, is contrary to the tone and spirit of our institutions, and to condemn the statesmanship which has advised the enactment of such a law, still notwithstanding such condemnation, the statute in question is the law and must be obeyed.' And this has, of course, become one of the uncontested trivia of treatises on the British constitution.[20]

[19] Willmoore Kendall, *John Locke and the Doctrine of Majority Rule,* Urbana, Ill., 1941. See also C. B. MacPherson, 'The Social Bearing of Locke's Political Theory,' *Western Political Quarterly,* vol. IX, 1954, pp. 1-22.
[20] Geoffrey Marshall, *Parliamentary Sovereignty in the Commonwealth,* London, 1957, p. 72.

British political thinkers occasionally worry about this, and pine for a strong second chamber as a constitutional barrier to the majority. Pollock years ago wanted to see some 'formal limitations of legislative power,' and expressed the hope that: 'It may be that some readers of these lines, if not the writer, will live to see such provisions in force at Westminster itself.' [21] Others have also sighed for the same moon, and some of them quote Cromwell in their support: 'I tell you that unless you have some such thing as a balance [i.e. on the Commons] *we cannot be safe.*' [22] Still others—e.g. G. M. Young—noting the absence from the English Constitution of any political thinking on the 'concept of fundamental law,' expect that it will come in with the growth of the 'welfare state.' British political philosophers do not, however, show any tendency to fall back upon judicial review to 'save the people from themselves,' although judicial review of legislation is not unknown in some unitary states. In Britain, judicial review has been abandoned in favor of Parliamentary sovereignty for more than 300 years.

> Mr. Charles Morgan, in a recent lecture, [urged] that we should reconsider, in the light of Montesquieu's doctrine, the old arguments in favour of legal limitations to arbitrary rule. Such a suggestion, however, seems to me wholly academic, and I cannot conceive that our modern parliamentary democracy would agree to accept the rigid constitutional checks of the American type of government. This originated as much from the practical need to satisfy the claims of the states, which necessitated a federal constitution, as from the political theories of Locke or Montesquieu. [23]

All democracies, then, do not try to set up constitutional checks against the elected majority of representatives. We need not consider such examples as voluntary organizations or town meetings

---

[21] Sir Frederick Pollock, *An Introduction to the History of the Science of Politics*, London, 1920, p. 113.

[22] J. J. Craik Henderson, 'Dangers of a Supreme Parliament,' in *Parliament: A Survey*, London, 1952. Readers of this slightly nostalgic book might well read, as an antidote, Chapter 3, 'Their Lordships Die in the Dark,' of George Dangerfield's *The Strange Death of Liberal England*, New York, 1935.

[23] J. W. Gough, op. cit. pp. 118-19. Occasionally, as with Lecky, suggestions have been made that the referendum be adopted for constitutional changes: to 'check unbridled democracy.'

or the Athenian model since these are direct democracies. But we may legitimately take such countries as Britain, Norway, or New Zealand, which have a supreme legislature, and this empirical testing does not support a charge of tyranny. One hears very little in these countries of 'fundamental law' beyond the legal reach of the legislative majority, but one hears much of Parliamentary or legislative supremacy. The British people are at the political mercy of the party majority in the House of Commons, and the theory of the electoral 'mandate,' in vogue now for a generation or more to justify sweeping social legislation, tends to confirm rather than refute the fact of Commons party supremacy when it clearly has a popular majority behind it. The way it is put is to say that '*Parliament* is the guardian of our liberties.'

The course of political thought and events ran somewhat differently among the British colonists in America in the 18th century. When they came to devise a new constitution, many of the Founding Fathers of the United States were suspicious of the majority (true, they thought of a wider franchise than Locke had) and talked a good deal, for instance, of 'elective despotisms.' So they put some rights in the constitution itself beyond the reach of a bare majority, and to make doubly and trebly certain that the majority could not prevail, they devised an ingenious mechanism of government that would make it difficult for any majority to get its way. Madison and others, however, had less faith in the constitutional devices and relied heavily on the size and diversity of the country—power restraining power—to prevent majority tyranny, though they also favored the legal checks.

It may seem a bit curious that these men, in the full stream of the Enlightenment, with their invincible optimism and faith in reason, should have displayed so little of Locke's faith in the ability of their fellow men to see and heed the self-evident truths and to exercise self-restraint. The full explanation is no doubt complex —there were several cross-currents of political philosophy at work —but three reasons were prominent: (a) they thought in terms of federalism and states' rights; (b) they drew not only from Locke but also from Montesquieu, and from English 17th-century theorists who were wary of the democratic idea of political equality and its logical consequences; (c) they were essentially 'conservative' revolutionaries greatly concerned with their property, which they thought might be an irresistible temptation to poor voters and a legislature under popular control. John Adams put the latter sentiment bluntly, and with a slightly blasphemous note: 'The idle, the vicious, the intemperate would rush into the utmost extravagance of debauchery, sell and spend all their share, and then demand a new division of those who purchased from them . . . Property is as sacred as the laws of God.' [24] (The Jeffersonians feared the opposite: that a national government removed from popular control would serve wealth and privilege.)

In the Declaration of Independence, the revolutionaries did not regard themselves as belonging to the same political population as His Majesty's subjects in Britain, by whom they would have been outnumbered. We do not really believe, for instance, that if the colonists had been granted representation—even over-representation—at Westminster they would have acquiesced in taxation. They wanted to avoid taxation and restrictive mercantile regulations, and were interested in the content of legislation more than in the form of government. It was, as we are told, a 'conservative' revolution, and that is why Americans were horrified at the French Revolution so soon afterwards, and why to this day the only kind of revolution Americans understand and feel sympathy for is a colonial revolt that leaves the social structure substantially unchanged. Despite its dynamic technology, 'America is a conservative country without any conservative ideology.' [25]

So they fell back from 'representation by population' and the majority principle, upon other justification for their rebellion. The majority principle, even for the colonists themselves, was avoided in the Declaration. Instead they put their case in terms of the famous self-evident truths, which linked them with cosmic law. The appeal to reason and abstract rights, though perfectly consistent for Jefferson was an irrelevant argument for conservatives, as Burke noted, but it was an impressive way of arguing for a minority, especially in the 18th century, and especially in the

[24] Cited in A. P. Grimes, *American Political Thought*, New York, 1955, p. 110.

[25] Cf. Louis Hartz, 'American Political Thought and the American Revolution,' in *American Political Science Review*, June 1952. The quotation is from C. Wright Mills, *The Power Elite*, p. 335.

colonies.[26] The Northern states did not use it much, however, when the South wished to secede: they emphasized not the inalienable rights of the individual, or self-determination, or even states' rights, but instead they emphasized the importance of union. And this was quite plainly an assertion of the majority 'will' *à l'outrance*. It is the same kind of dilemma which confronts many countries today where the force of nationalism clashes with the sectional loyalties known as 'communalism.'

Still, the Fathers did mix the ideas of will of the people, popular sovereignty, and political equality (and by implication, the majority principle) into the great compromise, the constitution and the system of government they set up. They could hardly have followed Locke and left it out, even though, as Louis Hartz has stressed, they lacked a feudal heritage.[27] Besides, many of the leaders and common folk who fought in the war (like the Levellers a century earlier) were under the impression that they were, in fact, fighting for the political equality of persons. The result, then, is two broad principles of policy-making which are often uneasy bedfellows—the majority principle and the 'No Trespassing' principle.

This is well-trodden ground, and many scholars have spoken of the constitution's inherent opposition to democracy. The conflict with the majority-principle part of democracy takes several forms: (a) states' rights—in the federal aspects of the constitution, notably in the Senate; (b) separation of powers and checks and balances (which would give divided government if adopted even in a unitary state); and (c) the 'higher law' method (i.e. the Bill of Rights, which contains both procedural and substantive rights).

American federalism is a patchwork quilt in which logic and uniformity seem to be largely ignored, a complex of *ad hoc* relationships replete with apparent inconsistencies. This is also a fair enough description of federalism when we view it historically . . .

Writing at the time of the Civil War, Lord Acton observed that the American federal system was not founded on principles but on

---

[26] In supporting the American rebels Burke argued not from colonial 'nationalism' or 'natural' rights, but from the constitutional rights of the colonists as British subjects.

[27] Louis Hartz, *The Liberal Tradition in America*, New York, 1955.

'momentary suspensions of war between opposite principles, neither of which could prevail.' [28]

A short excursus into the relation of the majority principle and documentary constitutions will be useful, in order to see how effective the method of putting constitutional checks in the way of the majority actually is. The thesis to be examined is that the legal barriers are not in fact the effective safeguards, but that these are moral and political. Consider first the Canadian constitution.

(c) THE MAJORITY PRINCIPLE IN THE CANADIAN AND UNITED STATES CONSTITUTIONS

One can easily argue that in Canada the majority party in the House of Commons is supreme, if one looks at political realities rather than at the constitutional facade. I say this in spite of the present barrier to the national majority party which judicial review puts in the way, by occasionally striking down federal legislation. The Supreme Court of Canada is a creation of the federal Parliament itself. It was first set up in 1875, and was enlarged to seven justices in 1927 and to nine in 1949. It may be legally altered or abolished by Parliament. Politically the court, like all courts, is in the last analysis subordinate to the elected legislative branch.

With regard to amending the Constitution, if one grants—as one must—that the action of the United Kingdom Parliament in amending the British North America Act, 1867 (the chief constitutional document), is only a formality, then it must be true that the effective power of amending the constitution lies with Canada. The action of the United Kingdom Parliament is, for these purposes, a delegated part of the mechanism of amendment. An amendment via the Imperial Parliament is normally secured by the passage of a joint address through the Commons and the

---

28 Robert G. McCloskey in *Approaches to the Study of Politics*, ed. R. A. Young, Evanston, Ill., 1958, pp. 169-70. Acton goes on (*Essays on Freedom and Power*, p. 203): 'The question on which the founders of the constitution really differed, and which has ever since divided, and at last dissolved the Union, was to determine how far the rights of the States were merged in the federal power, and how far they retained their independence.'

Senate, but since the Senate is chosen by the Prime Minister, it is possible for the majority party to get its way by appointment of amenable Senators. There might be some delay, and it might take two elections, by which time the high death rate among senators would give the opportunity to replace those recalcitrant senators who were appointed by the party formerly in office. An unwritten convention seems to require the consent of some, perhaps most, of the provinces to some amendments, but like all such usages it is somewhat obscure, and in any case has strength only because it is voluntarily followed by the majority party.

Even a Cabinet request to the Imperial Parliament—without a vote of the Canadian Parliament at all, or any consultation with the provinces—appears to be quite sufficient (because the United Kingdom Parliament will not go behind a Canadian 'request'); and clearly this puts the constitution entirely at the mercy of the party majority—by-passing Senate, Commons, and the rest. A province, in its turn, may alter its constitution by an ordinary act of the legislature, except for the office of Lieutenant-Governor, and naturally only within the limits of provincial authority; but the national supremacy can be maintained by the federal power of disallowance or veto. On certain other amendments, since 1949 a simple act of the federal Parliament alone will suffice.

The makers of the Canadian Constitution, not being children of the 18th-century Enlightenment but of hard-headed Victorian romanticism, were less philosophical than the American Founders. They did, however, put a few 'rights' into the B.N.A. Act. Yet the most sacrosanct of minority rights—with regard to denominational schools—is not only subject to amendment by way of the Imperial Parliament (as mentioned above), but is also subject to political fortunes, since the Governor General in Council (effectively, the Cabinet) is the final appeal body (except in the case of Newfoundland, the province added in 1949, for which an appeal lies to the Supreme Court). Does it not seem extraordinary at first sight, at least to anyone steeped in the legalistic American tradition, that a committee of the dominant party should be the guardian of minority rights?

In spite of all this, the majority principle in Canada has not led to majority tyranny. Temporary party or popular majorities do not bulldoze their way over minorities. As Mr. Pearson once put it:

> The fundamental principle which has guided statesmanship in Canada, since Confederation, has been that on important issues the nation's leaders should seek and pursue a policy which will commend itself to a majority of those in each main section of the country.

Or perhaps, more precisely:

> The basic minimum of provincial rights is protected by the hard fact that one province, Quebec, is dominantly French in language, social structure, and culture.[29]

This Calhoun-like principle once again has strength only because it is voluntarily followed by the great majority. The overwhelming majority of Canadians agree, for example, upon the important bi-cultural and school rights questions, and this is by choice, not because of constitutional law. The real safeguards for special minority treatment are moral and customary and political, in the nature of the political parties and processes including the federalized Cabinet, with the result that Canadians are among the freest people in the world. Canada, in short, is an example of a democracy where the majority principle is camouflaged by a coloring of legalisms.

The position in the United States is not so easily susceptible to a simple majority interpretation, because of the separation of powers, the checks and balances, the electoral college, Senate representation and filibuster, and the rest of it. But the Constitution is quite alterable by a special majority of Congress-and-state-legislatures in terms familiar to all through Article V of the Constitution. There is, then, no question that politically a special (large) majority of representatives and hence of people could get their way. Even a simple majority (or worse, a large minority) of the nation, if it were distributed appropriately in the right states and their legislatures, could—if my arithmetic is right—amend the

29 Lester B. Pearson, *Democracy in World Politics*, Princeton, 1945, p. 44. Henry F. Angus, 'Federal-State (Dominion-Provincial) Relations,' *Western Political Quarterly*, September 1957, p. 728.

Constitution even to the extent (*horresco referens!*) of writing in a new amending clause—for instance, putting future amendments on a simple Congressional majority basis. (The likelihood of doing so is nil, but that is not what is being discussed.)

Apart altogether from formal amendment, any constitution may be altered almost out of recognition by informal means, such as the growth of new usages, a commonplace which every political-science student knows. These usages only become usages when they are followed by the majority. Indeed, it may be said that only the informal usages which grow up make any constitution, and particularly the American, workable at all. Effective amendment or alteration goes on all the time, often in response to the majority demands, and is the price paid for retaining the literal document.

> For better or for worse, however, the Constitution has acquired a quality of sacred writ that renders it immune to examination *de novo*. Nothing seems more certain than that peaceful constitutional change in the United States will take place only in such fashion as to permit the continued existence of the fiction that the system remains essentially as it came to us from the Founding Fathers. A crisis so severe as to permit a wholesale revamping would be revolutionary in the most complete sense.[30]

Someone may point to the Supreme Court as a barrier to the national majority. An overwhelming case can be made, however, that it cannot stand in the way for very long. This is a well-worn subject and I need only make one or two points. No one doubts, with regard to ordinary legislation, that the national majority can prevail if the party majority is firm in Congress and the Presidency (though it would take a two-thirds majority to override a presidential veto). But if the Supreme Court follows the doctrine of judicial restraint in its attitude to federal law, as it appears to do so much nowadays, then what is constitutional and what ordinary legislation is much more a matter within the power of Congress than used to be supposed.[31] Many people have documented

30 David Truman, *The Governmental Process*, New York, 1951, p. 530.
31 John P. Roche, 'Judicial Self-Restraint,' in *American Political Science Review*, vol. XLIX, 1955, pp. 762-72.

the number and type of instances where the Court has struck down or not struck down federal legislation (analyzing the Court's decisions and personnel is a national pastime), and such evidence goes a long way to support our old friend, Mr. Dooley, in saying that the Supreme Court follows the election returns— even if they do not do so very promptly. Certainly many of the judges have thought so. One of them, Mr. Justice Jackson, has pointed out that for the Court to be supreme over the elected branches of government is a doctrine wholly incompatible with faith in democracy, that in case after case the issue has been the extent to which the majority principle will be set aside, and that although the Court has sometimes set it aside, sooner or later a firm national majority will get its way. The Court 'is subject to being stripped of jurisdiction or smothered with additional Justices any time such a disposition exists and is supported strongly enough by public opinion.' [32]

As to the Supreme Court as a protector of political rights and liberties against the national legislature:

> Thus there is not a single case in the history of this nation where the Supreme Court has struck down national legislation designed to curtail, rather than to expand, the key pre-requisites [of the freedoms of voting, speech, assembly, and press] to popular equality and popular sovereignty.[33]

The Icelanders at the time of the Munich crisis in September 1938 did not seem unduly perturbed about the danger of war and whether it might affect them. They were not worried about war, some of them said to visitors, because 'we have a law against it.' Having declared themselves neutral by law, they appeared to draw from this a great sense of security (as indeed did Americans with their neutrality laws of the 1930's). The federal states of Canada and the United States often indulge in the same unrealistic thinking, believing they can insulate certain things from

[32] Robert H. Jackson, *The Supreme Court in the American System of Government,* Cambridge, Mass., 1955, pp. 25, 58. Among the many works making the same point may be noted: Learned Hand, *The Spirit of Liberty,* ed. Irving Dillard, New York, 1952 and 1959; Commager, op. cit.; and Robert A. Dahl, op. cit. pp. 110ff.

[33] Dahl, op. cit. p. 59.

politics, or put them beyond a national majority by laws against interference. Hence the inveterate tendency to look to the courts to give political protection and promote political policies.[34] But 'the battles of democracy are not won in the courts.' Judicial review has been adopted not to promote democracy, nor even for reasons inherent in a federal system, as Lord Bryce pointed out long ago.[35]

A simple, lukewarm majority may be restrained by constitutional checks, but such protection is unnecessary, since tyranny does not come from the lukewarm but from the determined and the fanatical. The large majority, determined to get its way—the type against which protection is needed—is exactly the type which cannot be stopped. The legal checks are thus either superfluous or ineffective. (Perhaps one may make a case for them, as for a second chamber, in terms of a short delaying power.) When needed most for protection, they turn out to be 'children's huts of boughs and branches.'

I often wonder whether we do not rest our hopes too much upon constitutions, upon laws and upon courts. These are false hopes; believe me these are false hopes. Liberty lies in the hearts of men and women; when it dies there, no constitution, no law, no court can save it; no constitution, no law, no court can even do much to help it.[36]

If the majority principle does not seem to prevail in the United States or Canada, is it not because on many matters there is not in fact a clear political majority, and on others the majority is agreed in giving minorities their way and voluntarily refrains

[34] It is amusing to see how public attitudes shift toward the Supreme Court, and how inevitably this is so because court decisions get caught up in political dispute. One may propound a thesis: 'conservatives' favor the Court and the whole principle of judicial review against the legislature when 'progressive' or welfare legislation is enacted; the roles are reversed with 'liberals' favoring the court and condemning the legislature when the latter is in a conservative or reactionary phase (as in the notorious McCarthy period). Attitudes to administrative tribunals shift in a similar manner—see Walter Gellhorn, *Individual Freedom and Governmental Restraint*, Baton Rouge, La., 1956.

[35] James Bryce, *The American Commonwealth*, New York, 1910, vol. I, pp. 36, 259, 260.

[36] Learned Hand, op. cit. p. 144.

from exercising its numerical strength? But when the majority does want its way, and it is not the minority way, the coercion is evident enough. Was not the South compelled to stay in the Union, and is it not being coerced today with the policy of school integration? Neither the separation of powers nor all the other built-in protections can stand in the way of the majority 'will'— indeed the constitutional devices may have contributed to the Civil War by making compromise and peaceful solution impossible because the South thought it had a veto.[37] Were not the Mormons coerced, before and after Utah was admitted to the Union? Is not the very principle of the melting pot a method of enforcing uniformity on certain matters, no matter how much small minorities may protest (as they do, but quite ineffectually)? Did not the majority get such large issues as a graduated income tax, the direct election of Senators, prohibition, and the repeal of prohibition, settled in its favor after awhile? And in Canada, is not a majority agreed upon enforcing a bicultural as against a multicultural society (i.e. two melting pots instead of one)? I choose these examples, out of hundreds, because they go deeper than the froth of day-to-day political decisions, but they are nonetheless majority decisions of representatives and expressions of the 'will' of the popular majority. Are they all to be construed as examples of majority tyranny?

Even in some highly hierarchical or pyramidal organizations such as the military, the majority (even of subordinates) often exercises tacit and informal power. The support of the majority is always necessary to hold an organization and its policies together.

> One is tempted to say that no association, no matter how rigidly organized, is able to withstand the permanent pressure of a majority and that an organized majority is the most potent social force on earth. There is a certain authority in a majority which no hierarchy can wholly obliterate.[38]

[37] Cf. Wm. H. Riker, *Democracy in the United States*, New York, 1953, pp. 158ff. The lesson drawn by the author is that majorities get more impatient if frustrated in peaceful means to their goal; minorities get more intransigent if they can fall back on legal arguments

[38] Robert Bierstedt, op. cit. p. 707.

(d) FURTHER REFLECTIONS ON THE MAJORITY PRINCIPLE

What, then, is our protection from the majority of people and representatives? 'What indeed beyond the conviction of virtually the whole of the American people that things are simply not done that way?' In the United States as in Britain, 'constitutionalism goes deeper than formal checks and balances, judicial review, or guaranteed rights.' [39] There are no legal or constitutional barriers capable of standing in the way of a determined and persistent majority if they wish to breach them. For that matter, even 'against mass hysteria no plausible constitutional safeguard has yet been proposed ... It would seem that the problem here is sociological rather than political, in that social conditioning is more likely to be an effective remedy than a system of constitutional checks and balances.' [40]

Legal barriers could probably not stand in the way even of a minority party determined to overthrow a democratic constitution, by refusing, for instance, to yield office after an election. Indeed, an American President is not in the last analysis kept from being dictator by law (which he could override), while there is not even any facade of a legal barrier to dictatorship in a system with Parliamentary supremacy. The difference between the British and American democracies in their use of the majority principle and their safeguards against tyranny is small, the chief difference being that the legalism of the American system, and to a lesser degree the Canadian, tends to obscure the deeper and broader constitutionalism, and the checking of power by power in policy making.

The institutional arrangement (the 'constitution' in the broad sense) rests upon widespread beliefs and attitudes, upon usages and conscience, upon custom and 'traditions of civility.' These

---

39 John Swarthout, 'The Postulates of Res Publica,' in *Western Political Quarterly*, June 1957, p. 254; Thomas I. Cook and Malcolm Moos, *Power Through Purpose*, Baltimore, 1954, p. 185. As another student puts it: 'Somewhere along the line the public decided to read the Constitution as if it were a democratic document. This is infinitely the most important interpretation of the Constitution in our history.' E. E. Schattschneider, *Equilibrium and Change in American Politics*, College Park, Maryland, 1958, p. 8.

40 R. Wollheim, op. cit. p. 236.

are traditional and moral inhibitions upon the abuse of power, and of all limits they are the strongest. These are institutionalized and supplemented in the political system, which itself provides many safeguards—in cabinets, parties, pressure groups, and electorate; in the perpetual conflict of interests and opinion, the struggle for votes and political influence and of power against power (including property against numbers). And these are precisely the safeguards which exist in any democracy, including the unitary state with legislative supremacy, where it is far from true that the minority is always compelled to give way to the majority.

Taking them all together, these are in fact such effective safeguards that they often make it very difficult for the majority to get its way, except over a long period of time. Macaulay once called the American Constitution 'all sail and no anchor.' But when to the formal government is added the complicated political process, it is a heavy anchor with very little sail, open far more often in actual practice to the dangers of minority veto power than to unlimited 'majority rule.' '... in government, as in marriage, in the end the most insistent will prevails.' Doubtless Calhoun's theory of concurrent majorities, or minority veto, was an impossible one to put into *law*, but something closely resembling it is at work in the United States political system, the Canadian, and perhaps others. In politics, as in the use of the English language, there is no *Academie* to legislate, but usage is all.

The argument is sometimes heard that it is 'illogical' to give the majority power to abolish the majority principle. Hence a 'fallacy' is alleged to reside in something called 'Absolute Majority Rule.' But if minorities are subject to the majority principle, and cannot be protected by any legal barrier (see Appendix to this Chapter), then *a fortiori* it is surely futile to attempt to protect the majority from itself by constitutional law. This is a point on which there is almost endless confusion, wrought by good men as they have vainly tried to think up ways of preventing the majority from voting itself into slavery, of protecting free people from themselves.

If a community decides that some conduct is prejudicial to itself, and so decides by numbers sufficient to impose its will upon dissenters, I know of no principle which can stay its hand. I do not see how we can set any limits to legitimate coercion beyond those which our forbearance concedes.[41]

The majority principle is not the last word in politics—there is no last word—and what the majority will approve will always depend upon moral and political considerations, on which there will always be dispute and conflict in the give and take of democratic politics. It is at this point, although each vote counts for only one, that different intensities of feeling, of preferences for or against policies, make their impact upon government: those with strong feelings are powerfully motivated to political action in a large variety of ways. So far is such minority action effective that many decisions are not made which could almost certainly secure popular majority approval in any democracy. A plausible case can be made that having had minority veto, if not 'minority rule,' so long, we might well see an improvement with 'majority rule.'

> ...although no nation is more entirely committed than we are to republican government operated by majority vote, we have found more (and more ingenious) ways of moderating, delaying, sidestepping, and hamstringing the will of the majority than any other nation has thought it necessary or desirable to submit to.[42]

If the case above is sound, then we should alter somewhat the emphasis of our approach to democratic politics. The notion that anything can be taken out of politics by putting it into constitutional law ought to be exploded. No cows are sacred in politics or law except by popular agreement. The lessons of politics are political, not legal. If the majority principle is the legitimate, though sometimes concealed, method of political policy-making, and is in fact impossible to avoid in a democracy over the long run, then it ought not to be obscured in the analysis of the machinery of government, of Senate representation, of state and

[41] Learned Hand, op. cit. pp. 55-6.

[42] Carl Becker, *Freedom and Responsibility in the American Way of Life*, New York, 1951, p. 75. Cf. Edward Elliott, *American Government and Majority Rule*, Princeton, 1916, who wrote in order 'to point out the fact that the people of the United States have been hindered in the attainment of democracy, or the rule of the majority, by the form of government, through which they have been compelled to act.' p. iii.

provincial and minority rights, of loaded electoral laws; and above all not in the quasi-scholastic exercises in judicial review and constitutional law. How much energy goes down that drain!

Finally, if the argument above is sound, we ought to face forward into the future, not go reluctantly backward into it pining for what is not, never was, and never can be: a political system which permits the majority to do right but prevents it by law from doing wrong. Free political societies are afloat on the great ocean of majority decision-making, committed to we know not what, except a venture of faith in people with freedoms. The only channel between tyranny and anarchy is the majority principle in a democracy. Although the majority principle does not tell us where we are going or should go, it does give us the means —the only means—of getting to whatever destination a free people wish. There is no democratic answer to the old question *quis custodiet custodes* except 'we, the people.' Democrats can never imitate the example of Plato who, faced with the possibility that the constitutional government which he set up in *The Laws* might commit injustice, backed away from the constitution altogether, and called upon his 'god in the machine,' the horrible Nocturnal Council. But who was to maintain the purity and wisdom of the Council, he did not say.

From one point of view, it requires a tremendous faith in the majority to approve wise and just policies, over the long pull, a faith subject like any other to doubt and despair; but from another viewpoint the majority principle, with its concomitant freedoms, may be adopted because we do not trust any self-appointed minority to rule over us. The principle is thus suited alike to optimists who believe that human nature is inherently good and pessimists who believe in original and inescapable sin.

(e) SUMMARY AND CONCLUSIONS

This chapter has examined the justification of the democratic principle that political decisions should be made by a majority of freely elected representatives, and in the long run for the main lines of policy, presumably approved by the majority of the electorate. The question then arose of 'majority tyranny.' Cannot legal barriers be set up to prevent the majority from trespassing on certain fenced-off areas—natural rights, minority rights, political liberties, and the like?

I have argued that as a matter of political fact the majority, when determined and persistent, does get its way; obviously so in a democracy with Parliamentary supremacy, but no less so in systems where it does not appear to be true at first sight. The judiciary does not normally set itself for long against a national majority, and in any case the judiciary is politically appointed and dependent, while constitutional usages and ordinary legislation can give new meanings to any 'entrenched clauses' of a constitution. A special majority is often required for formal amendment of constitutions, but while this tells against a bare majority, it is conclusive evidence that the entire constitution is at the mercy of a substantial, determined majority. The rights and liberties we enjoy are therefore and can only be, in any democracy, at the pleasure of the large majority, or—what is the same thing—they exist because of moral and political restraints, voluntarily observed by the great majority of legislators and public.

A final point: although the argument above is valid as a matter of general principle, in practice it often has little political relevance, because of the difficulty of knowing what in fact a majority wants on any specific issue. The argument is true, that is, where a majority both large and persistent feels strongly, but not where majority opinion is lukewarm and uncertain. As a result, the policy decisions actually taken may seldom be those preferred by a majority, but merely those the popular majority will put up with from the representatives. Hence, to say that a majority *can* get its way is not the same as to say that a majority—even a large one—always or usually does so. If a large minority strongly resists a policy, it is unenforceable in a democracy. Fortunately—and it is the best we can hope for—because of the built-in political safeguards, the political system of a democracy very rarely sets intransigent majority over against irredentist minority.

APPENDIX | A NOTE ON MINORITIES

THE PERMANENT MINORITY

The foregoing theory has been couched in terms of the shifting popular majority. Hence it may be said that the only minority right built into the definition of democracy is the right to try to become a majority. But in every democracy there are some minorities that have no realistic hope of becoming a majority, and hence do not regard this one right as sufficient protection.

> I understand a minority to be a group of people who, because of a common racial, linguistic, religious, or national heritage which singles them out from the dominant group, fear that they may either be prevented from integrating themselves into the national community of their wish or be obliged to do so at the expense of their identity. I thus exclude from the definition political as well as socio-economic minorities. I am concerned only with cultural minorities.[1]

Of the two types of minority mentioned in this definition, the first such type of group minority (a minority by 'force') presents no special problem for democratic theory: these are the groups whose members desire nothing more than political equality with all their fellow citizens, 'to integrate themselves into the national community.' Examples are women, lodgers, and others before their enfranchisement, and Negroes in the United States. Equality more than liberty is their aim.

The second type is the permanent or cultural minority (sometimes called the 'out-group' or minority of 'will') which wants not equal treatment, but special treatment or privileges, for its language, religion, or other identifying characteristics. To such a minority it does not seem quite enough to say that it enjoys the usual political rights and liberties—freedom of speech, for ex-

---

[1] Jean La Ponce, 'The Protection of Minorities by the Electoral System,' in *Western Political Quarterly,* June 1957, p. 318. The minority in this cultural sense may even be a majority in an arithmetic sense, as the Negroes in South Africa.

ample, is inherently not equal for a linguistic minority—and so it commonly presses for constitutional and legal safeguards for its special minority rights. It seeks not the chance to become a majority but security in its 'rights' and identity.

If we bear in mind the previous argument about legal limits on the majority, it is fairly plain that a democratic system can give no certain guarantee that the cultural minority will be protected against majority pressure and 'integration.' Neither can any other system give any such guarantee beyond the reach of political forces. The only unique chance which a democracy offers is the opportunity for a minority to put its case, to share in policy making, to bring pressure to bear, and to influence votes. In short, the safeguards are moral and political as they are, within the democratic system itself, for the shifting and temporary minorities.

The cultural minority problem is particularly acute in the modern world in ex-colonies which have suddenly come to self-government and democracy. United against imperial rule by the spirit of nationalism and the struggle for independence, colonial people often find their unity fading when independence has been won, since the nationalism is often not strong enough to hold the majority and minority together. India with partition is a case in point. The secession of Pakistan was the answer to Indian independence; a solution which may always be the final refuge for 'national' minorities who want self-determination as a unit, not political equality of persons with the majority.[2]

If ex-colonies are not ready for the full majority principle, then 'fancy franchises,' special representation, or the constitutional checks of federalism may be all that is possible, short of secession.[3] Happy is the divided country that can work these compromise devices, where the majority is restrained enough to

[2] 'Not the South, not slavery, but Yale College and Litchfield Law School made Calhoun a nullifier. In the little classroom, Reeve at white heat and Gould with cold logic argued the 'right' of secession as the only refuge for minorities. Logically their argument was unimpeachable.' Margaret L. Coit, *John C. Calhoun, American Patriot*, Boston, 1950, p. 42.

[3] Some ex-British colonies, such as Ghana, have therefore adopted constitutional checks upon Parliament which are foreign to the normal British tradition. W. Ivor Jennings, *The Approach to Self Government*, Cambridge, 1956.

hold the allegiance of the minority. How long such transitional stages can last no one can say, but they must come first in many cases if full democracy is to come later. It is foolish to spurn partial democracy because the full system cannot be obtained at once. Even democracies like Switzerland and the United States have only attained their present workable systems after civil wars when the right of secession has been denied. Federalism, with its apparent guarantees of minority rights (comparable to treaties) will always make a strong appeal even though the safety it gives is largely illusory because (a) if it protects anything, federalism protects only 'state's rights,' and (b) even these 'treaty' guarantees (as we have seen) are at the mercy of the special national majority which can amend the constitution.[4] Multicultural states can live peaceably and to a large extent democratically, whether federalized or not, provided the right of secession is not insisted on, and the minority does not feel subject to 'tyranny'; conditions which seem easier to attain when political parties are inclusive, and not divided along 'cultural' or 'communal' lines.

Occasionally a permanent minority—especially if it is powerful socially or economically—may in fact play a leading if not dominant role politically. The question of intensity in politics comes in again at this point: a minority which feels ill-treated, or fears possible ill-treatment, is powerfully motivated to political action. Nothing is so impressive as a cultural minority fighting tenaciously for its 'rights.' [5] A small intense minority may thus sometimes get its way as much as a large, looser minority or majority.

There is also the fact that under any kind of government, whether it operates on the majority principle or not, sooner or later any one of us may be faced with the dilemma whether to obey the law or his conscience. As Alf Ross put it, in his splendid little book, 'there may come a time when we have to pass.' [6] When that point is reached, we must each make a fearful decision,

---

[4] Cf. La Ponce, op. cit.

[5] There may, however, be little sympathy for the claims of deviants if they are grotesque, or if the group is an irreligious minority. Yet, as Mr. Justice Jackson said: 'The day that this country ceases to be free for irreligion it will cease to be free for religion—except for the sect that can win political power.' Zorach v. Clauson, 343 U. S. 306, 325 (1952).

[6] *Why Democracy?* Cambridge, Mass., 1952, p. 119.

in the light of all the circumstances at the time. In the case of a minority the dilemma is much the same, except that the fearful decision will be made by the minority leaders and not by the individual rank and file. In the history of political philosophy the right to resist and rebel has often been discussed in collective (group) terms as well as in terms of individuals. But in spite of the innumerable volumes on this subject, it is impossible to lay down beforehand any except the most general principles, and these by themselves do not settle any political policy.

THE 'ANTI-DEMOCRATIC' MINORITY

The problem here is that of protecting democracy from an anti-democratic minority, a problem which has become especially acute in recent times because of fears aroused by communist and fascist parties. The problem is not posed entirely by these groups however, but is raised by every minority which wants to spread doctrines or adopt practices which are contrary to the principles of democracy. As a solution, it will not do merely to say: build a good society and those parties and groups will not arise. They exist everywhere, though no doubt they are not equally powerful or dangerous everywhere.

Historically, the question has been posed as one of toleration. In founding his Leviathan, Hobbes thought it 'rational' that a man should 'be contented with so much liberty against other men, as he would allow other men against himself.' It would be imprudent, irrational, even disastrous, to grant liberty to others if they would not reciprocate. This is, in a way, the whole case for not tolerating any organized party or minority that would abolish the political freedoms if ever it attained political office. It is more than mere prudence, it is also a question of mutual agreement to abide by the rules of the game; of that mutual trust indispensable to a secure social existence. In Hobbes' writings, the ruler enforced the same conditions upon all subjects, forcing them to respect one another's liberties and rights. A democracy, however, cannot call upon this *deus ex machina* since the rulers are the popular government, responsive and controllable; the people do not put their fate in the hands of a sovereign once and for all;

the sovereign fluctuates. We have rejected the stark Hobbesian alternatives of absolute power or anarchy.

Locke, too, would give an 'absolute and universal right to toleration,' only to those actions and opinions which did not concern politics and society at all; those which affected society could be prohibited by the magistrates, after due consideration, 'for the peace, safety or security of the people.' Mill, also, with his test of liberty being the line between the self-regarding and other-regarding actions—although on opinions, as distinct from action, he is very close to advocating absolute freedom, in his denial of a distinction between liberty and licentiousness—is no better guide to policy-makers. The great trouble often noted is: there is no way of separating the two types of actions and opinions, to say nothing of the initial difficulty in making the assumption that purely private actions exist.

From the enormous mass of controversial literature on this subject we may distill several relevant considerations: (a) Democracy has its rules of the game. Only those who abide by them are entitled as of right to play. Hence advocating overthrow of the freedoms of democracy may properly be prohibited by law, particularly when the anti-democratic minority is an organized movement. A democracy may or may not choose to be prudent, however; that is, it may choose not to repress or outlaw organizations which seek to abolish the freedoms and hence democracy itself. But it would not be illogical to adopt a repressive policy. (b) Even more obviously, the law may be used to control or suppress groups which use or advocate force to attain political power. Force and the threat of force may legitimately be met by force.[7] (c) Again, it is generally admitted that the community has rights. 'It can never concede to any of its members the right of behaving in such a way as to endanger its own existence.'[8] (We need not go so far as to hold that 'Liberty in its very nature is limited by

---

[7] Cf. the question of a democratic minority wishing to make a revolution against a 'tyranny.' 'No Englishman who is not a Jacobite, no Frenchman who is not a monarchist and no American who does not repudiate the Declaration of Independence can be logically consistent in objecting on principle to the use of armed force to overthrow an unpopular government.' Michael Lindsay, *China and the Cold War*, Melbourne, 1955, p. 102.

[8] Sir Thomas Murray Taylor, *The Discipline of Virtue*, Oxford, 1954, p. 49.

the supreme law of self-preservation which inheres in a state as well as in an individual.') [9] But there is an accepted doctrine of 'reasons of state,' or priority of the community over the individual and the minority, and this is made use of in every political system to justify internal security measures for the protection of the political system itself.

Despite the validity of these general considerations, they do not automatically point to any single policy. To suppress an anti-democratic movement may be logically impeccable, but it may also be psychologically and socially harmful in other ways. Nor do the general counter-arguments, on behalf of toleration for the anti-democratic minority, point to one and only one policy. For instance, the general argument is often heard that:

> Democracy cannot exist on inherited and unexplained tradition. It lives in the free air of nimble thought, and the discussion of principles is as vital to its life as the discussion of policies.[10]

And among the principles which may be challenged are those of democracy itself, just as a vote may be a vote of confidence in democracy when cast against an anti-democratic party.

When all the arguments based on principle are in, the question of policy is still open, and consequently we find different democracies pursuing quite different policies, and the same democracy adopting different policies at different times, in their toleration of or restrictions upon non-democratic minorities. One may employ the 'clear and present danger' test, another treat the problem entirely as one of military security, another—as in India—may move drastically against, for instance, a communist party. Many political and expedient factors peculiar to each democracy, as well as general principles and 'reasons of state,' influence the policy judgments made.

One such powerful force, helping to shape policy toward the anti-democratic minority, is the tradition of toleration, which in time becomes a moral quality, resting upon an optimistic forecast of the political consequences of freedom. To extend the demo-

---

[9] W. Torpey, *Judicial Doctrines of Religious Rights in America,* Chapel Hill, N. C., 1948, p. 36.
[10] Ernest Barker, *Greek Political Theory,* London, 1941, p. 4.

cratic freedoms to all, including those who would abolish them, implies a large faith in the ability of the democratic system to survive, and ultimately a faith in the people, (or perhaps with Milton a faith that 'truth will win in a free and open encounter.') It is a venture which not all democracies are ready for, especially if young or unstable, and so we cannot blame them if in their prudence they bias policy against liberty in favor of security. An older and more stable democracy on the other hand, may be taking little risk in tolerating the intolerant and even subversive party.

NINE | *Justification of Democracy: Its Values*

We have now examined the four broad principles characteristic of a democratic political system. If these principles of operation are followed, then the result is a democratic system. Policies are made by representatives, on the majority principle; the representatives are chosen and authorized to make the policies in free elections conducted on a universal franchise; the elections and the system in general are marked by the full range of political liberties. The result is popular government or policy-makers effectively controlled by the electorate.

A political system cannot be justified entirely by its constituent principles; its social performance must also be considered. Institutions are always judged by what is accomplished through them. Inevitably, then, we must raise the question of the conscious aims which democracies have actually pursued in the course of history or which it has been thought democracy should pursue. That task is undertaken in Chapter 10. In this chapter I propose a different enquiry: to examine the values which are inherent in or implied by *any* democracy; those values which follow logically or emerge from the actual working of a democratic system. Those values will then constitute a large part of the justification for democracy.

At first sight, it might appear that the democratic system outlined is on the whole compatible with any (well, almost any) conception of the purposes of government or the nature of its policies. We must say 'almost any' in order to rule out self-contradictory policies, i.e. those which would conflict with the success or self-perpetuation of the system, and with the separate principles which characterize it. These limits aside, democracy is often regarded as merely instrumental, to be used to achieve any ends which the majority of the representatives and voters wish to attain. The first objection to be met, then, is that democracy is 'value-free,' that logically as a system it neither aims at nor produces any particular values in the results actually achieved. In the ensuing discussion we return to the question of method and content, opened up briefly in the last part of Chapter 2.

IS ANY POLITICAL SYSTEM NEUTRAL AS TO RESULTS?

The initial doubt about the virtual neutrality of democracy which arises is this: can any system for political policy-making be strictly neutral or instrumental? In a purely technological sense, we say a tool is merely a tool and may be put to any use, but even here, since some tools are more specialized than others, all tools cannot be put to all uses; and surely democracy, even if 'merely a method,' must be put in the category of instruments which can be put only to certain uses. Moreover, it seems to be undeniable that the means employed can seldom, if ever, be entirely divorced from the results which actually occur, or which are intended. Means and ends frequently, perhaps always, affect one another, and there is a prima facie case that a complex political system like democracy must have important influences upon the kind of substantive results obtained or aimed at. Concern over procedure is frequently concern over substance, because the procedure so often determines the outcome. The form of church government has a considerable effect on the faith that is preached; types of voting—whether open or by secret ballot—often yield different results. Other examples, of procedure affecting the substantive result, may be found in the U.N. Security Council, in the choice of members of an arbitration board, of the date when an election is held, of the procedure for adopting constitutional amendments. In all these cases the method and content are inseparable.

A further clue may be found by a cautious analogy with the scientific enterprise. It seems clear enough that in science the methods and attitudes are all-important—they remain constant, so to speak, while any particular results achieved are always provisional. To be scientific is to be on the side of a method, which may be regarded only superficially as merely instrumental.

Another analogy, with the economic system, may be even more relevant. One may imagine a competitive economy based on private ownership, operating in either a poor or rich country. The results in one case may, for many reasons (e.g. lack of resources) be a low standard of living, and in the other a high one. Or we may imagine producers turning out and consumers buying quite different products from time to time. But although the results may differ in the level of living, types of products, and in other respects, surely we should say the *kind* of result is the same. The pattern of income distribution would be the same, the entrepreneur would be rewarded for his initiative, the investor for his thrift, consumers' sovereignty would prevail, and so forth. The values inherent in the free market economy are the same, wherever such an economy is found; they consist of all those prudential values and vices noted by Adam Smith in his defense of a commercial society.[1] One may, in principle, prefer a free market mechanism, even though another system yielded the same or better economic results.

Now, if such apparently neutral endeavors as scientific methods or a market economy are 'value-laden,' how much more likely that a political system so complex as democracy would have underlying value implications for the kind of results turned up or the goals pursued. Montesquieu said that every type of government has its distinctive principle: that of despotism is fear; that of monarchy is honor; that of a republic is civic virtue or public spirit. Our task is to identify this 'civic virtue' of the democratic system, and to see what bearing it has on the ends pursued or attained.

A seeming objection to the claim that democracies involve a family likeness of values arises from the allegation that from a method one cannot deduce the content. Hume, so it is said, cleared up this distinction between method and content—which Hegel later mixed up again to the great confusion of philosophy ever since. The argument from Hume is mistaken, however, since

---

[1] Cf. Joseph Cropsey, *Polity and Economy, An Interpretation of the Principles of Adam Smith,* The Hague, 1957.

his analysis has no relevance to a political method. Hume raised an objection that a purely logical operation, grounded upon purely logical premises—as in geometry, for instance—gave no necessary application to real life; and further that moral values could not logically be deduced from neutral premises. In this, he was surely right. So far as Hegel was concerned, however, there was never the sharp Humeian distinction between logic and life, fact and value; fact and value were intermingled in the premises of his theory. They were so to speak, 'value-facts.' He was not engaged in an attempt to deduce the content of history merely from its dialectical form, although sometimes he gave the impression of doing so. Indeed, he professed not to use ordinary logic at all, but a dialectical logic, which is certainly obscure and probably misleading. Fortunately Hegel is not our concern here.

DEMOCRACY IS 'FOR' THE PEOPLE

One broad implication of democracy almost inevitably follows from the system: government by the people is likely to aim also at government *for* the people, and not only because democracy is partly so defined, as in Lincoln's well-known phrase. The implication, though virtually irresistible, is not one of strict deductive logic. It is possible to imagine a democracy, by majority vote, devoting itself to some other end than the interests of its citizens— say the interests of the people on Mars or Madagascar.

Of itself, this does not take us very far—it merely puts the emphasis on the *people*. In some way, what is done to and for them is most important of all; the sights are trained on them, and not upon a collectivity, an organic state, a divine monarch, a particular class, or the like. The utilitarians in their emphasis on the happiness of the greatest number, and all democratic politicians in stressing the welfare or service of the people, belong in some sense to the same tradition of government for the people. Some of the support for democracy, and the opposition too, has come from those who hoped or feared, as the case might be, that it would turn out to be *for* the people.

So much has the idea of government *for* the people sunk into the modern mind that dictators nowadays profess to rule for the benefit of their people, a method of justification for despotism used far less often in earlier days. The definition of democracy given by Soviet spokesmen usually follows this line: if the policies of a government are for the benefit of the people, instead of for 'their most bitter enemies,' then the government is a democracy. But this definition will not do. It abolishes the distinction entirely between benevolent despotism and democracy, while in the absence of the political freedoms and effective choice—which are distinguishing features of democracy—we have only the dictator's word for it that his policies are in fact for the people.

The Soviet definition leads into two ancient errors: one is that the wishes of the people can be ascertained more accurately by some mysterious methods of intuition open to an elite rather than by allowing people to discuss and vote and decide freely. The other error goes deeper: that in some way the rulers know the 'real' interest of the people better than the people and their freely chosen leaders would know it themselves. All fanatics believe the same.

When Aristotle spoke of the state continuing that men might live well and said that the purpose of the *polis* was to promote the 'good' life, he too laid the democrat's emphasis on '*for* the people' (though in this case on a concept of their virtue). Historical experience shows, I think, a rather high positive correlation between rule *by* and *for* as representative democracy has broadened. After votes for women were secured, more women's-rights legislation of all kinds followed; with every widening of the franchise, more legislation followed to benefit the enfranchised voters. Common sense and a knowledge of political methods would confirm this: after all, a politician comes to office by bidding for votes, by offering something he believes the voters want. He has room for 'statesmanship' in the debate and competition, which give him the chance to persuade them to want what he thinks they need. The cynic might call this mass bribery, but it scarcely rivals the class bribery of the earlier limited franchise. There is too much evidence that special-interest legislation was a corrupt and delicate art, brought to a much finer flower of perfection in the days before universal suffrage.

Yet this first implication—that democracy works out for (or is designed for) the people—is undeniably vague. What sectional interest or policy, after all, is not defended on the ground that it is *for* the people? Yet vague as it is, it is not useless, and may be said to constitute one of the values of democracies, a value which many people rate highly. In this context, however, I shall treat it as a highly general, preliminary value, and proceed to identify more specific values of democracy.

THE SPECIFIC VALUES OF A DEMOCRATIC SYSTEM

The values of democracy are two-fold: (a) those underlying the principles considered separately; and (b) the values of the system as a whole. The task is to identify the values in both cases, so that, these being isolated, we may see what values we are committed to when we embrace democracy. In isolating these values we are not, of course, committing ourselves to every institution in every democracy, since obviously any actual democracy contains much that is unique and adventitious derived from its particular history.

The separate principles have been examined in Chapters 5 to 8, in both their operational and normative form. Each of these principles in its normative form may be taken as an ultimate; or else we may be persuaded to accept them because of the reasoned justification, the case, that was made for each. Democracy is, then, justified for those who accept the values in the ultimates, or the values in the justification—assuming that democracy is the system which best gives effect to these values.

As for the political system as a whole, we may grant that it is instrumental. But it is also 'more besides.' Like the pursuit of science, the free market economy, or an impartial judicial trial, the democratic system contains moral values (and perhaps an implied metaphysic as well). It is now my purpose to try to isolate the separate items in the cluster of values around an operating democratic system in order that we may estimate their appeal.

(1) *The first value is the peaceful voluntary adjustment of disputes.* Life in any human society contains a perpetual conflict of interests and opinions, whether the conflict is suppressed or

conducted openly. If anyone doubts this, let him look around him or read history. A democracy is unique in recognizing the political expression of such conflicts as legitimate, and in providing for their peaceful adjustment through the negotiations of politics, as an alternative to their settlement by force or fiat. Every political theory either provides means for this peaceful settlement within a political system, or else it must call upon a *deus ex machina* to impose order, an authority from outside the system of conflict, as Hobbes expected the monarch of the Leviathan to rule, as Bolingbroke looked to his Patriot King, as Plato looked to his Guardians, as the Germans looked to the Führer and as Marx once or twice spoke of the state as standing 'above society.'

Democracy makes unique provision for the peaceful adjustment of disputes, the maintenance of order, and the working out of public policies, by means of its 'honest broker' or compromise function. The policy compromises are worked out as the representatives bid for electoral support, amid the constant public debate, agitation, and politicking that go on in the context of political liberties, until in time many policies pass from dispute to virtual unanimity in settled law; or perhaps we may say from an equilibrium of forces to voluntary unity, although even a continuing equilibrium is in itself no small achievement. In speaking of equilibrium, however, I am not suggesting a neutral, general explanatory theory of democratic politics along the lines of 'dynamic equilibrium' comparable, say, to the equilibrium in mechanics, or to price determination in a competitive market.

No political system bases itself on the principle of forcible settlement. Even dictatorships try to rule by obtaining ideological support for their system and a favorable public opinion for their policies, as well as by resorting to force. The tragedy is that they often succeed in gaining popular support. In this sense all governments employ both coercion and persuasion, and may be said to rest upon both. Yet the difference between voluntary and enforced support is clear enough, even if, like everything else in practical politics, it may be a matter of degree in the borderline cases—questions of how frequently force is used, what channels exist for public debate and influence, how effective the choice of the policy-makers, whether 'consent' is final or provisional. Democracy does not, on principle, apply legal force to suppress political dissent, whereas dictatorship relies on legal compulsion, censorship, and the like, to suppress dissenting views which would undermine support for the system and its policies whenever the manipulation and conditioning failed. The use of coercion or force is not excluded and cannot be, in any political society, but is the last resort in any legal settlement in a democracy, and is not used at all in many political settlements.

Democracy is thus institutionalized peaceful settlement of conflict (ballots for bullets, a counting instead of a cracking of heads), a settlement arrived at *pro tem* with the widest possible participation because of the adult suffrage and the political freedoms. It is distinguished from elite systems or borderline cases (with *some* freedoms, *some* choice, etc.) by the difference in degree, by the recognition of the legitimacy of many diverse political interests and the extent of public participation in the settlement of disputes.

Here, then, is a value, characteristic of democracy, which will be prized by all who prefer voluntary to imposed adjustment and agreement. It is not a value, however, to those (if there are any such) who believe that force is preferable; nor would democracy be valued by those who believe that the ideally best policies are always preferable even if they have to be imposed from above.

(2) *The second value is that of ensuring peaceful change in a changing society*. This is so closely related that it may be regarded as an application of the first to the special circumstances of the modern world. The value makes a stronger appeal today than in earlier, more static, periods, that is, it has a greater element of plausibility now, because we accept the normality, even inevitability, of rapid technological change. Tomorrow the stars. (In suggesting that technology is an independent variable, initiating social and political changes though not fully determining their extent or direction, we need not ignore other determinants such as population changes or such mechanisms as the entrepreneurial function.)

We know from experience that social changes of many kinds inevitably follow the technological. The democratic political method—flexible, responsive to public opinion and to the influence of leadership, open to controversy—ensures political adaptation to this determinant of change. Almost by definition, because of the electoral changes of policy-makers, there is less 'political lag' in the many adjustments which are required in law and policy to meet rapidly changing circumstances.

We are all quite accustomed to the idea of change, and aware of the need to canalize it peacefully, despite occasional calls for a 'halt to inventions' and sporadic nostalgia for an earlier age or for a static society. In the modern world there is a surprisingly little of the attitude associated with Plato or Aristotle—suspicion of social change because of its disruptive political effects.

Whether industrialization can proceed democratically—even peacefully—in many parts of the world is in grave doubt; there is very probably a rate of change beyond which the democratic machinery will not work, particularly in countries where the appropriate historical tradition and other empirical conditions of successful democracy are weak or lacking. If so, the price may be a dictatorship, benevolent in intention, ruthless in method, for the 'emergency operation' of rapid industrialization and the modernization of the other aspects of society that go with it.

It seems a fair enough prediction that many poor countries will travel the road of forced, despotic industrialization, since no population nowadays is willing to wait for industrialization to spread of its own accord, to take the slow method which brought such countries as Britain and the United States to their industrial power. So far as economic development and the promise of 'plenty' are concerned, the world has moved from fatalism and *laissez faire* to conscious control, forced investment, and other short cuts; and the rate of such economic growth can in many places be rapid only under severe central direction. But the methods of emergency are not a safe guide to normal living, and do not seriously weaken the case for democracy, although they do indicate some of the social conditions without which democracy cannot work successfully. There is nothing in the case for the democratic system which requires us to maintain that it will work under any and every set of circumstances.

Today there is little serious argument against the value of

peaceful change as a normal process, particularly in a complex industrial society, so that it constitutes a powerful justification for democracy. Some writers, such as Merriam, have gone so far as to say that 'The greatest of all problems of government lies in the adaptation of traditions to changing times rapidly enough to clear with catastrophe.'[2] Even Marxists do not disparage this value; instead they usually deny the possibility of its realization in a capitalist democracy which they regard as a class society of irreconcilable antagonisms. (There are, however, hints here and there in some communist apologetics that democracy and its political liberties are only unrealistic in *backward* areas, where only communist regimes can force the pace of industry and social transformation.)

(3) *The third value is the orderly succession of rulers.* Democracy not only presides over social conflict and change, but at the same time solves an even older political problem: that of finding, peacefully, legitimate successors to the present rulers. Hobbes, for instance, thought that the problem of succession was the chief difficulty with a monarchical system. Democracy is pre-eminently an answer to the question which no alternative system can answer convincingly in the modern climate of opinion: how to find and change the rulers peaceably and legitimately. The methods of self-appointment, of hereditary succession, of co-option by an elite, and of the *coup d'état* are not contemporaneously plausible in their philosophic justifications, apart altogether from the practical difficulties inherent in them, to which abundant historical experience testifies.

It was with these three social values in mind—peaceful adjustment, change, succession—that Judge Learned Hand could write of democracy and free elections:

> It seems to me, with all its defects our system does just that. For, abuse it as you will, it gives a bloodless measure of social forces —bloodless, have you thought of that?—a means of continuity, a principle of stability, a relief from the paralyzing terror of revolution.[3]

[2] In *Ethics*, vol. LIV, 1943-4, p. 268.
[3] Learned Hand, *The Spirit of Liberty*, ed. Irving Dillard, New York, 1952 and 1959, p. 76.

(4) *The fourth value is that of the minimum of coercion.* A fourth value may be constructed by reference to the extent and quality of coercion involved in a democracy. (Again, the question of intensity of feeling in politics comes up, although we need not be so foolish as to try to measure *amounts* of coercion. Political thermometers are always operating even if we are not sure what they measure.) It is not only that almost by definition the greater number approves of the policy decisions, so that always the smaller number is coerced. This is the least of the argument, which depends much more on the existence of political freedoms and the way in which policies are made. For one thing there is great value in a safety valve, in being able to let off steam and to contribute to the debate and the politicking even though one is finally outvoted. We may follow the fashion and call it a catharsis, a working-off harmlessly of buried feelings of aggression, guilt, or the like. An ill-treated minority does normally feel differently—less coerced—if political equality is recognized and if it has to give only conditional obedience to policies which it may criticize and which it can entertain a reasonable hope of altering either by persuasion or by political influence. (This does not, however, always satisfy 'permanent' minorities, on which see Appendix to Chapter 8.) Here is the kernel of truth in Rousseau's account of the General Will: we may agree with the rightfulness of laws which we do not always like. It is also the position most of us are in when obeying laws or other policies of which we disapprove, for all of us are minorities on some policy or another.

We may go further. The normal democratic policy is in a sense a decision which gives no claimant everything he asks for; is not a mere mechanical compromise but a new policy, shaped from the continuing dialogue and struggle of the political process. Some go so far as to call the method 'creative discussion.' From this it is only a short step to saying that there is more value in decisions which we make, or help to make, than in having 'wiser' decisions made *for* us, and which we must be compelled to obey.

To try to force people to embrace something that is believed to be good and glorious but which they do not actually want, even though they may be expected to like it when they experience its results—is the very hall mark of anti-democratic belief.[4]

One might plausibly assume then that nearly everybody would accept this value—that *ceteris paribus*, it is better to coerce fewer people than more, to get voluntary observance rather than coerced obedience, to substitute what Wordsworth called the 'discipline of virtue' for the 'discipline of slavery': 'order else cannot subsist, nor confidence nor peace.' The notion of willing obedience reasonably, freely, and conditionally given would also agree with ideas of self-discipline, responsibility, and the like, of which we hear so much.

(5) *The fifth value is that of diversity.* The argument here depends initially on whether diversity of beliefs and action, and a wider area of choice, are of themselves good. Many will dispute their value, since diversity and variety can result in more of both the good and the bad, and free choice implies the freedom to choose badly. Ruskin thought that liberty of choice destroyed life and strength, and hence democracy was destructive. Human freedom has destructive as well as creative possibilities. But is there not at least some prima facie case for diversity and variety per se, as there is for freedom?

In the first place there is always diversity in any society, even if not to the extent of as many opinions as there are men. Democracy merely recognizes its existence, and legitimatizes the different opinions and interests. A psychological aspect of human nature often forgotten is relevant here, namely, the capacity to be bored, the common sense of which is incorporated in the old saying 'variety is the spice of life.' To quote Locke:

> It is not the Diversity of Opinions, (which cannot be avoided) but the Refusal of Toleration to those that are of different opinions, (which might have been granted) that has produced all the Bustles and Wars, that have been in the Christian World, upon account of Religion . . .

In the second place, the value of open channels and political liberties is that by implication an inevitable variety will result.

---

[4] Cf. A. D. Lindsay, *The Modern Democratic State*, Oxford, 1943, pp. 45, 241, 275. Schumpeter, op. cit. p. 237.

Here, too, as far as ideas are concerned, we may fall back upon the arguments used by Mill in his defense of liberty of opinion. We do rightly, on grounds of experience, to be suspicious of man's ability to know beforehand what new idea or proposal or way of behaving should be strangled at birth by the authorities and what allowed to live. The true and the good often repel in their very novelty.

In the third place, however, we can only say that 'other things being equal,' a wider choice is *ipso facto* good; it is a necessary condition for moral improvement, for reaching closer to the truth, (so long as we assume we have not already reached perfection or the *summum bonum*).[5]

Some comparison may be made here with the criterion often set up to measure progress in biological evolution. If we define biological progress with reference to the successful adaptation of the organism to the environment, then should a rapid change in environment occur, a perfectly adapted species may become extinct. Indeed, we are told that this has happened with dinosaurs and many other species, so that adaptation is not an adequate definition of progress (or efficiency) if it sometimes leads to extinction. But another criterion is possible. Evolution may be called progressive insofar as the adaptations and changes which are evolved, whatever they may be, *keep the future open* and make it possible for a species to adjust to future environmental changes. On this criterion man has progressed the more he has been able to control his social environment and continuously to adjust to natural environmental changes. The criterion is not mere survival at any given moment but, *ceteris paribus,* a large assurance of continued survival in the future. (The crude population test was given by Rousseau:)

[5] A subsidiary value from diversity may be formulated: a wider range of temptations gives more opportunities of strengthening the character. For this reason Morris Cohen could write: 'the very essence of civilization [is] that we should increase the temptation and with it the power of self-control.' *Reason and Law,* Glencoe, Ill., 1950, p. 52. Rousseau started from the same point: morality for the individual implies liberty of choice. Unfortunately, he tended to merge individual liberty in the community, though in this he was not far from one of the ideals of the Greek city-state.

All things being equal, the government under which, without external aids, without naturalization and without colonies, the citizens increase and multiply most, is infallibly the best. That under which a people diminishes and decays is the worst. Statisticians, it is now your business; reckon, measure, compare.

By maintaining an open society, democracy may then be called good because its freedoms give flexibility and a wide variety of choice. The argument may rest not only on the formal principles of democracy, but also on the empirical tendency for the political freedoms to extend beyond the purely political. The tendency is strong and ever present since political discussion includes the very topic of what is political, and because in their bidding for votes, parties and candidates tend to compete in granting substantive favors, including repeal of restrictive laws in some fields, and promotion of positive policies in others, e.g. on behalf of education, the arts and sciences. It is partly because of this tendency that democracy is sometimes called a 'way of life.'

The freedoms in a democracy may then be called good, as the increase in knowledge of self and society, and the mastery of nature, is good: they enlarge the possibilities open to man. They are not unconditionally good, because everything depends on what we do with the possibilities, but they are good so far as they go; they are an open doorway to an uncertain future. A means or condition of the good life is itself good to some extent. No single value—nor all the values taken together—in a political system can be considered unconditionally good; nor is (nor can be) any one value actually pursued to its 'absolute' limit, i.e. regardless of others. Looked at from this viewpoint, the fundamental problem of a democratic political system is to achieve a harmony of ends and values for the time being, while keeping a way open so that a better harmony may be achieved in response to higher and more sensitive demands when they arise. Diversity is never unlimited in any society—there is always a need for unity, for integration, for consensus, for community, however vague and unmeasurable these desiderata may be. There is always, in short, a pattern in the diversity, or limits beyond which variation cannot go.

Although the diversity and freedoms of democracy are sometimes made the basis of criticisms of democracy (by those who wish to exclude freedom once they have discovered the 'truth' or the best pattern), a much more common charge against democracy today is the very opposite: that the principle of political equality in democracy will kill freedom and progress.

One often hears, for instance, of the dilemma of democracy versus economic progress (sometimes put persuasively as freedom versus equality), as though the two were mutually exclusive alternatives and democracies by their nature were committed to the bad sides of the equation. The argument usually goes that economic freedom is necessary for economic progress, and the trend in democracies to equality, welfare, and security will destroy or reduce economic freedom and hence block the avenues of economic progress. The argument is impossible of conclusive proof or refutation. If we appeal to the history of democracies to refute it, by showing that they have been economically progressive and democratic, we are met with the assertion that equality and security have been less in the democracies of the past and hence the progress has been greater: democracies have been economically progressive because, so to speak, they were only partially democratic. If we appeal to the logical or practical implications of a democratic system—that the political freedoms are not necessarily hostile to economic freedom and progress, and they at least ensure that proposals for economic change or progress get ventilated —the political freedoms are dismissed as *only* political, and the argument is then shifted to a re-definition of democracy in terms of non-political egalitarianism. Now democracy has sometimes been defended by reference to its extra-political egalitarian tendencies—social equality, for instance—but it need not be: the political equality and the free participation make up the proper logic of the system.

In the end, we can only fall back upon common knowledge that progress is initiated by talent (by 'creative minorities') and flourishes in a favorable environment; that democracy—both the theoretical system and the working systems—does provide room for initiative and an environment for talent; and that the rate of technological innovation and economic change shows no sign of coming to a stop or even slowing down in the democracies. Nor can we seriously dismiss democracy as destructive of economic progress, without showing that the logical tendencies of alternative systems are less harmful. Hence we may conclude that the argument from the value of diversity is a perfectly valid one for democracy. Its strength and persuasiveness are another matter, and will depend upon how much we value diversity.

(6) *The sixth value is the attainment of justice.* Justice has been rated highly by political philosophers as a value to be attained in many societies. Its achievement is often regarded as the central core of political morality, and the defense of democracy on this ground must be that it is the system best able to produce justice. There are several relevant points in the case.

First let us grant that the best we can hope for in any practicable political system is not that injustice will never be committed (a perfectionist ideal) but that it can be seen, corrected if possible, and avoided the next time beforehand. (The dilemma could perhaps be avoided if democracy were by definition, or could be in practice, unanimous rule. There would then be no others within the system to judge the decisions to be unwise or unjust. But even then, a later generation could pass such judgment, as could persons in other states. Unanimity or universality is no guarantee of rightness or justice.) The link with democracy lies in the political liberties—the procedures, the publicity, and possibilities of redress. What the U. S. Supreme Court once said of liberty may be true of justice too: 'the history of liberty has largely been the history of the observance of procedural safeguards.'

No political system, lacking perfection, can be entitled to unconditional allegiance. There may come a time when any individual may feel bound in conscience to withhold his obedience; and it comes to much the same thing to say that no political system can lay down, beforehand, the institutional rules for justified disobedience or rebellion. In this respect, democracy again makes perhaps the best claim for obedience to an unjust law because of the political freedoms, provisional obedience, and chances of redress. It is certainly not illogical to obey a particular bad law if it is part of a general system of which we approve, and where we have the liberty of protest and persuasion, and the reasonable hope for redress. We must beware of posing the problem of obeying bad laws too sharply, and on this we may look to Locke for some sensible observations. Allegiance and obedience are never explainable on the ground that the political system gives us, as individuals, everything that we want.

Second, the likelihood of injustice under democracy is much less than where the political freedoms are suppressed, and where none of the usual political safeguards exist. Democracy provides some representation of all substantial groups and interests (though not always strictly in proportion to their numbers, and still less to their 'importance'); injured interests, being vocal and able to muster power through influencing votes and through many other recognized and legitimate ways, are seldom likely to be ignored when policy decisions are being made.

But this is a modern 'group' outlook on politics. The older democratic outlook towards the problem of injustice, in Athens for instance, was couched in individual terms. Rulers can be trusted with power only if they are removable from office, and injustice can be avoided only if all citizens are politically equal— if laws are administered impartially or equally, and above all if every citizen has his equal share in shaping the laws, both of these meanings being packed in the phrase 'equal laws' (*Isonomia*). A defender of democracy

> does not claim that the people's rule will be good because the people are just and wise. But only that their rule will be responsible and equal, assuming that it will be saved by this very fact from the *hybris,* which not even the best of monarchs can avoid.[6]

Third, democracy involves political compromise or harmony by the adjustment of conflicting claims. This may fairly enough be called 'relative' justice, even though it does not approach the kind of harmony or 'right relationship' of classes which constituted so much of Plato's idea of justice. In any case 'absolute' justice is an ideal beyond the reach of democratic politics, partly because it involves less than full satisfaction of some claims (or 'rights') but also partly because absolute justice in any other sense is beyond any system of government. Only relative justice, the relative at-

[6] Gregory Vlastos, 'Isonomia,' *American Journal of Philosophy,* vol. LXXIV, 1952-3, p. 359.

tainment of any of our highest ideals, is feasible in any political system. The best word to use perhaps is equity, with its connotation of both justice and flexibility.

In every society there is always a conflict between aspiration and reality. For instance, wealth may plausibly be said to be the operative social ideal of societies with a free market economy, yet relatively few can attain wealth and consequently there is bound to be perpetual frustration, so long as we hold to the ideal. So, too, if ideals concerning justice are pitched high, they may be more than frustrating, they may be dangerously disruptive. There may thus be less frustration, less 'anomie,' less friction, and more stability if ideals in a democracy are lower and attainable, i.e. only a little better than actual practice. For this reason the attainable compromises of democracy may take us further toward justice over the long run than an all-or-nothing attitude which is so characteristic of the fanatic or 'true believer.' For this reason too, justice may well be more feasible in a large democratic community where many diverse ideals must always be harmonized, than in a small community where substantially all are devoted to the same social ideals and the freedoms and dissent of democracy may appear to be enemies of the high ideals already reached. (If all men are by nature conservative or creatures of habit, as they are, then this, too, is an argument against trying to enforce ideal standards beyond the reach of the great majority, or even a large minority.)

Fourth, in practice, democracy almost inevitably leads to government *for* the people, as noted above. The effect is to widen the numbers over which justice applies, and restrict the numbers upon whom injustice can be wreaked.

Fifth, democracy and its majority principle may be expressed in Lincoln's words: '. . . faith in the ultimate justice of the people. Is there any better or equal hope in the world?' In the end this may be the best consolation that can be offered to those who feel unjustly treated for the time being; a consolation which gains strength when alternative political systems and alternative 'acts of faith' are considered.

(7) *A value often asserted on behalf of democracy is that it is the political system which best promotes science.* The argument rests on the prior assumption that science and its products are valued, an

assumption which it would be hard indeed to deny today. The social status of science is unimpeachable, the world having accepted almost unanimously the tangible fruits of science and technology. Ours is a science-shaped age, and one of the basic things any political system and theory must do is take this into account.[7]

The argument that democracy is especially favorable to science is often supported by reference to the Nazification of science, which almost certainly set the Germans back in many fields, while political dictation may also have set back the Soviet Union in some fields, genetics, psychology, and the social sciences being cases in point. Yet it is clearly possible for scientists to be left alone to use the universal scientific methods, in many if not in all fields, no matter how dictatorial the regime may be in other ways. The enormous strides in many branches of natural science in Russia are testimony to this. Moreover, science was born and grew in a substantially non-democratic political atmosphere, though it may be granted that in other ways much civil liberty existed in, for instance, England during the 17th to 19th centuries, or in France of the 18th century, during which much scientific advance was made. As Bryce noted:

> If we ask under what kinds of government letters and art and science have flourished, history answers, Under all kinds.

Further, there is nothing illogical in supposing an autocratic or even totalitarian regime devoting itself to science—using it as an instrument—to promote its ends; and this is precisely what the Soviet Union is doing. The results of scientific investigation may be used for any end: like the fire of Prometheus, it may benefit or destroy.

---

[7] I am not discussing the impact of science on society, or the responsibility of scientists for the social effects or uses of science. How far the faith in 'social science' and the willingness to be guided by its results have gone, may be seen from this example: American industry and, what is worse, American academics had to have a scientific experiment (the Hawthorne experiment of Elton Mayo) to prove that factory workers were human beings. These were greeted as tremendous revelations, as the Columbus discovery of 'the whole person,' etc. 'In reading these research reports one has a persistent vision of a modern dairy farm, managed to perfection, each cow in its gleaming stanchion, contentedly munching vitaminized food, milking machines barely audible through the piped-in Vienna Waltzes.' Dwight Waldo, 'Development of Theory of Public Administration,' *American Political Science Review*, XLVI, March 1952, p. 89.

Whether natural scientists can be given freedom of scientific investigation and discussion without, in time, some of the scientific freedom spilling over into politics, we simply do not know. On the one side is the apparent fact that an appreciation of natural science is certainly not necessarily correlated with moral or political sensitivity; while it is notorious that scientists do not carry over their careful methods or cautious attitudes into other fields. Moreover, 'scientists are curiously obtuse as to the special conditions which make possible their existence as a class.' [8] Sabine in his well-known *History of Political Theory*, New York, 1950, p. 904, notes another aspect of the difficulty:

> A government that aims at the maximum of military power and also a maximum of intellectual control commits its educational system to a peculiar experiment. Essentially it has to find out whether it can debauch the social studies and the humanities and yet keep the natural sciences vigorous enough to support the technology.

On the other side are plausible arguments that science and democracy are natural bedfellows. The first of these is that scientific methods and democracy share many of the same moral values. Now it is not an easy thing to agree upon the essentials of the scientific method or its 'values,' if any. Are scientific methods mere routine rules, dealing only with verification and proof, or do they also deal with discovery, with ordering concepts, and with the 'philosophy of science'? Sometimes they are said to consist of or imply such values as impartiality, persistence, honesty, tentativeness, integrity, fairness, loyalty to the scientific tradition, and the like. There is thus said to be a code of values which presses upon the conscience of every scientist, qua scientist, and which he learns as part of his profession. Hence—the argument runs—like the social sciences which are inevitably involved in morals ('value-laden'), so the scientific method is also essentially a moral enterprise. Democracy is also said to presuppose or imply these same values—in its public discussion, in voting, in the legislature, in the office-

[8] Harold A. Larrabee in *Scientific Spirit and Democratic Faith*, New York, 1943.

holders (whether politicians or administrators)—and to require loyalty to a similar tradition.

Second, both democracy and science are said to rest upon the same postulates of human nature—rationality and intelligence: in politics, that people can know and judge broadly their interests, by taking thought can judge the way to achieve them, and in fact can achieve them. Determinist theories of politics and science are alike rejected, despite the view (sometimes expressed by Engels) that science is 'determined' by social 'needs.'

Finally, the view of truth is said to be the same in both science and democracy—tentative, corrigible, approachable but never attained. It is a rejection of 'absolute' truth (except perhaps as some general ultimate ideal of little practical relevance), and a belief that open channels of expression and experiment are the best means of getting nearer the truth. The epistemological and metaphysical views involved may be summarized as a presupposition of the reality of truth, a reality which can never be known but is only approached by a number of tentative truths; the obligation of man to pursue it; and his capacity for it. All of these views could be regarded as the premises underlying science and also underlying the free society.

The same kind of case is argued in the writings of Michael Polanyi, especially in his *Science, Faith and Society* (London, 1946). The implications of the argument are very far reaching, for instance, if the moral values and the freedoms implied in the scientific method—to say nothing of the implied metaphysics—are the same as those identified as democratic then science is not only compatible with democracy, but the two also strongly support each other. (Occasionally one hears that science makes only one value judgment: that truth is good and always tentative. The undeniable aesthetic or intellectual pleasure which some scientists find in science has no necessary implications for political theory. One never hears the argument that 'virtue is knowledge' applied to science.) 9

9 Is all knowledge good? What of a knowledge of torture, and how could it be obtained except by torturing people? Cf. Douglas N. Morgan, 'An Interdisciplinary Program for Neopositivistic Social Science,' in *Ethics*, vol. LXVIII, July 1958, pp. 292 ff.

If one does grant these points—that science is a moral enterprise, involving moral values, a rational view of man, as well as a commitment to the pursuit of truth—then by necessary implication, so it may be argued, the scientist is committed to a society which honors these values, and in which science can flourish. In short the tenor of the argument is that the scientific pursuit implies a free society, and hence ultimately political freedoms and democracy. Conversely, a democracy is in principle the political system most favorable to science. (The immediate freedom of the scientist has two aspects: freedom of investigation as to the broad choice of subject—which can always be distorted by the supply of funds as well as by the fiat of political authority; and freedom of discussion and communication—which has clearly dwindled everywhere in recent years for reasons of national policy.)

No doubt something of a case can be built that democracy provides a favorable climate for science—they both went together in ancient Athens and have both grown together in the modern world:

> As time passed, a protective wall of tolerance was gradually built up around scientific pursuit, which became fortified to the extent that in a few of our most civilized countries the scholar's freedom became an unquestioned and almost unconscious part of our mores.[10]

Occasionally the argument for the kinship of science and democracy takes a different form: that the public ultimately or in the long run decides the controversies in science (and religion) as well as in politics. In sum, both science and democracy are committed to the values of public or popular decision, though full allowance can be made for mistakes—whether by temporary majorities, or by the consensus of scientists—by reason of the possibilities of correction which exist in both cases.

If the above line of thought is true—that science implies democracy and vice versa—then a social consequence of great importance follows. The scientific values and ideals may be in conflict with the other values and ideals in any unfree society; consequently, there will be continual tension: (a) as the political authorities are

---

[10] Gunnar Myrdal, *Value in Social Theory*, London, 1958, p. 20.

tempted to encroach upon science, as in the Lysenko case, and (b) as the scientific ideals tend to disrupt the different political and other values. The conflict is going on all the time in the Soviet Union—though not only there—with victory sometimes going to the scientists and sometimes to the political authorities. The hope, if not the expectation, is that in time the tension will be resolved in favor of science and democracy.

There are, however, several weak points in the reasoning above. To begin with, it is not at all clear that the moral and philosophical implications of the pursuit of science (let alone of democracy) have been worked out to general satisfaction or agreement. Then again, the argument almost certainly underestimates the capacity of men to 'compartmentalize' their lives. The same sort of conflict often goes on, and may go on indefinitely, in free societies within the consciences of sensitive scientists who, outside of their profession, embrace religious, political, and numerous other beliefs which apparently conflict with their scientific code.

Then, too, although the democratic system is one in which political liberties prevail, it is not illogical to hold that other substantive liberties may not be maintained, or that even science itself might be severely curtailed. Critics of democracy, like Sir Henry Maine, went so far as to argue that democracy would be opposed to science—although his example of Malthusian science was not very well chosen—and indeed, believed that democracy was an enemy of progress, new ideas, and the arts.

Finally and most important, science and democracy are unlike in several vital points. (a) Democracy has a different aim and motivation. It is not designed to pursue truth, but to arrive at rightful and acceptable political decisions for the time being. Scientists serve truth, but the politician serves the people. All political questions have at least two defensible sides, not one which is true while others are false. From Locke again:

> The Business of Laws is not to provide for the Truth of Opinions, but for the Safety and Security of the Commonwealth, and of every particular Man's Goods and Person.

(b) There is in science no central authority, such as government, which decides and has the last word for the time being. But in politics, the government decides and enforces its decision—often with heavy penalties, and often to control science itself.

It was this dependence of all the sciences on society that Aristotle had in mind when he said that politics is the architectonic art and science, the most authoritative of them all . . .[11]

(c) The 'decisions' in science—the validating of a new theory, a discovery, and the like—are made by a consensus of experts, of specialists. But there is no such impartial and qualified authority in politics, nor can there be, short of some quasi-Platonic Utopia.

Neither is there a social urgency about deciding for or against some of the disputed scientific theories (those remote from life). But in politics decisions often cannot wait or disputes be left open, even though information on hand may be scanty either about the facts of the case, the likely results, or the popular reaction. It would be absurd for science to proceed in this fashion.

Indeed it is possible to say that the scientific approach to a problem is an alternative method to the political. The reason is that a scientific problem is quite different in kind from a political (or economic) problem, and the scientist's contribution to it is only one element toward a solution. When he makes or influences policy, the scientist—like any other 'expert'—is stepping from a scientific into a political role for which his specialized interest and knowledge has given him no training, and which may indeed be a handicap.

Politics, especially the politics of a democracy, is most unscientific—sanctioning all opinions including the unverifiable, under its political liberties. Political methods of solving scientific problems would be ludicrous, a scientific solution of political problems would be a tyranny of scientists.

Even if we assumed that there were principles of law superior to the course of history, even if we eliminated from the discussion the power-hungry fanatic who does not care a fig if he is caught out in a blatant contradiction, even if we ignored the peculiarities of cultures which are incapable of communicating, political choice

[11] Richard McKeon, 'Democracy, Scientific Method, and Action,' in *Ethics*, vol. LV, July 1945, p. 241.

would still remain inseparable from particular circumstances, sometimes rational but never finally proved and never of the same nature as scientific truths or moral imperatives.[12]

To sum up: starting with the usual argument that democracy is to be valued because it best promotes science, we were led to the complementary proposition that science implies democracy. Both are comforting beliefs, highly plausible but unfortunately far from proven, and often further from being acted upon. Yet they are not worthless, they *may* be true, and for those who believe them (and many do) they will help to make the case for the democratic system.[13]

(8) *The eighth value consists of the freedoms found in a democracy.* Before constructing a defense of democracy in terms of the value of freedoms, a preliminary note on 'freedom' is in order, if only to avoid the worst of the confusions lurking behind that honorific word.

If freedom is not only a word, what is it? The literature of philosophy and politics abounds in answers to that question. And the answers are quite astonishingly various.[14]

First, we need not bog down in a tiresome discussion about free will and determinism, i.e. whether the 'will' is causally determined. Our problem is coercion, not philosophic determinism. I assume, with everyone else, that we may choose, in politics as elsewhere.

Second, we may rightly reject the notion that we are always free, and can never be otherwise, in the sense of always being able to choose death before dishonor. This variation on Hobson's choice has no relevance to a political theory, although it may have its uses in populating heaven with martyred saints. We are not free to choose, in any political sense, if as we say there is not a

[12] Raymond Aron, *The Opium of the Intellectuals,* New York, 1957, p. 158.

[13] For a substantial critique of the view that democracy and science are alike, see Richard McKeon, op. cit. pp. 238ff. For the other and, I think, weaker side of the argument, see James Feibleman, *Positive Democracy,* Chapel Hill, N.C., 1940.

[14] Maurice Cranston, *Freedom, A New Analysis,* London, 1954, p. 23. This is by far the best introduction to a difficult subject.

live option, if we are coerced or intimidated by other persons; though here as elsewhere a difference in the degree of penalty attached to free choice makes all the difference, since physical coercion shades off into other and milder social forms.

Third, we must also reject the monstrous doctrine that I am free if acting for my 'better' or 'true' or 'real' self, but not free merely when I choose what I want or what my own fallible conscience approves. The proper political answer to this doctrine is to say that democracy makes full allowance for all views to be heard on 'real' interests, 'true' selves, and the like, as well as on supposed interests or mere desires. This is the very stuff of political dispute. We reject, that is, the kind of view enunciated by Vishinsky in his *The Law of the Soviet State:* 'In our state naturally there can be no place for freedom of speech, press, and so on for the foes of socialism.' If there are experts on the 'real' interests of people or of the nation, they do not thereby enjoy a title to rule, but they may use the political processes of a democracy to try to put their policies into effect.

Fourth, we must in politics reject the closely related doctrine that I am free only if I do my duty, or what is right, but not free if I neglect my duty or do what is wrong. (Those who thus define freedom should logically hold—but seldom do—that since I am not free when doing wrong I am not therefore responsible for my acting.) Such a doctrine of freedom can easily turn into the dangerous belief that we are free only when we obey the laws, whether we must be coerced or not; and hence to the re-definition that 'freedom is willing obedience to the law,' a doctrine that owes much to Hegel's talk about 'compulsory rational freedom,' 'true' freedom being 'true' necessity, and the like.[15] Almost invariably, those who re-define freedom in this way contrast liberty (or 'true' liberty) with license (or 'false' liberty), and tend to equate freedom of choice with caprice and 'libertarianism'—both highly emotive 'boo' words.

Freedom can, of course, be abused, i.e. wrong and unwise choices

---

15 In Germany, with its different traditions, especially in philosophy, liberal theory seldom stood for freedom from the state, as in England, but defined freedom in moral terms, which led intentionally or not to a justification of obedience to and glorification of the state.

may be made, but only endless confusion can result from these stipulative and 'persuasive' definitions. They are semantic tricks that muddy the channels of communication.

Fifth, because, like the rest of animate and inanimate nature, we are subject to the natural laws of physics and chemistry and biology, it does not follow that man cannot be free in political and social life. In the words of Plato, in *Phaedo:*

> Of course I could not do as I wish without bones and sinews; but to say that I do as I do because of them and not from a choice of what I think is best, is an unreasonable way of speaking.

And in Learned Hand's inimitable lucidity:

> We must eat, sleep, be clothed and sheltered, and have our mates and our children. It is irrelevant that the Universe so often denies us these; we are considering hindrances by our fellows.[16]

The only germane point here is that our area of choice, of possible freedom, is always enlarged with increased knowledge and mastery of nature; but the choices made with increased knowledge may be good or bad.

Sixth, no matter how free, legally and politically, men may be, they are inevitably subject to other restraints imposed by society —custom, economic and social pressure, and so forth. Social existence is only possible on condition that some freedom of action is renounced. So much is a truism. Government restraints are thus not the only chains on the effective exercise of liberty of action and thought, although it is with reference to these restraints that a political theory must start. Hobbes said that 'the liberties of the subjects depend on the silence of the law,' and although this will barely do as a starting point, political theory must not fail to recognize the taboos in society no less restricting than law, although their sanctions are not legal. Anyone who has lived in a hidebound community and wished to break through its taboos can testify to both the controls and the strength of their sanctions. On this matter of 'social tyranny,' Mill was very sensitive, as we know.[17]

[16] *The Spirit of Liberty,* p. 111.

[17] There is the question here of how far economic, social, and even legal restrictions may be regarded as constraints on one's freedom, *if they are not*

(A related confusion is caused by mixing the notion of political and legal freedoms with that of possession of the economic means to exercise these liberties. The political freedoms are one thing, but economic security and the material means to use them effectively is another—they are conditions—though both are certainly necessary in a democracy.)

The case for democracy, on the ground that it promotes freedoms, is chiefly in terms of the political freedoms. Whether freedoms will be extended to other spheres is not guaranteed by the logic of the democratic system, but is merely a likelihood or probability, a tendency for the political freedoms to carry over into other spheres. The presumption is extremely strong that they will do so, as they did in Athens if we may take the word of Pericles on the social freedom which the citizens enjoyed. It is the same sort of (weaker) tendency by which equality tends to be carried over from the political to other spheres. As Duverger puts it (op. cit. p. 161):

> The history of the development of civil rights in France shows a link between the existence of a liberal regime and that of a democratic regime with free elections. This same link is to be found in most of the countries in the world, so that the following general statement may be formulated: civil rights in a country exist in direct proportion to the degree of democracy to be found there. This is not a logical connection but one based on actual fact.

The case can go somewhat deeper. The inescapable conditions of social life impose restrictions on one's freedom of action: freedoms conflict with other goods which we value highly, and sometimes with one another. The essential function of co-ordinating freedoms with one another and with other goods is performed by all governments, but the claim on behalf of democracy is that democratic co-ordination maximizes freedoms. And—paradoxical though it may sound—the maximizing of freedoms does not neces-

---

felt as constraints, but are, so to speak, what we prefer. Is a willing slave free? And there is T. H. Green: 'Progress, for Green, was the moral advance wherein that which must now be legally enforced might come increasingly to be done willingly, in which the realm of morality gradually diminished the sphere of law by transmuting enforced decisions into free choices.' Charles Vereker, *The Development of Political Theory*, London, 1957, p. 183.

sarily mean that the laws are few. To protect and even extend freedoms may demand an elaborate network of laws. We may start with Hobbes's dictum about the silence of the law, but a political theory cannot end there.

It is perhaps worth mentioning again (see Chapter 7) that the political freedoms of a democracy may be valued highly in their own right, and not only for the instrumental reason that they give citizens a share in political power, or are necessary to promote social welfare. There is eloquent testimony that such freedoms may be valued intrinsically, given by many refugees from Nazi Germany and from the Soviet Union and its satellites. Those of us living in democracies, having been born free, and never having been deprived, must often make a greater effort in order to appreciate our birthright. To those who value political freedoms, for whatever reason, the justification for democracy is strong; to those who place a higher intrinsic value upon *other* freedoms, it can at least be said that democracy has a marked tendency to extend the freedoms from the political to other spheres if only because there are channels for the political extension of freedoms.

(9) *Finally, a value may be constructed for democracy from the deficiencies of alternative systems.* Any alternative is inevitably a system in which some kind of minority makes the policy decisions —always of course a properly qualified minority, since no one advocates that the numerical minority should rule merely *because* they are a minority.

In the contemporary world there is a strong, almost universal aversion to the idea that any kind of minority has any right or title to rule. Not only are the almost unrecognized postulates of our political thinking against it, but also the rational objections: What minority? What credentials? Who will judge the credentials? Nor must we make the mistake of merely assuming that because democracy is imperfect, any minority alternative is better because it is made so by definition. We cannot get from a definition to a feasible and perfect political system.

COMMENTS ON THE JUSTIFICATION

Obviously, only those who prize those values listed above, and who believe they are inseparable from or most likely to be promoted by a democracy, will find the values cogent arguments for a democratic system. Thus, apart altogether from considerations of the social and other empirical conditions necessary for democracy, we have not proved that democracy is logically always and everywhere the best political system. I do not think it can be proved, in any logical sense of proof, and that is why I have not attempted it. Instead we may agree with Aristotle that the best form of government is relative to circumstances. The case for democracy is a case, not a demonstration like a Euclidean theorem. By taking this attitude we avoid making a political system itself into an absolute value, as well as the mistake of completely identifying any existing democracy with the theoretical model.

Again, all the values noted are not always and only found in actual democratic systems. Political systems do not always work as their distinguishing principles might lead us to think. Absolute monarchies, for instance, may occasionally be noted for the freedoms and diversity which they permit, as in the rich literary, artistic, and scientific life of 18th-century France. But those values noted above follow from the logic of a democratic system, whereas they do not follow from the logic of other systems. The empirical case for democracies or alternative systems is a different matter, beyond the scope of a theoretical inquiry, although I am inclined to think that those values listed can be plausibly supported by a historical inquiry, particularly if allowance is made for the greater or lesser deviations from the democratic model which are always found in real life.

In the foregoing justification of a democratic system by reference to its values, I have not suggested a theological defense of democracy, despite the pulpit oratory of today which so often equates democracy with this or that Christian sect, or holds that democracy best favors Christianity and vice versa. I avoid this defense because I do not find it at all convincing, and because it substitutes one sort of justification which is powerful but not conclusive (namely, an appeal to those values listed above) for another which, to say the least, is just as inconclusive (namely, the claims of one among several revealed religions). The theological defense of a political system, whatever the theology, carries conviction only to those who already accept the creeds.

Neither, so far as I am aware, have I committed myself to the skeptical argument, or the argument from man's ignorance, for democracy.

> According to this argument, it is impossible for anyone to discover what is the right course of action for the community, or where the true interests of its inhabitants reside. From this it follows that everyone in the community should be allowed to do what he wants to do as far as is socially possible...
>
> It seems to be certainly the case that scepticism does involve Democracy—even if the link is not as rigorous or as formal as some would believe. It does not follow from this, though—as certain critics of Democracy would have us believe—that Democracy involves scepticism.[18]

I have also refrained from pressing the 'natural rights' case for democracy, convincing as so many people appear to find it:

> ...it is maintained that everyone has a natural right to control government and that this right is recognized only in Democracy: therefore Democracy is the best form of government.[19]

Finally, it will have been noted that I have not included among the values that of promoting the equal moral dignity and worth of the human personality. Yet perhaps the most common argument for democracy is couched in phrases such as the 'moral equality and intrinsic value of all men.' This inquiry is treated in the following chapter.

[18] R. Wollheim, 'Democracy,' *Journal of the History of Ideas*, April 1958, pp. 241-2.
[19] Ibid.

TEN | *Justification of Democracy: Its Alleged Purposes*

The justification of democracy given in the preceding chapter was based upon the values which we may logically expect any working democratic system to realize. They are analogous to the values which may be found in any one kind of economic system regardless of the type of goods and services produced. Such values are often taken for granted, because they are inherent or implied, and are not usually held as conscious aims (or intentions) by the participants in a democracy. They belong to the system as it may be viewed from the outside by an observer.

As viewed by the participants, the citizens, these 'functional values' may not be what makes democracy attractive. Historically, for example, one or other of the separate principles of the system (e.g. political equality or freedoms) may have been the reason for the popular support, and for the establishment (or growth) of democracies, while other support has been forthcoming—perhaps more commonly—because democracy seemed the best means to promote certain ends, such as national independence or religious freedom. As Bryce put it:

> Popular government has been usually sought and won and valued, not as a good thing in itself, but as a means of getting rid of tangible grievances or securing tangible benefits, and when these objects had been attained, the interest in it has gradually tended to decline.

Historically, too, the main stream of political philosophy has started, not with the *how* of political systems, but with their functions and purposes: with *what* they do and should do rather than with *how* they do it, with the substantive content of policies and laws rather than with how they are made and executed. (On this see also Chapter 2, last part; and Chapter 9, first part.)

Clearly, then, the justification of democracy cannot depend only upon the separate operating principles (examined in Chapters 5 to 8), nor upon those values which result from the operation of the whole system (examined in Chapter 9). A final judgment must depend also upon the conscious purposes or aims which democracy sets itself, and the policies through which these are promoted. It is then to an examination of the purposes which democracy logically serves, or is likely to serve, or should serve, that I now turn. We may lead into the subject through a preliminary examination of function.

FUNCTIONS OF A POLITICAL SYSTEM

All social institutions exist to fulfill their own particular function, whether it be religious, educational, economic, artistic, or anything else. Government, we say, has the governing function. To put it differently: all governments, whether democratic or not, consciously fulfill certain purposes and find a common rationale in so doing. There is, so to say, a common case for government as against anarchy. The case may be put in terms of broad general goals (justice, peace, the good life, etc.) or in such agreed and more observable services as external defense, internal order, the co-ordinating of sectional and individual interests, the settlement of disputes. These are indeed the minimum services performed by all governments, to promote which policies are adopted.

Most of the earlier political philosophers attempted to justify the institution of government in general, and not merely a particular form of government. Plato and Aristotle, Augustine and Aquinas, Hobbes and Rousseau—to mention only a sample—all included this inquiry in their political theory. It is a type of inquiry, however, which has gone out of fashion in the modern world, except insofar as it may be engaged in by the anthropologist, and the case for government is taken for granted, as being so obvious that no sensible person would deny it.

Stripped of the awe and traditional mystification which has

often surrounded the concept of 'state,' government is merely another of the social institutions by which sophisticated societies operate. Regarding it in this way as a social institution with a unique function, or as an agent of society or of the citizens, then we do find it perfectly possible to speak also of the agent—the government—having purposes. They are those given to it by the principal, i.e. the citizens. Hobbes was a clear exponent of this point of view of the ruler as the purposive agent, and the same concept has been employed in every social contract theory.

The few specific services performed by all governments have been of slow historical growth, seldom deliberately invented or adopted. Other services may be added from time to time, and when added, the demand for them usually originates outside the political system itself. They may be found in a number of sources: in religion, morals, philosophy, economics, or elsewhere. Originating outside politics, they are translated into action by politics; they must become political if they are to be realized through government.

We may also say, I think, that the policies which the political system carries out are both common and individual. The use of government to serve individual purposes is, of course, a commonplace in the democracies because of their heritage of individual rights and economic freedoms. But all political philosophers have talked also of *common* purposes and common ends without which civilized life would be impossible. The Greek city-state typically thought of individuals co-operating for common purposes beyond defense and order—the erection of public buildings, the encouragement of artistic creations, the promotion of justice through a good judicial system, and so forth. These services were common in the sense of being valued by all or virtually all, and of being public, not private, property, though some might benefit from them more than others. (The concept of common vs. individual purposes is analogous to that of group welfare vs. individual welfare, or to 'national income' vs. the total of personal incomes, and similar concepts in welfare economics.)

We cannot, simply on the basis of their ostensible objectives, distinguish between political systems. Many of the objectives of the Soviet Union, for instance, are strikingly like those of western democracies—mass education, industrialization, a high standard of living, the elimination of disease, the promotion of public welfare, nuclear research, the rush to outer space. Conversely, it is possible for the same kind of political system—Nazism and Communism (totalitarian), or all democracies—to pursue many different objectives.

Where the broad objectives of government are the same in different political systems, the differences lie elsewhere—in how the objectives and implementing policies are arrived at, in the principles of operation of the systems, in how the policies are carried through, and in the 'meanings' which they have to the citizens. What appear superficially as identical goals may hold widely different meanings or significance to the participants. In one case, the goals are decided beforehand and the implementing policies are imposed on the public by a manipulating of popular approval; in the other, they become campaign issues, are an outcome of public discussion and debate, and are adopted by majority agreement voluntarily reached. In the democratic case, too, the ends are usually less ambitious and hierarchical, more flexible, and freely open to modification in response to criticism. The difference is that between total and piecemeal planning.

When government is identified with the 'state' and the 'state' with all of society, we hear much of its intrinsic purpose, or its 'ultimate and true' end, as if we analyzed the concept 'state' long enough we should arrive at its very essence and so extract 'a philosophy from a definition.' There is much of this type of thought in Hegel and his concept of the state, something, too, in Rousseau with his General Will, and a trace of it in Burke when he calls up feelings of reverence by referring to a 'divine tactic' in history.

But while we may say that a political system (which is only a part of any society) may perform certain functions and pursue certain purposes, can we say that a 'state,' or a society as a whole, can have a purpose? We can only do so, I think, on the same logic by which one ascribes a meaning or purpose to the universe as a whole, or by which one justifies human existence per se. It seems to me that an illicit logic is involved in the use of the word 'purpose' by comparing the purposes assigned by human beings to a social institution with the divine 'purpose' of the universe, or the 'purpose of human existence.' Aristotle and many other Greeks thought in teleological terms of the state, the purpose of the state being derived from the end for man; that end being found in a moral concept of the good life. Such a view, if it regards the end as debatable, is perfectly reconcilable with a conception of government as existing to serve the purposes assigned to it by the citizens (though at a deeper level any teleological concept—implying as it does, inevitability—is probably inconsistent with freedom or choice). (It is of course not illogical to imagine a state devoting itself to some end outside itself—a cosmic purpose, the 'white man's burden,' and so forth. Nor need we deny that any social institution may become an end in itself.)

What purposes, then, does a democracy seek to pursue? One thing is fairly plain at the start: since democracy encourages a diversity of interests and beliefs, and all policies are compromises, it is unlikely that we shall find any democracy committed to one all-consuming purpose (except temporarily as in war, during which it is more accurate to say that democracy is largely suspended). Democracy will be a fox, not a hedgehog. A fox knows many things, a hedgehog knows one big thing—that is, he finds one master principle which explains everything.[1] Foxes have been Machiavelli, Locke, Jefferson; hedgehogs have been Plato, Hegel, Marx. Tolstoy was a fox by nature who believed in being a hedgehog—a recipe calculated to produce much mental turmoil. If a government is dedicated to one overriding objective—for instance, war, self-sufficiency, or rapid industrialization—democracy may well not be the most efficient means to the end; planning, regimentation, and ruthless 'social engineering' may be more effective.

One firm, historical answer to the question of the unique purposes of a democracy is simply that democracy has and should have none. Apart from the minimum functions of all governments—defense, order, and the preservation of the system itself, which might almost be said to define government—democracy has no overriding purpose to promote. Only individuals, either singly or in combination, have purposes or goals, and the democratic system merely holds the ring and leaves individuals and groups

[1] Isaiah Berlin, *The Hedgehog and the Fox*, London, 1954.

alone to find and pursue their own purposes. In short, this doctrine is that a democracy is a political system devoted to no goals as such—though realizing incidentally those values noted in Chapter 9—but providing the machinery and opportunity for individuals to pursue their own private ends.

What we are thus given, in the reference to individual purposes and a negative government, is a doctrine of individualism which in the modern world has chiefly taken two forms: (a) of Manchester liberalism and a theory of natural economic harmony, and (b) of individual rights against the state. A brief glance at these two negative purposes of politics and government will be useful.

THE PURPOSE OF DEMOCRACY: THE MAINTENANCE OF A FREE ECONOMY

The view that the services rendered by government should be very few has been supported by a social doctrine of great historical influence. There is a sphere in which a 'natural harmony' reigns, and government action is 'interference' which can only make matters worse. Such a theory has a neutral, scientific flavor, whether grounded upon empirical psychological premises or a belief in an economic version of 'natural law.' The political theory which follows from it thus appears to be removed from the realm of moral exhortation. (Even a doctrine of individual, natural rights which governments should leave alone must have an implicit doctrine of 'natural harmony' of some kind, perhaps like that which Locke posited for his moral 'state of nature.')

The political and social theory is substantially that of Adam Smith. Self-interest under free competition is the 'system of natural liberty' of which Adam Smith spoke. Others—misreading Darwin—were more ruthless, and spoke of 'the beneficent private war which makes one man strive to climb on the shoulders of another and remain there through the law of the survival of the fittest.' Smith did not advocate democracy, but limited representative government (with a 'natural aristocracy' whose ambitions, not its virtues, would be the support of the state), yet logically his policy prescription can be adapted to any kind of government: to serve as a means to the maintenance of a commercially free economy. The purpose of government is thus to refrain from governing in most of life.

A similar broader idea, that the non-political and non-governmental is the most important part of life and will presumably look after itself if left alone—with the corollaries of self-sufficiency, withdrawal, and hostility to the state—has a much longer ancestry and goes back at least to the Cynics and the disintegration of the Greek *polis*. It is all a very far cry from the Athenian democracy, or from Plato and Aristotle with their emphasis on the common life of the city-state.

Thomas Paine and others also rested their case for 'the government is best which governs least' upon a distinction between the state and society. Whereas society exists because of man's virtues, the state is instituted because of man's vices. Society—a generic name for all of social life except the political—is good because it is voluntary, fraternal, a community, and 'natural.' The state is bad because it is coercive, arbitrary, artificial, and is set over and against its subjects. Paine did not, however, draw the anarchic conclusion toward which his logic pointed, but instead took the view that the state was a necessary and justified evil, i.e. necessary for the few traditional services. But the rationale for these services, and for these only, was never clear and has become even more blurred in time. The sharp contrast between bad government and good society, between the bad political and the good non-political, is in fact an arbitrary one, and has plagued and confused mankind far too long.

The laissez-faire argument, in its extreme form, is today seldom encountered except in ceremonial speeches, and we need not waste time discussing anything so irrelevant. It is not a live option, nor is it possible to call back mankind to belief in that temporary aberration of thought, the doctrine of a natural economic harmony. The really important question, and one much debated, is the relation of the government to the economy, in particular whether the free market economy is a *sine qua non* for political democracy. Is it, for instance, a historical accident that democratic government grew up with a free market economy, or are the two causally linked together? (It is agreed that democracy does not *mean* capitalism or socialism; and the debate therefore is whether one or the other of these economic systems may be more favorable, as a condition of political democracy.)

Oceans of ink have been spilled on this heated controversy and everything has already been said many times over.[2] The initial almost insuperable difficulty is familiar: when two events are linked together in history, how are we to isolate the causal connection if any? This aside, a few bald conclusions, widely agreed on, must suffice. A privately-run economy may be combined with political absolutism, as in Czarist Russia—granted. But today those countries which are democratic have also the bulk of their economic life carried on by private business— granted. Further, the only fully-planned, publicly-owned economy, that of the Soviet Union, is not democratic—also granted. These considerations do make some kind of case on empirical grounds, but it is far from conclusive, so that we cannot be sure that a free economy is a necessary (it is clearly not a sufficient) condition of a democratic system; or conversely that economic planning leads to dictatorship. The time sequence in modern times has in fact been exactly the reverse: the politically absolute rule came first and then moved on to ownership and management of the economy, as with the Communists in Russia and China, and with the Nazis and the Fascists until the latter regimes met a well-deserved and ignominious end. Dictatorship was a part of the political theory of all three, from the beginning. We cannot point to any country which has drifted into dictatorship because of economic regulation, but there is on the contrary a very strong case that in some countries dictatorship took over because the governments preceding them did too little regulation.[3]

The mixed 'political economy' in every democracy, with government and the economy hopelessly and increasingly enmeshed, has come about in response to public demands, especially those from business itself, which democratic politicians cannot ignore. It is not owing, as many Americans appear to believe, to 'alien'

---

[2] For a comprehensive discussion see Hans Kelsen, 'Foundations of Democracy,' in Supplement to *Ethics*, vol. LXVI, October 1955.

[3] Cf. John D. Lewis, 'The Elements of Democracy,' *American Political Science Review*, vol. XXXIV, June 1940.

ideologies or a softening of the rugged frontier character. (At the same time that the economy is more subsidized and regulated the term 'free' enterprise has been invented to describe it.) Since there is no sign that public demands will alter, or that the powerful trends can be stopped or reversed, those who value freedoms ought to employ their thought not in nostalgic dreams, but in finding ways of maintaining and extending freedoms in the face of what Max Weber called 'the twin dangers of capitalism and bureaucracy.'

We may perhaps conclude that there is a continuum, from democratic capitalism on one end to democratic socialism on the other, but no one knows how far the trend can go in either direction before unrestrained *laissez faire* would break down in social revolution on the one hand, as Marx predicted; or before socialism would cease to be compatible with political liberties on the other.

With the argument from history inconclusive, we are forced back upon theory, and here the logic seems to be against the necessary relation of the market economy and democracy, unless we lapse into some form of economic determinism. Any theory which draws a sharp distinction, for policy purposes, between the economic and the governmental presupposes that some rationale is available to distinguish the private from the public or political sphere.[4] Only on such an assumption does it make sense to argue that government can be limited to non-economic action. But what rationale shall we use that will do duty once we give up the optimistic and untenable theory of a natural economic harmony? Indeed, what principle can we find that in society as a whole—looking beyond the narrowly economic—will enable us in any given context to identify the spheres of the spontaneous and the governmental, to separate the claims of voluntary organizations from those of the state? There is no such fixed principle, or at least none that is not highly political and debatable, and we ought to stop deluding ourselves that Adam Smith, or Mill, or Professor Hayek, or anyone else has discovered one. (Even population—both numbers and quality—is not left entirely to individ-

[4] On the difficulty of separating business and government see W. Hamilton, *The Politics of Industry*, New York, 1957.

ual decision nowadays, but is becoming more and more a matter of public policy. And what is at once more personal and private than procreating, and more charged with social consequences?)

There is in fact only a political criterion by which to distinguish the two, with the boundary shifting from time to time and place to place as the political authorities decide: providing a harmony, a common purpose, a public interest, that does not emerge automatically like mechanical equilibrium or biological homeostasis, but must be worked for and created in the political process itself. Many current political disputes take place in every democracy over economic policies, until it is scarcely too much to say that most of our substantive law deals with economic matters. The dispute and its settlement must be political, and not purely economic, because the very things which cannot be offered for sale on the market itself are the values of the economic system. It is now plain that in plumping for a free market economy, we are choosing a congeries of values, as a glance at any of the literature on welfare economics will show. No economic system is value-free, much as we may have fooled ourselves on this point in the past, in the preoccupation with positive or 'scientific' economics.[5] If then, any of these economic values conflict with any of the values of the democratic system itself, or with the values in any policies adopted, the conflict can only be settled politically.

> The most decisive argument for the market mechanism, however, may be political rather than economic. A complicated control system necessarily means increased bureaucratic control.[6]

The same view would I think be held by Galbraith, who points out in his *American Capitalism* (p. 112) that the *economic* decisions of government in the U. S. do very little damage (or very little good): 'The consequences for general economic welfare of most government decisions has been imperceptible.'

Yet those who rate the market economy highly—and there is an understandably strong bias in favor of it in the western world —may reasonably support democracy on the ground that through

---

[5] Cf. J. de V. Graaff, *Theoretical Welfare Economics*, Cambridge, 1957.

[6] *Economics and Public Policy*, The Brookings Lectures, Washington, 1955, p. 20.

democratic politics they are likely to retain more economic freedoms than under alternative systems. There is, however, an opposing view which, if widely believed, would make every anti-socialist an anti-democrat as well. It was put clearly by the author of 'Parkinson's Law'—but is not to be taken as humor:

> Democracy was tried repeatedly, in different places, and for differing periods of time, and if any one conclusion can be reached from a study of the results it is that democracy will lead, sooner or later, to socialism.[7]

THE PURPOSE OF DEMOCRACY: THE PRESERVATION OF INDIVIDUAL RIGHTS

Another commonly-alleged goal for democracy is that of the protection of individual rights, a purpose which may be best examined through the older doctrines of liberalism.[8] The liberal attitude has traditionally been: man is free in those spheres of action where he is left alone by government—including trade and commerce, religion and 'culture,' and part, at least, of morality. Freedom from legal restraint was the core of the traditional liberal concern, and the Manchester variety of liberalism was concerned almost exclusively with freedom of trade and production, being anti-government from the start, with *laissez faire* as its logical end, Adam Smith its prophet, and Herbert Spencer its evangelist.

The inconsistency of liberalism, and of utilitarianism which was largely incorporated into it, is notorious, since liberalism came to display also a generous and humane concern for individual rights which does not lead by inevitable logic to a negative approach to governments. Even if we grant that some rights should be left alone, others need protection, and others as certainly need much positive promotion. No one can tell where protection leaves off and interference and promotion begins. As experience has taught us this, the emphasis accordingly is increasingly upon government action to *promote,* which may be

---

[7] C. N. Parkinson, *The Evolution of Political Thought,* Boston, 1958, p. 180.
[8] See Maurice Cranston, *Freedom, A New Analysis,* London, 1953, p. 67, for a brief history of the word 'liberalism.'

far-reaching indeed, even if, like the early liberals, we are nervous about it. While economic liberalism makes freedom from government the prior assumption, the tradition of humanitarian liberalism does not do so. The humanitarian element in liberalism, whether drawing its strength from religion or a social conscience, was frequently pro-government. When the French Revolutionaries said 'the end [goal] of politics is the preservation of these rights of man,' they were not arguing for a negative state. The logic of any doctrine of individual rights, which it is the purpose of the political system to protect and promote, is only accidentally linked with a 'let-alone' policy. Consequently one wing of liberalism verges on socialism, and another toward *laissez faire* or status quo conservatism.[9]

Must we say, then, that democracy may or may not happen to leave alone, to protect, or to promote individual rights (that is, beyond those political rights or liberties which are part of democracy?) Many are not satisfied with this lack of a guarantee that democracy will protect private rights. As they press their case, they speak of 'natural' rights which are objective, absolute, eternal—to which all political systems should be dedicated. Democratic systems can and sometimes do accommodate a good deal of this type of thinking.

Now, it sounds more confidently certain to talk of natural rights rather than of a moral 'ought' (e.g. men have a 'natural right' to property, rather than men ought to be allowed to own some property), especially to those who feel unjustly treated. The lot of man is so miserable that it is no wonder he 'objectifies' his ideals, and reads them into the cosmos, a tendency reinforced every time he looks within himself and realizes how much he

---

9 Cf. the remarks on 'Liberal Socialism' in L. T. Hobhouse, *Liberalism*, London, 1911. The United States Bill of Rights is mainly negative, restraining the national government from interfering with certain rights. But individual rights would be in a sorry state if the national government alone refrained from encroaching upon them. Consequently the national government (including the Supreme Court) also protects many individual rights from state and local governments—which infringe upon them more often than the national goverment—and is under heavy pressure more actively to promote rights. The language of rights has grown ever more common, as the United States government has become less negative in its attitude toward rights.

needs external strength to keep from falling even further below his ideals. If natural rights did not exist we should, so to speak, be compelled to invent them. They have always been a powerful plea against oppression and special privilege, and sometimes—when they have included political rights—they have promoted democracy.

Nowadays it has become fashionable in the United States to argue that men have somehow forgotten natural rights and 'values' (the two being often lumped together, with natural law and theology often tossed in for good measure), and the prime question is put as:

> How can natural rights become once again a matter of profound and unshakable conviction? It may be to Aquinas and not to Rousseau that one must look for light . . .
>
> The hollow way in which so many of the Czechs, presumably the most liberty-loving people of Central or Eastern Europe, have cynically or in helpless fashion voted Communist or surrendered to force and are now cheering their enslavers, itself shows how thin the veneer-like loyalty to liberty really is when it has no theological conviction back of it.[10]

Natural rights doctrines provided, in the 18th and early 19th centuries, the radical and typical, although not universal, standard of judgment for governments, and were not displaced as a standard until the rise of utilitarianism, which also drew its criteria from outside the values of the political system—from the happiness and welfare of individuals. Both theories—natural rights and utilitarianism—thus have much in common, since both look upon the state only as a convenience, rejecting organic and divine theories; and both theories consider consequences (as, for example, an intuitional moral theory might not do). Both theories are, of course, in wide circulation today, so much so that they are frequently taken to be the two doctrines most characteristic of modern democracies.

The language of natural rights—whether these are grounded upon theology or metaphysics or not—does emphasize that the claims or moral principles which they cover are in some way (in

[10] Ernest S. Griffith, in *Research in Political Science*, p. 223.

some societies) regarded as *basic* moral and social values, which a good government would acknowledge and promote. The values they express may properly be regarded as elements of the 'good society,' slowly evolved, seldom deliberately chosen. And we *can* tell the difference between societies where rights are observed and those where they are not. They enable us—depending on which rights we value more—to pass the moral judgment upon a given democracy whether it is good or bad; but we are here concerned with the democratic system per se, not with the uses to which it may, or perhaps will, be put in different democracies.

As with the relation of democracy and the free economy, the question arises: is the association of doctrines of individual rights with democracy historically accidental? It would not be true that the two were linked in Athens, where the concept of individual rights as we think of it was lacking. Yet something may be said for the view that modern democracy has historically been inspired by a belief in natural individual rights, even though, as Professor Sabine noted:

> The individualism of all social theory between Locke and John Stuart Mill depended less on logic than on its agreement with the interests of the class that mainly produced it.

The case could be made, for example, from the fact that traditionally political freedoms have been associated with substantive freedoms and rights of other kinds—of religion, of conscience, etc.; and from some of the speakers in the Putney Debates who argued very near the position that political equality—the equal right to vote—was part of nature's law; from Locke; and from the American and French Revolutionaries. The case is strong, but whether there is a causal or necessary relation must, I think, be left a trifle doubtful. It could not be supported by the democracies which do not talk the language of natural rights, though they talk nonetheless in moral terms. Morley's sentiment is roughly typical of the English attitude:

> I never said a word about 'Natural Rights' in any piece of practical public business in all my life; and when that famous phrase again made its naked appearance on the platform three or four

years ago, it gave me as much surprise and dismay as if I were this afternoon to meet a deinotherium shambling down Parliament Street.[11]

Democracy is not logically antipathetic to most doctrines of natural rights, fundamental or higher law, individual rights, or any similar ideals—but merely asks citizens to take note of the fact that the preservation of these rights rests with the majority, in political processes, and does not depend upon a legal or constitutional Maginot line. Democracy may, then, be supported by believers in individual rights providing they believe that rights—or any transcendental ends—are likely to be better safeguarded under such a system. Support for democracy on such instrumental grounds may, of course, lead to the dilemma of loyalty to the system vs. loyalty to a natural right—but the same kind of dilemma may arise for anyone, over any prized value, and in any political system, and is insoluble in advance.

There is unanimous agreement that—as a matter of fact and law, not of conjecture—no single right can be realized, except at the expense of other rights and claims. For that reason their absolute status, in some philosophic sense, is of little political relevance. Political policies involve much more than very general principles or rights.

> The main error of the older natural rights school was not that it had an absolute right, but that it had too many absolute rights ... There must be compromise, and as any compromise destroys the claim to absoluteness, the natural outcome of experience was the repudiation of all of them. And now the name of 'natural right' can only creep into sight with the reassuring placard, 'changing content guaranteed.' [12]

'Their abstract perfection is their political defect,' as Burke put it. Rights are relative to other rights and other values; to claims, duties, and the special circumstances of time and place. They are not self-interpreting, any more than any other general moral principles are. (Think of Albert Schweitzer's principle: 'It is good to

11 John Morley, *Oracles on Man and Government*, London, 1923, p. 238.
12 W. E. Hocking, in *Philosophical Problems*, eds. M. Mandelbaum et al., New York, 1957, p. 511.

maintain and promote life; it is bad to destroy life or to obstruct it.') Nor is it at all easy to see how any doctrine of inalienable, natural, individual rights can be reconciled with a political doctrine of common consent—except in an anarchist society, or one of saints. Every natural right ever put forward, and the lists are elusive and capricious, is every day invaded by governments, in the public interest and with widespread public approval.

To talk of relatively attainable justice or rights in politics is not to plump for a moral relativism—in the sense that all values are equally good. But while values may be objective, the specific value judgments and policies are inevitably relative to a context, and it is only when a judgment divorces context from general principle that it looks like moral relativism. Neither, of course, does the fact of moral diversity invalidate all moral rules.

Any political system, then, deals only with relatively attainable rights, as with relative justice and freedoms. Hence we may differ in given instances on specific policies, despite agreement on broad basic principles such as a right or a moral 'ought'; and per contra, we may agree on specific policies while differing on fundamental principles or long-range objectives or natural rights. Politics and through politics, law and policies, give these rights—and moral principles—their substance and limits. There is no getting away from the political nature of this or any other prescriptive ideal in a free society.

Some philosophers argue that in fact we are agreed about 'ends,' and political discussion is therefore only about means. This seems to be the position taken by Yves R. Simon in *The Philosophy of Democratic Government* (Chicago, 1951). I do not see how this case can be sustained unless the 'ends' are defined so broadly and are so long-range as to be almost meaningless—like the agreed formulas that are issued at the close of international conferences which have obviously broken down. (See also the question of consensus in Chapter 11.)

> . . . in politics agreement on very specific descriptions of long range objectives is seldom possible, and these are apt to be left in general terms. But for any political action to be effective it is necessary for a number of people to be able to agree on sufficiently

specific descriptions of short-range objectives for them to be able to have a policy.[13]

But to say all this is not to deny that the democratic system exists to serve human purposes. What other purposes could it serve? But we must say, I think, that the logic of the democratic system does not justify the conclusion that democracy is necessarily committed to the alleged ends of a free economy or of substantive individual rights (beyond the political rights). Yet democracy may reasonably be supported on the ground that it is not against individual rights, and—more positively—that it is likely to give the utmost in relatively attainable 'absolute' rights for the largest number of people. I turn now to examine the plausible case that the purpose of democracy is to 'develop the personality.'

The Purpose of Democracy: To Develop the Personality

The 'essential' purpose of democracy is often expressed as the 'fulfillment of the personality,' a purpose sometimes couched in such related terms as emphasis on human dignity, on self-respect, on the moral, responsible person, and in many similar ways. For instance:

> A democratic community is one in which human dignity is realized in theory and fact.

Or again:

> We assume the basic moral postulate of the intrinsic worth of the individual, which derives from Christianity, and we assume with the Greeks that we should strive for perfection of intellect and character, and with pleasure, in the end of man's activity.

And still again:

> We must define democracy as that form of government and of society which is inspired above every other with the feeling and consciousness of the dignity of man.[14]

[13] Dorothy M. Emmett, *Function, Purpose and Powers*, London, 1958, pp. 115-16.

[14] *The Political Writings of Harold D. Lasswell*, Glencoe, Ill., 1951, p. 473; B. E. Lippincott, in *Contemporary Political Science*, Paris, 1950, p. 222; Thomas Mann, *The Coming Victory of Democracy*, New York, 1938, p. 19.

There is almost no end to the similar expressions of this purpose to which it is said democracy, by its nature or by definition, is dedicated. It is one of the staples of luncheon-club oratory, though it is not perhaps on that account wholly false. Some put it as broadly as 'to ensure universal self-respect.' For discussion purposes, we may sum up the ideal as 'self-realization' or 'development of personality' or—in older language—'developing souls.'

Now, all this is very fine and inspiring. Who is not for virtue and against sin? But the political problem is to give this high general ideal enough content to make it useful for policy decisions —not an easy thing to do since, as Morris Cohen said, 'alas, even great philosophers announce principles that have great emotional uplift but little definite consequences.' If we cannot agree upon specifying the ideal in particular policies, we cannot judge between the promise and the performance of a democracy. How, then, can we pass the verdict—as many do—that the gap between the two is the chief problem of democracies? The content of the ideal, the specific policies and legislation, can only be worked out in the political process, a process in which both the highest and the lowest ideals, he good and the bad, come before the bar of decision. The problem of theory is to put enough flesh on the skeleton of general principles that they may reach the political level, although this does not mean that theory alone will dictate policies. Let us try to sort out some of the problems thus raised.

The first question is whether democracy builds upon a doctrine of human nature. Many political theories have purported to rest upon a construct or model of human nature: what it is, and what it should be—the two being identified in some theories. Sometimes it has been ostensibly a morally neutral postulate of human behavior, as in the case of Hobbes; or an alleged empirical concept, as with the pleasure-pain principle of the utilitarians. More often, perhaps always, such theories have combined a neutral postulate or empirical premise with certain moral premises about human behavior, as in the case of Locke or (though scarcely admitted) Bentham, and (more openly moral) Mill. Sometimes, indeed, the moral element has been implicit and unrecognized, as with Marx. To this first question we must answer, however, that the democratic system, as outlined, did not start with a concept of human nature and then proceed to show that democracy best promotes it, or follows logically therefrom. Very few, if any, of the concepts of human nature put forward by political philosophers have led, logically, to one and only one type of political system. We can all see the fallacy in Aristotle's argument that man is by nature a political animal, if by this he meant that man is naturally adapted to, and only to, life in the *polis*.

The second question is whether the democratic system *implies* a particular view of human nature? The answer here must be yes, since any political system does entail or involve at least a partial view of human nature. The Athenians, for instance, were astute enough in seeing that their democracy turned out one type of character, while Sparta and other states turned out a different sort. Demosthenes spoke of a city's laws as its 'character,' and Aristotle repeated often in his *Politics* that the citizen must be educated in the spirit of the constitution under which he lives. Part of the political inquiry for the Greek philosophers was always that of the relation of the *polis* to character, and hence—as in Plato—the subject of education played a large part in their political theory. Plato's *Republic* is almost as much a treatise on the education designed to adapt the citizen to the *polis* as one on how to train the rulers. John Stuart Mill was eloquent on the education and character of the democrat, while Sir Ernest Barker has said that 'the theory of education is essentially a part of political theory.'

Before we explore this point further, two preliminary cautions are necessary because they conceal points so easily and often overlooked. One is that character is not determined by the political system alone, but is affected by all parts of a society, although no doubt there will be a tendency, where politics is important and widely valued, to carry over the political type of character into the rest of society. Hence democracy, which requires a 'politicized' society par excellence (though not necessarily a governmentalized society), is often associated with an attitude, or 'way of life,' as well as with a political system. In Athens 'there embodied in the city, in its laws, customs and institutions, a pattern and ideal of life for the citizens.'[15] Yet, bearing in mind that only a small fraction of the citizens in any modern democratic society is or need be politically active, we should not expect, and do not find, that all people in a democracy have the démocratic attitudes or character.

The other caution is that although democracies will tend to turn out the same type of character in some respects, it does not follow that there will not be much variation in 'national character.' (a) The history of all democracies contains political traditions other than the democratic; (b) democracies may vary a great deal within the broad scope of the principles of their political system; and (c) all democracies have non-democratic compartments in their non-political life—i.e. in the economic, social, military, religious, educational, or family compartments.[16] For these reasons alone, it is bound to be difficult to draw conclusions about the influence, and requirements, of a political system upon character, when we cannot isolate this influence from the rest of the society.

Democracy, then, both presupposes and tends to promote a particular type of character or personality; or alternatively we may say—since character is a slippery concept—that the system relies on certain attitudes or dispositions or behavior patterns and these it tends to foster because they contribute to the working of the system. The nub of our inquiry, undertaken with all caution, then becomes: what is the view of human character entailed by democracy?

Although democracy has existed in a number of countries in western culture for more than a century, its psychological and ethical base has not been sufficiently investigated. There has been no adequate statement of a conception of human nature, and of the secondary attitudes, that lie at the base of democracy.[17]

15 Sir Frederick Pollock, *An Introduction to the History of the Science of Politics*, London, 1920, p. 10.

16 Much research of the type which purports to show that an authoritarian family implies an authoritarian political regime is based upon a slim number of examples, and the conclusions are highly tentative. Again, we may question much of the theorizing on the relation of child care to democracy, of psychosis to advocates of world government, etc., as in such articles as that by D. W. Winnicott, 'Some Thoughts on the Meaning of the Word Democracy,' *Human Relations*, vol. III, June 1950.

17 B. E. Lippincott, loc. cit.

One approach to the construction of a 'model' is to bring together the kind of qualities, attitudes, pre-dispositions and beliefs —i.e. broadly the kind of character or personality—which a working democracy presupposes. That is, we may try to construct the kind of personality which is likely to be able to work the democratic system successfully, and this is the approach taken here. Alternatively, we could begin by examining the kind of character which the democratic system does in fact produce, and to do this we could launch an empirical inquiry into existing democracies, after first agreeing on those characteristics which are typical of the democratic personality. Some inquiries of the latter type have been made, and there is an extensive literature, but much of it is vitiated by a preliminary lack of agreement on the essentials of a democratic character. Whichever approach is followed, the democratic personality or character, when delineated, may then be held up as admirable—as our 'model'—and democracy can then be justified on the grounds that it best produces this kind of character. Though it would, I think, be going much too far to say that the production of a special type of character has been the conscious purpose of any democracy. (To complete the answer, no doubt one should go further into moral philosophy and justify the character so delineated.)

Let us, then, try to list a set of attitudes which democracy requires, and which together make up a kind of synthetic character. Having such a character before us, we should be able better to judge the virtues and defects of democracy because of seeing the consequences, in imagination, upon individuals; while in addition, a guide to specific policy-making is provided—in education, for instance—since in any system there will presumably be a conscious effort to build after the model. Politics, personality, and other cultural patterns should be some kind of unified whole, as they are in any homogeneous 'culture.' The kind of character we are taught to admire—the model again—sums up the whole of any society's ideas about itself, though an examination of the actual character types produced in any society would be necessary in order to see how closely the ideal is reached. Like Spinoza, we call good that which 'is a means by which we may approach nearer and nearer to the model of human nature we set before us.' In political terms—as Harrington said—'the foundation of government is the creation of a political creature after the image of a philosophical creature.' Or, more modestly, we seek those characteristics of the ideal or typical democrat, rather as the days of chivalry set up the knightly ideal, or the 18th century its ideal gentleman, or W. S. Gilbert the 'very model of a modern major-general.'

If, then, we try to construct the characteristics of the personality required of a democracy, we are often told that they will run along these lines, though we need not presuppose many 'pure types.'

(1) First and most obvious must be a desire to be self-governing, on which Mill said some useful things. The democrat will value political freedoms for themselves, as well as for the objectives which he wishes to achieve by using them. He will like to make his influence felt, and be averse to political decisions which he has not helped to shape, even if indirectly. It follows that he will not be averse to responsibility, nor regard freedoms or voting as a 'dreadful burden.'

(2) The active democrat will presumably possess an inquiring, independent, rational attitude. This is the attitude required to equip him to judge and defend his own interests, and to judge the competing claims of parties and candidates at elections. His political loyalty will be in a sense intelligent, although we must be cautious here and not make the absurd assumption that he is always above emotion, or behaving with the rationality of the prudent economic man. Neither does this attitude tell us whether he will incline towards being conservative or radical.

(3) To behave as a political animal, he must enjoy a feeling of confidence in the political system and its policies. Only if secure and confident can he take part in politics, by expressing opinions and the like, free from the fear of reprisals or victimization. He must feel that he counts, or he will be apathetic or hostile to the system. Some have held that only if he is personally secure and free from anxiety can he release and direct his energy into individual purposes socially sanctioned, and into group and common purposes freely chosen or worked out.

(4) He must also be sympathetic to the claims of others, with a

low 'will to power' or 'will to dominate,' or he will not as a citizen admit the principle of political equality, or as a politician
bow to the verdict of the voters. There is a certain deference, of
one to all others, in democracies which 'must be given in order to
be got. This is the secret of democratic honor.' [18] It is also the
secret of restraint on the part of the majority, and of obedience
on the part of the minority. Yet we need not assume that a democrat is wholly altruistic and bubbling over with the milk of human kindness. A sympathy and fellow-feeling for men, as men, is
one thing, but it need not lead to pacifism or self-abnegation. It is
much more a question of respecting the sincerity of conscience of
others, though we may have a different conscience ourselves, on
the issue in dispute.

Bryce captured the spirit that is indicated here when he wrote:

> The adjective [democratic] is used to describe a person of a simple
> and friendly spirit and genial manners, 'a good mixer,' one who,
> whatever his wealth or status, makes no assumption of superiority,
> and carefully keeps himself on the level of his poorer or less emi-
> nent neighbours. I have heard a monarch described as 'a demo-
> cratic king.' [19]

Beyond the gregariousness common to all men must be the
recognition that, despite all differences of wealth, talents, education, and social class, the things in which men are and should be
alike—their capacities to choose and lead a moral life, their equal
political and legal rights—are, in politics, more important and
valid than the differences.[20] (The argument is analogous to the
religious view that in the sight of God all men are equal.) A democrat need not and probably will not, in any personal sense, love
or be charitable toward his political enemies, but he will tolerate

[18] T. V. Smith in *Philosophy of American Democracy*, ed. C. M. Perry,
Chicago, 1943, p. 152.

[19] James Bryce, *Modern Democracies*, New York, 1921, vol. II, p. 23.

[20] 'To the modern mind, criticism of this kind of philosophy comes easy,
long skilled as we are in exploiting the classic position that the differences
between men are more significant than their similarities and that society
should operate by the rule of observing classified distinctions, not philan-
thropic exchanges.' Eric A. Havelock, *The Liberal Temper in Greek Politics*,
London, 1957, p. 398.

them or at least not wish to suppress them and their political proposals.

(5) He will probably have a tendency to express, rather than repress, emotions and opinions, because the opportunity is there —in the political freedoms—and he is constantly encouraged to choose and participate.[21] The vigilance necessary to assert rights and preserve freedoms is unlikely to be maintained by the shy and the retiring. (Whether this tendency is necessary, or whether if present it promotes democracy, is doubtful, I think. The Russians are said to be very extrovert, like Americans; while on the other hand the Englishman, though a democrat, does not tell his personal troubles to every casual acquaintance.)

(6) He must possess a considerable willingness to compromise, to acquiesce in a political policy which is not his first preference. He must thus tend to be 'tolerant of ambiguity,' since he will recognize that few political questions are black or white. As with Mr. Justice Holmes, the tolerance may rest upon a personal modesty, 'the great act of faith' that one is 'not God'—or for that matter, God's appointed. He will thus not be a fanatic for any substantive matter, though he may well be so from a keen sense of 'fairness' or attachment to democracy, on behalf of the procedural freedoms and the other 'rules of the game,' i.e. the methods and principles of democracy itself. A certain number of such procedural fanatics may be indispensable, to call others to rethink from time to time the fundamentals of the democratic system. A 'procedural fastidiousness' runs deep in democratic societies—it is often said, for example, that concern for procedures is keener than for substantive liberties in the United States.

(7) As a counterpart to the virtue of compromise—or perhaps as a substitute—he will place a high value on peace and order achieved as common purposes through the political freedoms; and upon those other values of the system sketched in Chapter 9, as against the promotion of his special interests. Inclined to com-

---

[21] Lasswell has suggested (*Democratic Character, op. cit.*) that the democratic personality will: (1) have an 'open' ego, (2) be multivalued (not fanatic), (3) have confidence in the benevolent potentialities of man, and (4) be free from anxiety and automatic compulsions, so that he may tap the energy of the unconscious, instead of being in conflict with it.

promise, or value peace, the democrat is less likely to be on the extreme ends of any radical-conservative continuum of attitudes, whether he happens to be with the minority or the majority on any specific policy. It is the same attitude which is expressed in such phrases as 'respect for law.'

(8) He will not be inclined to extreme optimism or pessimism. The view of politics which democracy presupposes does not lend itself to the optimism of the anarchist and other purveyors of panaceas. This helps to turn the edge of the criticism that democracy is wedded to an unrealistic doctrine of the immediate or political perfectibility of man. It is, however, unquestionably a benevolent, even optimistic view of man, encompassing as it does a faith in the individual and the long-run future, given political equality and freedoms—a faith that although there is no 'natural' harmony, yet one can be worked out, and individual and common interests reconciled; but it is also tough-minded enough to recognize limitations, set-backs, and the need for special conditions. On the pessimistic side, the democrat may value the system *because,* like the ancient Athenians, he distrusts men with irresponsible power. In this respect, democracy fits into today's climate of opinion, since we are not in the market for utopias or theories based wholly upon the inherent goodness of man.[22] We can say, following Niebuhr, that man is at once *good* enough to make democracy possible, and *bad* enough to make it necessary.

IS THE CHARACTER FEASIBLE?

The set of attitudes put forward very tentatively above does not, I think, furnish a complete and adequate 'conception of human nature,' since it is confined to political attitudes. Yet there is a kind of logic to democracy by which it tends to grow in a society. Despite our ambivalent attitudes to politicians, public service

---

[22] A more unflattering view of the psychology of a democrat is the following: 'The democratic doctrine is, in its essence, an unconscious expression of envy of anything superior to self, and a vague aspiration for a state of society in which there should be no contrasts between one man's lot and another's—though the crier for fraternity generally wants the elder brother's place.' Lord Norton, in *Nineteenth Century Opinion,* ed. Michael Goodwin, Harmondsworth, Middlesex, 1951, p. 179.

carries prestige; and the democrat tends to take his personal attitudes into other than political fields. The very methods—discussion, participation, equality, freedoms, negotiation, compromise, the majority principle—tend to get carried over into other associations and the making of other decisions. What is political is itself debatable so that, with free speech, the door is open for treating many matters in the democratic political spirit. Again, apart altogether from the sphere of politics, we can speak of and identify a democratic method of decision-making, and democratic values, and—what is more relevant here—democratic attitudes and personality. There exists what the psychologist calls 'the generalized nature of responses in the attitude field'; our attitudes affect learning, remembering, reasoning and perception itself. So the pressures build up for the democratic society to cohere; there is a powerful 'strain to consistency' within a democracy. (But the *logical* consistency may easily be overrated; while it is probably also true that non-democratic attitudes elsewhere in society tend to grow into the political.)

Although we may avoid making an ambitious inquiry into an 'adequate conception of human nature,' we cannot avoid the narrower question whether the set of attitudes taken together is feasible. For instance, a common opinion has it that democracy has lost much of its appeal in the modern world because its attitudes or character are thought not to agree with the findings of psychology. At any rate, there is a substantial corpus of pessimistic writing to that effect.

For one thing, it is alleged that a whole body of psychological doctrine, starting with Freud, has undermined belief in the rationality of man by showing that much of our behavior is determined at the unconscious mental level. If political decisions cannot be partly rational—in both the economic sense of means to ends and the sense of choosing ends—it is hard to see how we can justify democracy. Another fashionable school of thought purports to show that people are 'naturally' and not 'culturally' afraid of what Gide called the 'anguish of freedom'—of choice, self-discipline, and the responsibility that the democratic method presupposes.

Then, again, so it is said, sociology and the discovery of 'iron laws of oligarchy' in virtually every type of large-scale social organization including political parties tend to the same pessimistic conclusion of the inherent unsuitability of democratic principles and attitudes for any large-scale organization, and *a fortiori* for one as large as a political system. This kind of social determinism is seen at its most determinist and pessimistic in the classic by Michels on *Political Parties:* the iron law of oligarchy is 'the fundamental sociological law of political parties.' No remedy can be found: all organizations in time will become oligarchic. The charge of inevitable oligarchy, or something very similar, is brought not only by Michels but also by writers such as Pareto, Mosca, and Burnham, and is supported by much empirical evidence drawn from the study of political parties, trade unions, and business organizations. The charge is based on different concepts such as that of the 'managerial elite,' the inevitable trends to bureaucracy, the 'organization man,' the nature of large-scale technology, and so forth. The concept of the 'sociology of knowledge' has contributed also to the same end—e.g. here and there in the works of Karl Mannheim—by suggesting that social factors determine man's beliefs and actions.

What are we to say to these impressive arguments? For myself, I do not find that they support the anti-democratic conclusions so often drawn. Take the 'iron law of oligarchy.' There is nothing in democratic theory which cannot come to terms with leadership in organizations, political or any other kind. It is no great news that large-scale organizations are led by the leaders. This sociological finding, for which so many—sometimes conflicting—causes are given and from which different conclusions are drawn, is only devastating to a primitive or direct type of democratic system, and scarcely affects a representative system. A democracy does not require everyone to be politically active, or show all the democratic attitudes, and can make full allowance for the realities of leadership and parties. (A democracy does, however, presuppose that political action is not determinist, but that human choice and attitudes do count, causally; that human choice can control and mold the impersonal forces at work in society, and within limits shape them to human ends.)

A fuller answer may be attempted to the charge based upon

psychology. We can, in the first place, readily admit that any democracy may contain a proportion of undemocratic personalities, judged by the standards set forth above or by other standards. How high the proportion can get before a democracy becomes unworkable, we simply do not know. Doubtless the proportion will vary with the kind of political circumstances at different times, including the urgency and magnitude of the policies to be made, the quality of political leadership, and so forth. We do know, however, that democracy need not presuppose any large proportion of the politically active, or even a high proportion of voters. Despite Aristotle, not every man is (or need be) a political animal.

Then, too, we can point to the going democracies, some of which have been successful for a considerable time; and to the many attempts at self-government—even those that have failed—all of which must be explained away by the psychological pessimists. Those who assert that man is not psychologically able to work democracy often forget that full representative democracy is, for all practical purposes, a comparatively new political system. It takes time for the masses of men to adjust to new political forms, and to adapt to the ideas and the moral climate which accompanies democracy—the autonomy, the discussion, the political equality and freedoms, and the majority principle—until they become 'second nature.' Life in the past seems to have been lived more by 'instinct' (or custom) and government has been more readily accepted with resignation, instead of approached with the idea that it can be popularly created and controlled. Every democracy trails clouds of these older traditions into the present. Democracy, as Morley said, 'stands for a remarkable revolution in human affairs.' Then, too, there is still the cogent point that so much of man's 'unfitness' for democracy may be simply his 'unfitness' for, or painful adjustment to, a scientific and industrial urban way of living.

In pointing thus to experience with democracy and self-government, we do not need to posit any primitive 'instinct to freedom,' nor yet to assume any universal psychological or other needs which only democracy can satisfy. There is a set of psychological *wants* that are democratic, but they are a function of the values of democracy, i.e. they are culturally learned and (as yet) certainly not universal. Men may come to democracy to fulfill different needs —as they go to religion for different reasons. It is enough if the needs thus fulfilled, in their overt expression as wants, are compatible with democracy. (Those who have been led to take a pessimistic view of man's capacity for democracy have, I think, been led astray by making two additional mistakes: first, by founding their psychological theory upon clinical experience with the unfit; and second, by assuming that democracy presupposes that all, or even a large proportion of, citizens need be politically active. They have been better at their psychology, their technical expertise, than in their understanding of politics.)

We can also point to the psychological evidence in *favor* of man's capacity for democracy—including those persons who value the procedures of democracy more highly than any of its substantive objectives. While it may be true that 'every man bears within himself a dormant fascist,' it is equally true that we are all animals in our unconscious. It is what is in our consciousness that counts, and the business of any society is to make a civilized consciousness.

Our conclusions can be modest. We need conclude only that there is nothing in the demands which democracy makes upon men, or in the kind of personality which it requires and promotes, that is at variance with what we know with a fair degree of reliability of psychology. This may not be saying much, because we may not know much for certain; most psychology is local and western and not universal. On the other hand, if we do not know much, it is hard to feel that arguments drawn from psychological theories are very damaging to democracy. We must assume, however, that the democratic character 'does not form against the grain' in enough people to work the system successfully. Compatibility, then, is a justifiable assumption, and a quite sufficient one. 'Man has no nature: what he has is ... history.' (And it may help to recall that anthropology finds something very like democracy in some early primitive societies, whence some assert that democracy is the oldest form of government, while some make the cheerful assumption that democracy is the norm at which the political animal most naturally will arrive.)

The objection to democracy based on psychological grounds often goes somewhat deeper than pessimism, and has a more direct application to politics. The objection rests upon the implicit assumption that we can get from science (psychology, cultural anthropology, and the like) to the 'real' human nature or personality; and given this, we can then promote its attainment as we do other scientific goals, by scientific means. Behind the idea of ascertaining the real or basic human nature by science lies the old assumption that the 'natural is best' which, like so many seminal ideas, both good and bad, is originally Greek.[23] In later times the language has changed, and the 'natural' often takes the form of basic 'needs,' whether biological or psychological. But even if we knew all these 'needs,' they would give no guidance on which wants to pursue in order to satisfy the 'needs,' i.e. they would not answer —though they are relevant to—the problems of social and political living, which are always those of choice: which wants to satisfy, and how, and which to deny.

> ... the conception of biological need is so general as to be sterile; there are so many ways in which a society could fulfill the need for survival that this by itself tells us little about why it should have some institutions rather than others.[24]

As the ancient Sophist said:

> By nature we are all equally adapted to be barbarians or Greeks, the natural needs of men are much the same, all breathe with mouths and nostrils.

The same objection applies to concepts of 'maturity,' of which many patterns are possible, and on which (it seems to me) the social psychologists write much naïve philosophy.

[23] Mill wrote a sustained and savage attack upon 'Nature's immorality' in his *Three Essays on Religion* (reprinted in *Nature, Utility and Religion*, ed. G. Nakhnikian, New York, 1958): 'the course of natural phenomena is replete with everything that when committed by human beings is most worthy of abhorrence; so that any one who endeavoured in his actions to imitate the natural course of things, would be universally seen and acknowledged to be the wickedest of men.' Back-to-nature philosophers might take note.

[24] Emmett, op. cit. p. 99. As for anyone who professes to derive moral ideals from man's 'needs,' he 'is misleading himself and others since the "needs" on which moral ideals are allegedly based are already charged with moral meaning.' H. B. Acton, *The Illusion of the Epoch*, London, 1955, p. 113.

If it were really true that we could get from the sciences the 'real' human nature and the means to attain it, it would follow, I think, that democratic politics—all politics, except perhaps those of competing scientists—would be virtually superfluous. The psychologist or other expert, the man who knows the 'real' human nature, should be put in charge of society to perform the governing (administrative) function. Those who did not then assent would be not merely perverse or wicked, as they would be in violating a moral rule, but pathological—as conscientious objectors are said to have been sent to mental hospitals, instead of prisons, in Germany during the First World War.[25] If we go outside politics to the scientific expert to find an end or goal for man, and to manipulate him, then politics and conflict become 'disease,' and the dissenter must be 'treated,' not met in argument or his claims compromised.[26] On this kind of view, political activity of a kind could at the very most be justified as purely expedient, acting perhaps as a psychological safety valve for dissenters while they were treated for their mental ill health.

Professor Lasswell came close to lending support—perhaps unintentionally—to this sort of view when he generalized from his study of pathological politicians in his *Psychopathology and Politics* (1930). But as one student has pointed out:

> Pathology however is not physiology and a study of neurotic politicians may no more explain sane statesmen than a study of corrupt elections explains the democratic process.[27]

and another:

> ... primary motives are [said to be] 'displaced on public object rationalized in terms of public interest.' This must mean that

[25] 'Complete rationality in this field would consist in handing over the treatment of crime, criminal and punitive, or, better, reformatory measures to the medico-socio-educational expert. Since he, as an expert, has the best scientific insight into the problems involved, as well as the best possible solutions for them, he would be able to deal with crime as it should be dealt with, namely, as a problem of "social engineering."' John H. Hertz, *Political Realism and Political Idealism*, Chicago, 1951, p. 159.

[26] Cf. Isaiah Berlin, 'Political Thought in the 20th Century,' *Foreign Affairs*, April 1950.

[27] D. E. Butler, *The Study of Political Behaviour*, London, 1958, p. 81.

politics is not an adult activity, but a means of seeking compensation for infantile deprivations ... Would not this have to mean that the motive which leads people to enter political life would have gone, so that we should presumably have to look forward to a situation where there would be no more politics? [28]

There is not much prospect, however, that we shall be able in any foreseeable future to get any one scientifically validated end or model for man, and so the problems of politics remain. They will remain no matter what scientists may discover about man and his important attitudes and drives, of which we know so little. The chief reason why we cannot go to the scientific experts for final answers is that politics involves choice and conflict and raises moral questions—not merely technical problems. '... the proper study of politics is not man but institutions.' [29] The pattern of maturity, of personality, of harmony, in both individual man and society, is worked out, not discovered, is a function of the moral evaluation we use when intellect works upon 'needs' and desires.[30] There is no escaping morality and choice in all our policies. The role for the scientific specialist is thus that of advisor: he knows one aspect of the problems posed by politics. But like the expert in 'human relations' or administration, or organization—whose work is so largely inspired by a desire to manipulate people— his knowledge can be used for good or evil purposes. To reduce the problems of politics to problems of scientific management is to abolish politics and democracy altogether.

The place for the so-called experts on political 'wisdom,' too, whoever they may be, is also subordinate—that of advocating policy, leading this or that party or pressure-group. But if any one type of expert—scientific or other—is put in charge, and is not

[28] Emmett, op. cit. p. 119.

[29] J. P. Plamenatz, *Consent, Freedom, and Political Obligation*, Oxford, 1938, p. 309. Cf. also '... for political theory individuals must always be taken as they exist in society, on the one hand, and on the other, that political society is simply a feeling of relationship in the minds of individuals. This is the primary fact for the political theorist, who thus starts by assuming neither the rights of individuals nor the rights of the State.' Alfred Cobban, *Edmund Burke and the Revolt against the Eighteenth Century*, London, 1929, p. 272.

[30] H. R. G. Greaves, *The Foundations of Political Theory*, London, 1958, Chapter 3.

accountable as politicians are, they will, as Plato's guardians did, compel men to live their way. Consent then becomes irrelevant, or something to be engineered, not worked out in the public debate of a political system.

> Scientism would take the politics out of politics. Moralism would destroy it if necessary as the enemy of virtue. In the unsophisticated view of both scientism and moralism, politics is literally a means ... They are motivated by a common urge, the passion for certitude. For the mortal enemy of one is the mortal enemy of the other: the stubborn persistence of complexities and ambiguities in human existence.[31]

What, after all, would be the practical difference between Plato's statecraft and Stalin's 'engineering of the soul'? In both cases self-appointed guardians with vision and knowledge mold human beings from the highest motives toward what they regard as the highest goals. Regeneration in both cases is by means of the state —a classical, ancient, and non-Christian notion; although it was later adapted to Christian purposes, as when it was incorporated into the political Puritanism of Calvin's Geneva and that of early Massachusetts, with forced external piety: an inferior copy of the saints in heaven.

There are no experts—or rather there are too many—on the 'ends' and proper character for man, or the purposes and policies which government should pursue. There are many deeply held and conflicting convictions about the 'true ends' which democracy should aim at, and still more on the policies to attain them. In the absence of knowledge from any source, the great virtue of democracy is that while giving the people what they want for the time being, it keeps the future open: this is the check on the conflicting experts of all kinds. We cannot afford to treat as axioms 'what politics leaves free for discussion and amendment.'[32] We cannot afford to believe that knowledge, from any source, will relieve us of the burden of moral and political choice.

The assumption of democratic politics has no place for scientifi-

[31] Norman Jacobson in Young (ed.), op. cit. pp. 117-18.
[32] Cf. Henry S. Kariel, 'The Normative Pattern of Erich Fromm's Escape from Freedom,' *Journal of Politics*, November 1957, p. 652.

cally ascertained character or goals, for Platonic guardians, for 'ends' and policies beyond partisanship and beyond relaxation. Democracy sets up no scientifically ascertained 'end' for man, has no all-consuming purpose, no Form of the Good, no final ultimate to serve. It has its operating principles and their values; it has the values inherent in the system; and it has a typical character which it both presupposes and promotes. Within these limits a democracy may be used to pursue aims which change from time to time—aims and purposes which are worked out and form a pattern of policy by a complicated interplay of the many forces at work in the political processes, the chief of which is the interplay of politicians and public. The realm of political and social purposes in a democracy is open and indeterminate, unless they are very general and thus permit political dispute over policies.

> The purposes of many associations can be clearly defined and set forth in articles of association . . .
> This conception of an association is expressed in what Maitland calls the trust theory of associations . . .
> It is perfectly adequate, for example, to the limited liability company. But there are other associations to which this theory will not apply so satisfactorily. They can best be described as associations whose purposes are essentially such that they have a natural development of their own . . .
> It is by living together that men learn what they want and conceive purposes to which they will devote themselves, by playing complementary parts in a society of which they are all members.[33]

If legal and political philosophy may be divided into two broad streams, as they often are—one finding the binding character of law in its aim and content (it is only legal if 'right'), the other in its source or the legitimacy of the legislator (it is legal if legally made)—then democracy is unquestionably in the second stream.

The same general point which I have argued above is often made by saying that democracy is not an ideology, but is above all ideologies in the sense of competing bodies of doctrine advocating this or that policy or purpose. Hence we can say that democratic government is the 'voluntary acceptance of a central agency

[33] A. D. Lindsay, *The Modern Democratic State*, Oxford, 1943, pp. 43, 240.

of intimidation, designed for the attainment of the desires of the public.'[34]

To those for whom the 'ends' of government are felt to be determinate, and violated by democratic policies, there may always arise the eternal dilemma of the incompatibility of 'good' government and democracy, of due process and substantive 'right' —a dilemma which can never be entirely absent from political life, because no matter how fair the procedures, there may come a time in the life of any of us when we may have to make the decision whether to obey or resist. The problem of individual conscience becomes inevitably also a social and political problem, because 'no man is an islande.' There is, of course, more to a society than its political system; there are community and the innumerable bonds of men in society, and to these we now turn for their relation to politics.

[34] W. J. Baumol, *Welfare Economics and the Theory of the State*, London, 1952, p. 35.

ELEVEN | *Critics and Problems*

The problems of any political system and its theory are often best brought out by its critics. Indeed, political systems and their theories can scarcely be understood without taking into account the criticisms brought against them. Arguments and illustrations in favor of democracy can always be found by those who live in democracies, but a special effort of thought must be made to find answers to the critics, an effort which always yields fresh understanding.

Criticisms of democracy take two forms, not always easily distinguishable: of the working system, and of the theory. Criticisms of the theory in turn are directed at the explanatory principles—e.g. denying that the system works as the principles assert; or at the justifying principles—e.g. denying the validity of political equality, or the values realized by the system, or else, accepting these values as good but alleging that they are offset by other, undesirable values, or are purchased at too high a price.

In the foregoing chapters, a number of criticisms have been noted and treated cursorily. Two strands of criticism were treated in slightly more detail in Chapter 10, namely the criticism based on psychology (that democracy is forever impossible because it is 'unnatural' to man); and the sociological criticism (that democracy is impossible because of the 'iron law of oligarchy'). There is no need to repeat here these criticisms, or the kind of answers which can be made to them in defense of democracy. Apart from those, however, two other classes of contemporary criticism also deserve mention.

THE MARXIST CRITICISM

The first of these is the Marxist, the most militant and systematic of the contemporary attacks upon the democratic system. Its main outline is well known. Starting with the familiar proposition that the political is determined by the economic, or is merely a part of the social superstructure erected upon the economic foundation, the criticism consists in applying this formula to democracy. Being the political system of a class society, democracy —it is said—cannot help but reflect the interests and wishes of the bourgeois or dominant class, which bases itself on private ownership of productive property; and so long as class society (i.e. capitalism) endures, democracy cannot be converted into an instrument of genuine majority rule by the proletariat, since by definition the minority (the *bourgeoisie*) make the political decisions, either openly or behind the scenes. The economic power and decisions are the important ones, and these are merely ratified on the stage of politics where the game of pretense is played out. At its most generous, Marxism concedes that capitalist democracy is a 'real' democracy for the rich, but is only a sham for the poor; though on the whole it may be better than Fascism or other non-democratic capitalist forms if only because under democracy Marxist parties may operate.

Marxism is thus a sustained and uncompromising critique of both the democratic system and of the theory which explains its operation, but not necessarily of its justifying theory. If it could be conceded *per impossibile* that the democratic method could 'really' work in a capitalist society to achieve the desires and interests of the majority, would the Marxist continue to criticize? Probably not, but his answer is: the question does not arise; capitalism by its very nature cannot be a 'real' democracy for the majority—the proletariat. Marxism is a long and strenuous denial of the efficacy and primacy of politics, and Marxist parties are interested in the destruction of the political and economic system of 'bourgeois democracy,' not in the alleged futility of political methods in a class society.

As to the normative theory which justifies democracy, there are many kind words in the writings of Marx and Engels for the *idea* of democracy, conceived as a wide suffrage, free elections, and political liberties, while in the original Marxist concept the communist party was expected to be 'real' democracy for the great majority of its membership. But when we leave classical Marxism for the Leninist, Stalinist, and later versions of orthodoxy, the democratic elements in the party dwindle to vanishing point, and are replaced by 'democratic centralism.' In the alternative system which Marxism offers in the Soviet Union and China —unquestionably the chief rival system of democracy today—a few of the superficial features of democracy are present, but none of the essential features. In the communist system the wide franchise prevails, but free elections and political liberties are lacking, and the social meaning or function of the voting is transformed. The dictatorship of the proletariat, which in Marx was expected to follow the revolution temporarily, becomes an apparently permanent dictatorship of the party, or more accurately an oligarchy of a small party executive, and in the extreme case (under Stalin) a dictatorship.

Later communist theory must, then, explain away the differences between the earlier Marxist concepts and the current reality, and in doing so it displays considerable ambivalence—hovering between a frank admission of class (if not party) dictatorship in communist states on the one hand, and on the other a re-definition of their dictatorship and oligarchy as 'democracy' in order to capitalize on the good will which still exists, even in the communist world, for the humane ideas traditionally associated with democracy.

In the ultimate ideals of the classless, stateless society of abundance, there are several affinities in Marxism with the ideals of traditional liberal and democratic theory. But one—the vital one —is absent: the importance of politics, and with it the need for government. All political and governmental problems vanish in the classless society, and we are left with virtual anarchism. The contrast between dream and reality is given by the Soviet Union, where politics and democracy are not so much assumed away as frankly suppressed in favor of the absolute, the governmental, and the administrative.

There are many refutations of the Marxist critique on the

market, drawing their arguments both from defects in the theoretical analysis of Marxism and from empirical evidence in the existing democracies, so that it would be a work of supererogation to write another here.[1] Neither is it my purpose to examine the alternative system proposed by Marx, or that established by later communist movements in Russia and China, or the problems of internal and foreign policy posed for democracies by the existence and challenges of communist systems.

THE CHARGE OF INCOMPETENCE

The second class of contemporary criticism, commanding a wide following, may for convenience be grouped under the head of 'incompetence.' A host of such specific charges used to be directed at the existing democracies before World War II, most of them being associated with Fascism and Nazism, both of which despised democracy but avoided the Marxist diagnosis of putting the blame on the capitalists and the economic system. The charges were focused instead around the allegation that democracy is incompetent and inefficient—in dealing with serious economic problems, in its unstable domestic and foreign policies, and in its inability to prepare for war. The breakdown of democracy in Germany and Italy, and its relative economic failure everywhere in the depression of the 1930's, was usually adduced as supporting evidence of incompetence. (The Marxist criticism is almost the opposite, that democracy *is* efficient in terms of its own 'real' underlying principles—giving the *bourgeoisie* their way, and maintaining class rule for the time being.)

The alleged incompetence of democracy is accounted for in several ways. For one thing, the democratic system is inevitably slow—taking too long to act, to hammer out a policy in the endless debates, electioneering, and politicking. This slow method is quite unsuited for dealing with emergencies requiring quick decision. Nothing gets done, except during a war, and then only at the cost of suspending democracy.

For another, the political system of democracy is said to be

[1] See, for example, H. B. Mayo, *Introduction to Marxist Theory*, New York, 1960.

inherently unsuited to the complexities and large scale of the modern world, whatever may perhaps have been its usefulness in a simpler age, when political units were small or when *laissez faire* prevailed and the services provided by government were few. When a government does a few things, mistakes hardly matter; but when many things, failures are always serious and may be calamitous. This particular criticism is indeed made the basis of pessimistic predictions of the prospects of democracy by both its friends and its enemies: by its friends who fear that 'increasing' government may destroy democracy, and by its enemies who hope that it will do so.

Then again, democracy is said to fail on the score of leadership. The talents for vote-getting are not those of ruling—of making 'wise' decisions. Democracy emphasizes and rewards the former, and bonuses opportunism of parties and politicians as they have the money or cunning to influence the votes. But good government, wise policies, are needed to ensure the success of any system, and only good leaders can provide these desiderata.

Moreover, even if competent leaders should occasionally find themselves in office—combining the roles of politicians and statesmen—they are hopelessly handicapped by the methods of democratic politics. Democracy diffuses responsibility for policies, whereas responsibility must be concentrated in order to 'get things done,' i.e. to decide policies, to make them into a consistent pattern, and to see they are carried out efficiently. A casual reference to the near-chaos or deadlock in some multi-party systems—usually that of France—is taken to be enough to document the case against democratic leadership.

The very principle of compromise which is, so to speak, built into the democratic system further militates against efficiency, consistency, and 'good' government. Compromise is also made the basis of the charge that democracy lacks 'principle' (compromise is said to be the exaltation of 'no principle'), while in addition it stands for and invites unlimited sectionalism, pressures, and group selfishness. Alternatively, democracy is sometimes accused of being organized deceit and hypocrisy—professing high principles and the public interest but always deviating from them in the compromises of politics—an inevitable tendency (so it is said), since, not being able to accomplish anything important, politicians must pretend that the trivial things they actually do are important.

Democracy is also confusing to the citizens, who cannot understand the complexities and subtleties of its policy-making or methods of operation. It has, moreover, no ideology, no body of agreed and simple doctrine, no great aims or purposes, by which to inspire devotion and sacrifice and to command the enthusiastic loyalty, if not the understanding, of the masses. The result is bound to be disillusion and apathy among the public, and in the end a collapse of the system from its own defects—to give way to more militant, inspiring, and demanding faiths, supporting other newer systems which are the 'wave of the future.' Where the democratic system has worked, after a fashion, its success is accounted for by extraneous or fortuitous factors which have, as it were, managed to keep a bumbling and incompetent system afloat in spite of its defects.

The case is familiar and at first sight formidable. (I pass over the virtues sometimes grudgingly granted to democracy, e.g. that it solves the problem of peaceful succession of rulers.) And it would obviously be foolish to deny an element of truth here and there in these criticisms. Before coming to grips with the main charge of incompetence, two oft-forgotten points of considerable importance should be recalled.

(a) Much of democratic government—though by no means all—is conducted in the white glare of publicity, and faults are exaggerated. The very function of an opposition is to oppose, and to do so as noisily and as effectively as possible. Because of the political liberties allowed, every democracy produces critics of the system and of its most fundamental principles. Mistakes of policy and abuses of the system, both real and imaginary, are freely ventilated—often to loud and profitable applause. By contrast, only praise and flattery are allowed in a dictatorship, and since the mistakes and evils go uncriticized, one tends to assume they are nonexistent. The old observation is still true that under a popular government everyone speaks ill of the people with freedom and without fear; whereas no one speaks of an absolute prince without a thousand fears and precautions.

(b) The critics of democracy all too often fail to apply the same standards to democracy as to *its* rivals. The very highest, often perfectionist, standards are used to judge democracy—as when moral purists attack the United States for the mote and make generous excuses for the Soviet beam, or denounce the scandals of democratic politics, forgetting the institutionalized corruption of other political systems. (This kind of criticism also subtly shifts the ground of attack from incompetence to moral turpitude.)

Nevertheless, even when due allowance has been made for the exaggeration of faults and the use of the double standard, the charge of incompetence raises a question which goes to the very root of the theory of democratic politics. Incompetence, or the lack of political wisdom, constitutes in fact the gravamen of the most serious charge (other than the Marxist) and is also the oldest of the criticisms against democracy—modern versions being seldom more than glosses on Plato, with a few topical illustrations added. In the end, the quasi-Platonic criticism is directed against the principle of political equality, and rests upon a particular view of the nature of politics. This principle of political equality, so it is said, is based on the assumption of equality of political wisdom among the citizens—which is absurd. Political wisdom is distributed unequally, and some obviously know more than others. The masses of the citizens are ignorant, and even if most of them can be made technically literate, their judgment on public policy (if it can be called judgment) is necessarily incomplete and faulty.

Whatever validity Plato's critique of the assumption of equal political wisdom had against Athenian democracy, the modern version has far less force against the indirect, representative democracy with which we are familiar. Political wisdom of a high order on every complex issue is not required of all citizens in a system where the people do not make the policy decisions, but instead elect and authorize representatives to do this for them. The wisdom is needed by the leaders (though there is admittedly the problem of how the leaders may persuade the citizens to follow them). The modern criticism ought, then, to be directed against the democratic method of choosing its leaders (politicians). And often it is in fact so directed—as when it becomes an attack upon the universal suffrage, which is alleged to have been responsible for the rise of Hitler, to make the conduct of enlightened foreign policy impossible, to lower and destroy moral and cultural values alike.[2]

Democracy, like any other political system, must produce 'adequate' leaders, adequate to ensure the continuance of the system, and thus to realize its values; adequate to meet the short- and long-term problems, whether economic or international or whatever they may be. Democracy obviously stands or falls by its method of selecting its leaders, and rests on the explicit assumption that elections are the best, or least bad, method of choosing the wisest and best. Behind the elections there is, of course, the pre-selection of candidates by parties—using all the political criteria of 'availability,' electoral appeal, and so forth; an elaborate and severely competitive pre-selection process that is usually ignored by the critics.

Let us grant that we need more investigations into democratic leadership: how it is in fact found and brought forward; in what political 'talent' consists; whether there is a large stock of 'talent'; whether the system does in fact make good use of its 'talent'; whether a traditional ruling class is necessary (as Schumpeter argued); whether businessmen as a class are inherently poor political leaders (as Adam Smith believed); whether democratic leadership tends to compare unfavorably with leadership in other systems, and many similar questions. H. L. Mencken was much more severe than Adam Smith on what he called the plutocracy. Bryce too, a friendly critic, thought that the chief fault of democracies was 'The power of money to pervert administration or legislation.'

The theoretical argument against democratic wisdom is not, however, to be turned aside by empirical studies of leadership, even if their results should happen to be favorable to democracy. Questions of philosophy and principle are also at stake. Plato, it

---

[2] For a survey of the criticisms of democracy on cultural grounds by Carlyle, Ruskin, Arnold, Stephen, Maine, and Lecky see Benjamin E. Lippincott, *Victorian Critics of Democracy*, Minneapolis, 1938. Tocqueville and Henry Adams should also be consulted.

will be recalled, supported his critique by extended argument on the kind of knowledge required, and hence on the difficulty of acquiring wisdom, and on the training and qualifications of the guardians. The philosopher-rulers were to be an aristocracy in the better sense of the word, who by a combination of experience and knowledge received their title to rule just because they *were* qualified.

Fundamentally, two quite different views of the nature of politics and government—the question of what politics and political leadership are *about*—are involved. In the one case, the 'proper end' and the implementing policies can only be known with difficulty, by the philosophers; in the democratic view the ends and policies are many and conflicting, the task of ruling is not conceived as holding society, willy-nilly, to the highest ideals, but of achieving the tolerable and the acceptable for the time being, of permitting progress to whatever ideals may be cherished and which the public may be persuaded to accept. Knowledge of the *summum bonum* is not excluded from a democracy, but it must be married to political persuasion in the politician or pressure group.

It is, however, when we come to consider practical minority-rule alternatives to democracy that the nature of the elite critique is more clearly revealed. Not only do all such critiques start by assuming differences in political capacity and wisdom—so much is admitted to exist—but they go on to assert that the 'wise elite' can be identified and their rule validated. This is precisely the insuperable difficulty, since there are no accepted credentials for such wisdom.

> Nor will I forsake the faith of our fathers in democracy, however I must transmute it, and make it unlovely to their eyes, were they here to see their strangely perverse disciple. If you will give me scales by which to weigh Tom and Dick and Harry as to their fitness to rule, and tell me how much each shall count, I will talk with you about some other kind of organization. Plato jumped hurdles that are too high for my legs . . .[3]

[3] Learned Hand, *The Spirit of Liberty,* ed. Irving Dillard, New York, 1952 and 1959, p. 77. See also Charles E. Merriam, *Systematic Politics,* Chicago, 1945, pp. 187ff.

Even if an elite is once selected, methods of continuing its recruitment and training must be invented. (The nearest approach to a dominant elite today is the self-selected communist party in some countries.) The selection of an elite cannot be done by mass voting, or else we should be back again at democracy, yet somehow the whole of the citizens must be able to recognize the presence of such wisdom and the rulers who have it; and must accept and continue to accept the validity of their rule, i.e. its legitimacy. It is no wonder that even Plato flinched at this task, and resorted to his 'myths' and 'conditioning' once the initial philosopher-kings were installed. Nor can it be seriously maintained today that we can accept the rule of some kind of aristocracy based on and validated by wealth, blood, intellect, military prowess, or priestly power. (Think of the difficulty of getting an I.Q. rating accepted as conferring a right to rule.) We know that none of these is necessarily accompanied by political wisdom.

Further, the elite alternative assumes that the wisest and best, once found, will accept rule and responsibility, and will continue to exercise it wisely, their virtue and judgment alike remaining incorruptible by power. These are large assumptions, for which we are not in the market. Architects of Utopia may ignore the peril, but we know too much today about the corrupting influence of power upon those aloof from and out of touch with the governed, exacting obedience, yet unaccountable to anyone except their consciences or their God. It is for this reason that it seems so true that 'Great men are nearly always bad men.' In the end such rulers can only reduce the stature of their subjects, and they are left trying vainly—as Mill put it—to 'do great things with little people.' Only a democracy provides institutional safeguards against the corruption of power in an elite, by its freedoms and elections answering the old question *quis custodiet ipsos custodes?* Elites and dictators both good and bad, are shrewd enough not to take chances by asking for a free renewal of their mandate. They fall a prey to all the evils of the 'cult of the individual,' having 'no remedy for the personality defects which they may bring into their exalted station.' [4]

4 F. Hermens, op. cit. p. 83.

PROBLEMS IN THE THEORY AND PRACTICE OF DEMOCRACY

By now it is plain that the problems of any complete political theory are of two kinds. The first is that of explanatory theory—how the system operates—and here, so far as democracy is concerned, the chief critics to answer are the Marxists. These are met with relative ease, as long as we employ the same terms of discourse and are willing to rely on normal empirical evidence, and do not, as Marxists so often do, fall back on doctrines of 'essences' of capitalism and bourgeois democracy.

The Marxist criticisms aside, it must be confessed that there are still large gaps in our knowledge of the actual working of democracies, and consequently many of our lesser generalizations in theory must be regarded as tentative and suggestive rather than well-established. If they can be better established by empirical studies, well and good—and there is certainly much room for such studies. Yet we must not make the mistake of believing that every separate generalization, and still less every theoretical construction, is useless if it does not exactly 'fit the facts.' Explanatory theories are of several possible kinds. Only one of them consists of easily verifiable generalizations.

Others are 'idealized' models, approximated but never reached in real life—like the frictionless machine or the pure chemical in the natural sciences. Such theories—or in our case, an orderly set of principles of operation—must make contact with practice here and there (i.e. be empirically verifiable either in their assumptions or deduced consequences), but even though imperfectly testable, they contribute greatly to understanding (explanation) of the system. Some of the problems of a theory of democracy can be solved, if at all, only by those who turn away from the 'great issues' and center their attention upon building the analytical tools and the theoretical constructions—of power, equilibrium, game theory, and others.

The second kind of problem in the theory of democracy is that of normative justification. Here the job is first to examine critically the kind of case which may be made for the principles and values of the system in moral terms. Only by a return to the assumptions of democratic politics can the theoretical charge of incompetence and related defects be met. But the assumptions may be taken much further and raise 'more ultimate' questions than those touched upon in this brief essay. At this point arise those unanswered and fundamental questions concerned not only with the justification of democracy (its separate principles and its systemic values) by reference to a few simple moral principles, but also with justification in terms of a deeper philosophical analysis: of the democratic logic, political wisdom, moral principles in politics, and the status of knowledge itself, especially knowledge of man and society. Although not perhaps of wide contemporary interest—we are so much caught up in a demand for immediate practical results—these questions are nonetheless basic to a theory of democracy which is intellectually satisfactory and yet explicit enough to be relevant to policy decisions. In short, my point is that in order to justify democracy in any depth we need much further investigation into the relation of democratic theory to the various branches of philosophy.

Moreover, in order to deal with problems of politics, with policies, we must always come back to the moral and justifying component of the theory. There is, for example, always much dispute about what constitutes the 'important' practical problems which any political system has to face, and toward which it should shape its policies. In identifying these problems everything depends on the standpoint of analysis and principle from which we survey the political landscape. To one the 'central' problem may be defined as the relation of authority to the individual, to another (following Plato) the nature of justice, to others the control and distribution of power, and so forth. Yet even should we agree on the problem, and the desirable aim, the question of the feasible always confronts us, as it confronts us with the feasibility of democracy itself.

Consider the charge that democracies are in fact inept, from the very nature of the system, and that consequently they must fail. The questions thus raised cannot be answered *a priori* when they deal with feasibility—with the conditions for democracy. In order that the system may be feasible, i.e. work successfully, it is obvious that certain external, empirical conditions are necessary. It is not enough to show desirability, that the theoretical virtues are attractive, or even that the system would work under specified ideal conditions. A political system must work, or be a success, since it will inevitably be judged by its results, as every philosophy must in a certain sense be a 'success' philosophy.

Why are some democracies successful? Why have some collapsed? Where successful, has this been due to luck, or to undemocratic elements within the system? What kind of soil—social, economic, religious—is favorable to the growth of democracy? It can hardly be denied that inquiries into such questions are of the first importance, both to preserve and improve democracies which are going concerns, and to encourage the spread of democracy elsewhere. 'The question of the conditions of Democracy, i.e. what must exist for Democracy to exist, is one of the great problems of the age.'[5]

To try to specify the conditions and circumstances favorable to democracy, and to derive causal relations, is to explore almost unknown territory.[6] Although we know, for instance, that there must be a 'sufficient' number of persons with the democratic character in order to start the system and to keep it running, we have no idea of what constitutes 'sufficient,' and not very much on how to promote such character. Again, despite all the writing on the subject, we know very little about the type and extent of support for a political system that must be forthcoming from the alleged 'intellectuals.'

Nor have we much reliable knowledge on the minimum, or optimum, economic conditions that are necessary, e.g. what standard of living is required. (We must avoid economic determinism. Athens was poor, and one may always say with the Athenian:

[5] R. Wollheim, 'Democracy,' *Journal of the History of Ideas*, April 1958, p. 237. Studies in the history of democracy are also badly needed.

[6] There are a few works on the subject. E.g. Norman L. Stamps, *Why Democracies Fail*, Notre Dame, 1957; John D. Montgomery, *Forced to be Free, The Artificial Revolution in Germany and Japan*, Chicago, 1957; and W. Ivor Jennings, *The Approach to Self-Government*, Cambridge, 1956. The Montgomery book is the result of careful field studies, and the Jennings book is based on long experience of colonial and ex-colonial constitution-making.

'Poverty under democracy is better than any prosperity under oligarchy.') Some put the remarkable economic expansion of the 19th century as the chief 'cause' of democracy—in that it promoted a higher living standard, and generated faith in 'progress' which in turn led to a widening of the franchise and the growth of political liberties. The thesis of David Potter in *People of Plenty* (Chicago, 1954) virtually amounts to saying that modern democracy is possible only with an economy of abundance, although the author tries to avoid a rigidly determinist relationship between the economic and the political. Many other observers have also recorded their conviction that the uniqueness of American society lies in its productivity and affluence, and that these in turn account for its freedoms and its democratic system. One has said that the U. S. is 'not so much a democracy as a huge commercial company for the discovery, cultivation, and capitalisation of its enormous territory,' and Professor Karl Lowenstein writes of the American government (*Political Power and the Governmental Process*, Chicago, 1957, p. 114):

> That it worked at all is a near-miracle, explainable only by the abundance of a nation that could afford a cumbrous and wasteful governmental system.

The economic problems of all political systems are exacerbated today because of the enormous and quite fantastic growth of world population, which has been so large in recent times that it may be truly called an 'explosion.' Population growth expresses itself in the first instance as an economic problem—of pressure upon standards of living. But the problem is inevitably also political—revolutions occur, new parties and leaders lead new regimes—and the questions arise: can economic growth be pushed fast enough to raise living standards, or alternatively, will population be limited in order to achieve the same end? Can either of these policies be carried through democratically?

Other aspects or consequences of the economic problem multiply themselves: can democracy, even among 'people of plenty,' adapt to an ever-growing apparatus of economic planning and controls, and all the apparatus of the 'service' state? What kind and extent of 'pluralism'—of other centers of power—must exist? What of the problem of rapid technological and economic change? So large and so pressing are these political-cum-economic problems that it is no wonder many people believe that any political system today is tested most of all by its handling of its economic problems.

When we leave the more narrowly economic, other realms of unanswered questions lie before us. What rate of social change or degree of social stability can democracy accommodate? What are the social and cultural prerequisites in terms of traditions, legal systems, ethnic unity, social structure, and the like? Is democracy more, or less, feasible in an urban and interdependent industrial society of large scale and with a large bureaucracy? Does the spread of the scientific attitude throughout society aid or handicap democracy? What kind of educational programs are best calculated to promote democratic attitudes?

If limiting conditions to successful democracy are admitted (even though we are ignorant of the limits and cannot distinguish the necessary from the favorable conditions), then we should not expect all democratic experiments to be successful—and indeed obviously some have been abortive in some countries, and will very probably not be successful in others. There is, in fact, every prospect that democratic systems will be for a long time in a minority among the states of the world. And even for those countries which have newly come to independence by colonial revolt, or have tried to promote reform after a social revolution, 'guided democracy' may be the best that can be achieved. This may sound cynical, but is surely only common sense; it may sound discouraging, and is meant to, as an antidote to so much easy democratic optimism. Fortunately, therefore, a more realistic attitude toward the 'export' and prospects of democracy is making itself felt.

Though the sample is too small to give a high degree of certainty to any generalisation, the empirical evidence does suggest that progress towards democracy in societies which start with no democratic institutions and a low degree of political education has been most successful where there has been a period of political tutelage, either under a colonial power or else under some native dictatorship, as in Turkey.[7]

One practical problem of democracies is especially acute. Whatever disputes may exist over the conditions for democracy, or the 'central problem' of democratic politics, one cannot deny that the problems of international politics are extraordinarily pressing today. The world lives in the shadow of an annihilating war which threatens to destroy urban civilization, if not all human societies. The prospects of democracy are thus bound up with the prospects of civilization in a more literal manner than ever before. What has a theory of democracy to say upon this international crisis? Have its principles and its values any direct relevance?

If we look back upon Athenian democracy, it is plain that Athens did not solve its 'international' problem—a failure which some put as the fatal defect of all the Greek city-states. It was for the incompetence of its foreign and imperial policy that Thucydides criticized the Athenian democracy—not altogether fairly—though it is perfectly true that any democracy encounters special difficulties in the formation and conduct of its foreign policy.[8]

The failure of Athens was in political philosophy as well as in organization. Little attention was given to interstate questions, except in wartime, when practical matters were to the forefront—while the very greatest of the philosophers, Plato and Aristotle, did not see beyond the *polis*. Federalism, for instance, was not seriously considered, either by the democracy or its critics. Is our political theory, including that of democracy, equally defective and backward-looking today? Do our traditional categories of political thought correspond any more closely to the desperate needs arising from the contemporary desperate dangers? In our think-

[7] Michael Lindsay, *China and the Cold War*, Melbourne, 1955, p. 104. And David Potter, op. cit. p. 127: '... when America, out of her abundance, preaches the gospel of democracy to countries which see no means of attaining abundance, the message does not carry the meaning which it is meant to convey. No other part of American activity has been so consistently and so completely a failure as our attempt to export democracy.'

[8] Cf. A. H. M. Jones, *Athenian Democracy*, Oxford, 1957, 62ff. Max Beloff, *Foreign Policy and the Democratic Process*, Oxford, 1955.

ing for the most part in terms of autonomous states, which now threaten to destroy one another, are we much ahead of the Greeks who thought of the *polis* while Philip and Alexander—and others even earlier—were destroying its very basis? Are we not caught in the dilemma of Woodrow Wilson—torn between the policy of encouraging democracy abroad and the principle of self-determination, which forbids all interference in the affairs of other states? International politics is focused upon the *political* relations between states, but although all states find themselves willy-nilly in the political relationship, it is a relationship lacking the sanctions of a law-enforcing authority; the analogy on the domestic scene would be pressure groups without a government.

The end of the period of the nation-state has, formally, much in common with its beginning. At the close of the middle ages the serious theoretical difficulty was to try to understand a political world of embryonic nation-states within the conceptual framework of an empire sharing authority with a universal church. Today we are beset with the troublesome task of comprehending a nascent inter-national society with the help of political concepts almost wholly limited to the needs of national sovereignty.[9]

The principles and values of democracy are, it is true, humane and potentially universal—especially those of peace, order, compromise, and political equality—extending beyond the western tradition out of which democracy grew. They do not exclude themselves from the international plane because they are not by definition or practical necessity nationalist, racial, religious, or based on any other exclusive premise dividing men from men. In this, democracy is like economic theory, which also knows nothing of territorial boundaries, although again like economic systems, democracy has received its fullest application within the unit of the nation-state. Moreover, economic liberalism—still a powerful ingredient in the democracies—has always been highly internationalist, even if its belief that trade would unite the world was a naïve and utopian assumption, the kind of easy free-trade pacifist assumption made by middle-class traders from time immemorial.

[9] Charles Vereker, *The Development of Political Theory*, London, 1957, p. 221.

Other bodies of modern thought—secular humanitarianism, Marxism, socialism—regardless of how internationalist their principles, have also been unable to prevent war. Neither, for that matter, has religious unity or theology been able to do so. (It is, of course, open to anyone to argue that some or all of these systems of thought do in fact contain recipes for permanent peace if only men would choose to apply them.) The principles and values of democracy, however potentially universal, are clearly not enough to ensure peace, even if all the countries of the world became democracies. It is possible for a democracy to be nationalist and aggressive as well as internationalist and pacific. There is a strain of criticism of democracy which goes much further, asserting that democracies are inherently warlike, and especially prone to trouble in their international relations. In Sir Robert Filmer's words:

> As it [democracy] is begot by sedition, so it is nourished by arms: it can never stand without wars, either with an enemy abroad, or with friends at home. The only way to preserve it is to have some powerful enemy near . . . for the common danger of an enemy keeps them in better unity than the laws they make themselves.[10]

What is needed here is reliable knowledge of the conditions, if not for peace, then for avoiding war—again an essentially empirical type of knowledge. Is a world jural order feasible, with enforcement and sanctions voluntarily accepted? Would it be effective? Or is a common authority necessary, whose legitimacy must be universally accepted? Can democracies combine with dictatorships in close union? Or was Demosthenes right when he said 'it is not possible for those who exercise arbitrary power to be trustworthy friends of men who choose to live on terms of freedom and equality?' Is union feasible, for instance, as a federation with a large element of democracy? Can the principles and techniques of representative democracy be applied on a scale as large as the world? The feasibility of world democracy involves the same problems as that of democracy within one state, with additional complications: e.g. patriotism may strengthen a democracy,

[10] John Locke, *Two Treatises of Government,* with a supplement *Patriarcha,* ed. by Thomas I. Cook, New York, 1947, p. 247.

but xenophobia weakens a world organization; the incentives are different in the two organizations; and the penalties for failure may be very much higher on an international level. Whether we are or shall be sufficiently impressed by a sense of impending catastrophe is an open question.

One conclusion from all this seems safe enough. The broader perspective must be taken for the near future of a world containing both democracies and non-democracies, all poised precariously on the edge of an abyss. It is the predicament of mankind, not only of democracy, which is most urgent. And it would surely be out of place here to do more than mention this vast subject. The prospects and the conditions of democracy are, then, bound up with the prospects for civilization, and these in turn depend on the prospects of avoiding war, which are not bright. We are

> Wandering between two worlds, one dead,
> The other powerless to be born.

International politics aside, a few elements in judging the prospects and conditions for democracy are well known. In the first place, its achievements must not be judged by reference to Utopia but by reference to feasible alternatives:

> 'In order to love mankind,' said Helvetius, 'one must not expect too much from them.' And fairly to appreciate institutions you must not hold them up against the light that blazes in Utopia; you must not expect them to satisfy microscopic analysis, nor judge their working, which is inevitably rough, awkward, clumsy, and second-best, by the fastidious standards of closet logic.[11]

In the second place, a political system is not necessarily successful because of its theoretical principles and the popular support which these generate. Humanitarianism and patriotism, old ideals and 'spiritual resources,' or merely the luck of history or economic resources, may account far more for the success of democracy than any conscious theory. In the third place, '... it is the lesson of two World Wars that democracy can stand the test. In both these wars it was the totalitarian state that best organized

[11] John Morley, *Oracles on Man and Government.* London, 1923, p. 73.

all its resources, and when it failed to achieve a swift victory, it was the first to come to the end of them.' [12]

THE QUESTION OF CONSENSUS

An essay on theory cannot specify in advance answers to all empirical questions. There is, however, one theoretical-cum-practical question which theory cannot avoid, and on which something may usefully be said—that of consensus.

The question of consensus, or the minimum agreement on 'fundamental' beliefs which may be necessary in order that the democratic system may work smoothly, or work at all, is much debated. There are, broadly, two opposing views: one, that a consensus on 'fundamentals' is necessary; the other, that democracy can work well, and is perhaps the only system that can do so, without a unity of underlying beliefs. There must be, of course, agreement on the system itself—so much goes without saying—so that the problem becomes that of finding what additional agreement, if any, is required before there can be agreement on the political system.

According to the first and more common view, 'government by discussion and majority vote, works best when there is nothing of profound importance to discuss...' and when there is plenty of time to discuss it.[13] Matters in the consensus are by definition beyond 'politics' and approach virtual unanimity, and these are taken to be the only important matters, and consequently only trivial matters are left to be disputed. Political unity is viewed as resting upon other social bonds and homogeneity. Hence we have opinions such as the following:

> Perhaps it is only when parties can treat politics as a game and not as a war that parliamentary government is possible. This may mean that they must agree about fundamentals, and differ only about less radical matters. Their refusal or inability to do so is one of the excuses for distatorship.[14]

[12] Sir Bernard Pares, *A Wandering Student*, Syracuse, 1948, p. 407.
[13] Carl L. Becker, *Modern Democracy*, New Haven, 1941, p. 88.
[14] J. W. Gough, *Locke's Political Philosophy*, Oxford, 1950, p. 53.

Again:

> The breakdown of democracy comes when this community of values and interests disintegrates, when common agreement on fundamentals no longer exists, when partisans no longer endeavor to work through the state but to become the state.[15]

Political parties in successful and stable democracies, so it is said, appeal to an underlying consensus, and when they do so the parties will inevitably approach each other as they bid for votes: they will tend to combine many interests, to be broad and not monolithic or narrowly doctrinal. Of the United States, for example, it is said that 'both parties represent a spectrum of opinion, and the centers of the two spectra constitute a majority and embody consensus.'[16] The Marxist argument is also that political disputes in a 'bourgeois democracy' are not over 'fundamentals'—the latter being defined as the ownership of the means of production—but this is only one possible 'fundamental,' and it is hard to see that parties which divide over other issues, foreign or domestic, are conducting a trivial dispute.

France is often cited as a country with a low consensus, where consequently the democratic machinery works badly, and much governing is done by the civil service, i.e. at the non-political level. The nation is badly divided, with many conflicting traditions—of the revolution, the *coup d'état,* republicanism, royalism, clericalism, anti-clericalism, and perhaps others—each of them commanding strong sectional loyalty. The same concept of legitimate authority ('let the majority decide') is not shared by large minorities which *in toto* make up the majority of the nation; so that extremists are encouraged in their intransigence, which is enhanced, too, by the electoral system. With a consensus lacking, the parties tend to become more hostile, to become single-interest and hard-core ideological parties.[17] And yet Duverger can say, with truth (op. cit. p. 163),

[15] John Hallowell, 'Compromise as a Political Ideal,' in *Ethics*, vol. LIV, 1943-4, p. 164.

[16] Thomas I. Cook and Malcolm Moos, *Power Through Purpose*, Baltimore, 1954, p. 185.

[17] Cf. Anthony Downs, *An Economic Theory of Democracy*, New York, 1957, pp. 126ff.

For the last 50 years there has been, as we have seen, a struggle between two or three irreconcilable concepts concerning the form of the government, its philosophical basis, and its methods of wielding power. The present opposition between Communists and the rest of the French is in many respects no greater than that between conservatives and liberals immediately after the Revolution of 1789 and during the whole of the nineteenth century. Thus the French have learned to live surrounded by radically contradictory political philosophies, with the result that they now believe that the co-existence of such philosophies is one of the essential conditions of freedom.

The *second* or alternative view on consensus starts with the fact of the diversity that exists in any democracy, and holds that political unity may cover differences of many other kinds. The 'will to believe' has a smorgasbord of 'fundamental' beliefs to choose from in any democracy—religious, philosophical, economic, and so forth —to say nothing of the conflicting economic interests or the divisions which may exist along ethnic, linguistic, or cultural lines. All that is required in a democracy is 'disagreement without distrust,' or agreement on the system itself—the principles and the 'rules of the game,' including the majority principle—rather than on substantive policies. On this view, we may say:

> ... the democratic procedures for coming to agreement provide for the possibility of concurrence in action without the preliminary necessity of shared religion, moral conviction, or political program.[18]

Formally, this view of consensus is impeccable; and there is no *logical* reason why democracy cannot work in a divided society, providing one of two conditions are observed. Either (a) if 'fundamental' beliefs (or interests) enter into politics and divide the electorate and representatives, the disagreement is not pressed to the breakdown of the system; or (b) the 'fundamental' divisions are kept out of politics by common or tacit agreement. (Once more we come to the proviso of either majority restraint or minority obedience.)

[18] Richard McKeon, 'Democracy, Scientific Method, and Action,' in *Ethics*, vol. LV, July 1945, p. 286.

Of these two conditions for democracy when the (non-political) consensus is low—that of compromise through politics, or that of leaving the conflicting 'fundamentals' outside of politics—we do not know which is more feasible. The experience of states like the Hapsburg Empire, or better still of federations, where many matters of great importance are not entrusted to the central government (i.e. are not put into the arena of national politics) but instead are retained by the state or local unit in which the consensus is high, would appear to show that leaving some matters out of politics may be the easier solution. The difficulty which arises—as shown by the current dispute over segregated schools in the United States—is that sooner or later even the most local and 'reserved' subject may be injected into national politics. For that reason, any democracy may at any time be compelled to fall back upon compromise or minority obedience.

What is regarded as 'fundamental'—at any rate to the point of provoking strong partisanship—changes through time. For that reason, among others, we may argue that party conflicts can be bitter, and center upon 'fundamental' principles, just *because* there is a political consensus on, for instance, the maintenance of democracy. A country can afford bickering and bitter political strife, under such conditions of widespread agreement on the unwritten constitution, without falling apart. In Lord Balfour's words:

> Our alternating Cabinets, though belonging to different Parties, have never differed about the foundations of society. And it is evident that our whole political machinery presupposes a people so fundamentally at one that they can safely afford to bicker; and so sure of their own moderation that they are not dangerously disturbed by the never-ending din of political conflict.[19]

Aneurin Bevan, for instance, is as British as Churchill or the monarchy—a point which is well understood in Britain but often misjudged abroad—because the 'spirit of concord' and the agreement on democracy are deeply ingrained. (May this be why the United States is more politically legalistic than, for instance, the United

---

[19] Introduction to Bagehot's *The English Constitution*, World's Classics, London, 1942, p. xxvi.

Kingdom or New Zealand, in which the consensus runs somewhat deeper and the political procedures or unwritten constitution can be more readily taken for granted?)

Compromise or acceptance of a political settlement even over differing 'fundamentals' injected into politics is thus possible; loyalty to the 'rules' alone is feasible—in appropriate circumstances. Yet one is inclined to think that agreement on the 'rules' alone is not likely to be powerful enough, in practice, to support compromise and a continuing democracy, if the system actually works to the grave disadvantage of a permanent minority, i.e. frequently and perhaps severely infringes upon what they deeply regard as 'fundamentals' or ultimate values. The question of 'faith' in or loyalty to democracy, regardless of the ends it pursues, is sometimes expressed as the problem of getting 'enough' respect for the principle of mediation and compromise, of recognizing that—in the words of T. V. Smith: 'Democracy is whatever can be arrived at democratically and not another thing.' Yet—as suggested above —unconditional commitment to a procedural system hardly seems psychologically sound, although it must be confessed that this area of motivation is not well explored.

The problem of consensus and conditions of compromise (beyond a statement of the formal conditions) is thus empirical and unanswerable in advance by general theory. It is a question in each case of finding those 'common understandings,' that matrix of tradition and attitudes which makes up the informal constitution and which exists, and must exist, in the working democracies to support agreement on the system. It becomes, then, an empirical and analytical problem of isolating these binding ties, causally, from other fortuitous factors where they exist; of trying to weigh the strength of the community's cohesion against its tendency to fall apart, without waiting for such crucial tests as passive or active resistance, rebellion, secession, or civil war. Politically, it is the problem of achieving unity voluntarily, as against a coerced unity such as is found in a dictatorship. (An organic theory of the state solves this problem, but does not necessarily give rise to a feasible or stable system.)

Now, there is a common 'something' in every democracy— namely, the system, its principles and values, the reliance it places on procedures and liberties. These—like the democratic attitudes mentioned in Chapter 10—go some way toward making up a 'way of life' of shared values (what some call 'a faith for living') even though there is not an unconditional commitment to any one of them or to all of them combined. The rules of procedure in a democracy are not 'value-free' or indifferent, as they may be in games or routine traffic laws; most policies and laws, as well as the system itself, are also mixed with values—which is one of the reasons why systems clash, as on the international scene. In its doctrine of political equality, democracy emphasizes the common features of men, their 'needs, physical and spiritual, for amity and friendship with their own species.'

> ... the democratic consensus, however approximate, is therefore a natural and historical condition by which all societies operate and function to greater or less degree. 'It is in democracies that amity is maximized ...' Indeed amity is enough without justice, but what use justice without amity? [20]

Although we cannot go far into the non-logical, fraternal, psychological, anthropological, and other 'understandings' which make up the social consensus and which bind men together so tightly that political disputes do not sunder them, a few important lessons of history seem clear and relevant enough.

(1) The first of these is that a democracy cannot work with diverse religions, unless there is religious toleration, an agreement to live and let live on creeds. In earlier days it would have seemed intolerable to imagine different faiths dwelling peaceably together. The early New England colonists, for example, were not the first to argue that different religions could not settle peaceably in the same civil society because they divided the people on 'fundamentals.' Since religious toleration comes hard to the devout believer, then, *ceteris paribus,* a common religion is no doubt a factor favorable to democracy (providing it is a religion not antipathetic to democracy). Common religions are rare, however, in most countries today, and so there is nothing but toleration left as a practicable democratic alternative.

[20] Eric A. Havelock, *The Liberal Temper in Greek Politics,* London, 1957, pp. 40, 391. Cf. this idea of 'amity' with de Jouvenel's 'social friendship.'

Toleration need not be regarded as a positive religious virtue, but as a political virtue, an expedient, and as such may reasonably be supported: for instance, as a consequence of a strong attachment to peace and order; or from the realization of the fact that minorities can seldom find new lands today to set up a new state and establish their religious unity. Even if the minority is one individual, he cannot leave the state as he would a voluntary organization. Toleration from expediency led Lord Acton to support Mill's conclusion for liberty of opinion. Nor does this imply that peace and order or other democratic values are the highest values of all, as some philosophers appear to think. Some people, whether in a large or small minority, will always have to make the decision whether to obey or resist in the particular case—i.e. to decide which value they rate higher—a decision which can scarcely be provided for beforehand, but which must be decided in each case, not only in the light of the principles held but also of all the circumstances when they arise. Clashes of pure principle rarely, if ever, occur in politics.

The experience of practically every democracy certainly confirms that the system may work without religious homogeneity; and hence gives us reasons for believing that other clashing ultimates may also continue to live together in a democracy, since it is hard to see what differences could be more 'fundamental' than those of religion. Philosophies and religions may not be capable of ultimate reconciliation, but they may co-exist peaceably. Cosmic ultimates must be interpreted if they are to affect daily life, and there is a surprising amount of agreement in practice even among different religions. From different premises and for different reasons it is possible to come to agreement on the same policies. The common agreement to differ, or to compromise, or to tolerate from expediency—in short to regard the democratic system as 'above' the doctrinal disputes—appears to be the only workable answer.

(2) Another lesson from history is that much of the ideological unity within democracies is national rather than religious homogeneity.[21] Patriotism has bridged many gulfs and still does so.

---

[21] 'Confidence in democratic rule has been accompanied by two broad forces for integration, namely, nationalism and an expanding economic system.'

With this bond has often gone a unifying hatred of a common enemy—for instance, an imperial power—the test of political unity coming later when the foreign yoke has been thrown off. One thinks of India and Pakistan. The test for democracy also comes after national independence is achieved. Not every nationalism is democratic, as witness Mussolini and Hitler, and not every movement for 'self-determination' is democratic, as we see from those numerous colonies which threw off Spanish rule in Latin America. Even the 'invention' of a common enemy or scapegoat in order to promote unity is not unknown in political history. Hence also the suggestion that we may best unite the peoples of earth in face of an invasion from Mars or the Moon, as the people of Camus' novel *The Plague* were united by a common danger.

Failing such non-logical and traditional bonds (which are probably strongest and should probably be forged in the early childhood years), in a democracy there can only be a 'rational consensus, which ... requires agreement upon values.' Hence the need, in some cases, for a political theory that first makes its values plain and only then calls upon emotional aids. The moral imperatives of democracy may be agreed upon as a result of discussion, or the system may be agreed upon as the best means to ultimate, diverse ends. Indeed, in any rapidly changing society which is also becoming diverse, the order and agreement must either be imposed, as in Russia, or reached by choice as it is worked out in political discussion and politics.

(3) In view of the doubt about the feasibility or propriety of an unconditional loyalty to democracy (mentioned above), we are often told that we must have some other enthusiastic faith or creed to match that of Communism. The international tension seems to be the chief stimulus to such demands.

A great enthusiasm, a bright hope, a glowing faith are necessary if liberal democracy is to survive in Europe or Great Britain.

Pendleton Herring, op. cit. p. 57. That democracy bred nationalism, aggressive and soul-destroying, and worshipping either the state or the masses or both is a charge of many critics of democracy. In virtually every such case, however, 'democracy' is defined as Jacobinism or Messianic Utopianism—or sometimes— as 'direct democracy.' Cf. Talmon and Lord Percy of Newcastle, cited in Chapter 8.

Earlier generations could believe in Progress, as Russians and Americans do still; we may envy them the enthusiasms of youth; we cannot share their confidence.[22]

The call for such a faith rests, I think, on a mistaken view. Democracy has been 'conditionally' justified in earlier chapters: if one approves its values, then democracy is valued for their realization, either for themselves, or as means to an end. But democracy offers no clear goals or dynamic collective purpose, no act of government to deliver us into Utopia. The call for a creed, on the other hand, is for 'unconditional' commitment, comparable to a religious commitment.

The attempt to find a faith often takes the form of seeking an essential logical connection between democracy and religion—for instance, a religious justification for democracy—whence it would appear that an unconditional commitment would then be reached, since 'The sacred may be defined as that which is deemed to be of infinite worth or to impose an unqualified obligation. For a man's religion may be defined as that for which he is prepared to die.'[23]

The thesis of a logical or other essential connection between religion and democracy needs to be examined with great care.[24] It presents, indeed, one of the topical and debated problems of democratic theory, resembling the attempts to found democracy upon a particular philosophy—empiricism, pragmatism, instrumentalism, idealism—and to show its incompatibility with other philosophies. Although the close logical affinity of Christianity and democracy may be justifiably doubted, it is enough for present purposes if we assume compatibility, without making the gratuitous assumption of religious unity as a prerequisite for democracy.

(4) A related argument often encountered is that democracy

[22] Nathaniel Micklem, *The Idea of Liberal Democracy*, London, 1957, p. 129.

[23] Ibid. p. 103.

[24] Hans Kelsen, in 'Foundations of Democracy,' Supplement to *Ethics*, vol. LXVI, October 1955, surveys some of the attempts to justify democracy on Christian grounds. Cf. A. D. Lindsay, op. cit. p. 255: 'However true it may be that modern democracy could not have come into being without the influence of these Christian ideals, these ideals are clearly not enough in themselves to produce democracy.'

needs religion because of the political and social utility of the latter—its ability to generate loyalty and enthusiasm for democracy through the habits, attitudes, etc., which are inculcated. 'It is to religion we must look for the moral dynamic that will spur men to that life of virtue which the State desiderates.' [25] According to the same reasoning, the democratic system fails, where it does fail, because of a 'moral vacuum' left when religious faith declines; secularism invites totalitarianism, and only religion can resist tyranny. The reverse connection is sometimes alleged—that democratic systems are more conducive to the practice of Christian morality—a proposition that may well be true, and if believed may strengthen support for democracy.

It is risky, however, to sound the call on behalf of religion for political, instead of religious, reasons since it may so easily tempt the State to use religion for its purposes. And is it not degrading to any religion to say that it should be embraced because it is the only or best alternative to Communism? The mistake of the appeal is that it tends to equate the dissimilar: a secular political system with spiritual truth. This is not to argue for the neutrality of Christianity in all political disputes, but to suggest that the Church's role is only marginally political.

(5) Does democracy presuppose or rest upon a doctrine of progress? That is, is such a belief necessary, even if not sufficient? Morley thought so, though he was not eager to define progress:

> ... what guides, inspires, and sustains modern democracy is conviction of upward and onward progress in the destinies of mankind. It is startling to think how new is this conviction; to how many of the world's masterminds what to us is the most familiar and most fortifying of all great commonplaces, was unknown.[26]

Some kind of case can doubtless be made for progress in the modern world (though pessimism seems more common in the 20th century) by calling attention to such facts as these: the increase of scientific truth; more people (Rousseau's quantitative test); the health, welfare, education, longevity, and relief from pain enjoyed by more people; the fact that although dictators exist, they are

25 Micklem, op. cit., p. 92.
26 Morley, op. cit. p. 127.

widely regarded as 'monsters,' not venerated as gods. Even if such a case—and it could be extended—is granted, however, the causal relation, if any, to democracy is obscure. Two opposing views are possible on the relation of democracy to a belief in progress.

On the one hand, a pessimistic philosophy of man and his future can logically be combined with almost any political theory; one may embrace democracy because one does not trust irresponsible power, without thereby expecting very much of democracy and its leaders. Every political theory must look ahead, regardless of whether or not we are Augustinians in our view of history. In practice, however, one is inclined to think that 'a general sense of improvement is ... a necessary condition for political and social stability,' and for democracy.[27] But this is a far cry from a doctrine of inevitable progress, which no one could possibly entertain after Guernica, the Siberian labor camps, and Buchenwald.

On the other hand, optimistic doctrines of the historical inevitability of democracy must be rejected. There is no guarantee of success or failure for any political system, and so democracy, too, must be regarded as a 'calculated risk.' And democrats will merely fall into the same pit of irrationality as any fanatic if they adopt the dogma that evolution will underwrite the values of democracy. '... we can feel no assurance that the peculiar arrangements that define the American system will hold some special place in the affections of an indulgent Providence.'[28] Yet although there need be no such implied belief as Tocqueville's—that democracy is inevitable—the democrat must obviously believe democracy possible and even probable, and that men are capable of it.

We may draw to a close this discussion on the question of consensus, and on the theory of democracy in general. As to consensus, the extreme of 'too little' consensus raises the danger of the destruction of democracy from within by social, economic, cultural, and other conflicts. The other extreme of a 'complete' consensus is a social conformity that makes liberties meaningless. Democracy

[27] *Economics and Public Policy*, The Brookings Lectures, Washington, 1954, p. 15.

[28] David Truman, *The Governmental Process*, New York, 1951, p. 535.

hovers forever between these two poles. In most of the existing democracies the danger is perhaps greatest, in a time of international crisis like this, from too much stress on consensus and unity. One thinks, for instance, of the damaging effects of self-conscious 'Americanism' upon liberties during the last decade. At any rate, we do well to fear that we may be reading our own future in the features of totalitarian states, whenever, like them, we stress unity at the expense of freedom. So it is not out of place to deplore the frenzied search for a unifying creed in the democracies.

The free world would be guilty of a fatal error if it thought that it possessed a unique ideology comparable to Marxist-Leninism.[29]

Aggressive myths and the search for certitude may be the marks of a political theory and system unsure of itself, a point made by Daniel J. Boostin, as he notes the decline 'in the sense of "giveness"' in the American tradition, and the absence of a unique American philosophy which can be exported.[30]

As to the theory of democracy in general, the tenor of this essay has been that democracy is best thought of as a political system together with its explanatory and justifying theory. Democracy in this view is not a unique ideology, comparable, say to Marxism-Leninism with its interpretation of history and its recipe for Utopia. That is, it is not a comprehensive philosophy embracing all of life and pointing the way to invariable ideals by means of a fixed policy program.

Democracy does have its principles and values, as we have seen in earlier chapters. Within the limits of these, democracy recognizes the legitimacy of whatever ideals or fundamental beliefs—different and even conflicting—that the citizens may cherish. It is a political system and a theory in which men may freely pursue their dreams and purposes, and try to convert them into reality through politics. Lacking the certainties of a closed system, democracy provides the greater challenge, the wider opportunities; but not repose, since 'repose is not the destiny of man.'

[29] Raymond Aron, op. cit. p. 316. Cf. also Mabbot, op. cit. p. 170: 'It is a sign of our political maturity that we have no such creed; it is a pathological symptom when such a creed sweeps a State...'

[30] Daniel J. Boostin, *The Genius of American Politics*, Chicago, 1953, p. 168.